INTERMARRIAGE IN NEW YORK CITY

A STATISTICAL STUDY
OF THE
AMALGAMATION OF EUROPEAN PEOPLES

SUBMITTED IN PARTIAL FULFILMENT
OF THE
REQUIREMENTS FOR THE DEGREE
OF DOCTOR OF PHILOSOPHY
IN THE
FACULTY OF POLITICAL SCIENCE
COLUMBIA UNIVERSITY

JULIUS DRACHSLER, M. A.
ASSISTANT PROFESSOR OF ECONOMICS
AND SOCIOLOGY
IN
SMITH COLLEGE

New York
1921

PREFACE

This monograph is a first attempt in a field of sociological research that has thus far been cultivated only to a very limited degree, and in which careful and exhaustive work would, without doubt, bring substantial results.

The problem of the amalgamation of ethnic groups in the United States is of deep interest not only to the student of group life and group interaction, but also to the practical worker in the field of Americanization. Because of the intensely controversial nature of the whole question, it has seemed to me that nothing is more important for a scientific apprehension of the problem than the effort to secure *basic facts first,* and then proceed cautiously with the elaboration of theories of assimilation and amalgamation.

In this monograph some of these basic facts are presented, and their wider bearings upon public policies of assimilation indicated. In a companion volume entitled *Democracy and Assimilation: The Blending of Immigrant Heritages in America,* published by The Macmillan Company, 1920, I have ventured a more popular discussion and interpretation of the data in this study. The two publications are distinct not only in purpose, but to a large extent also in form and in content. The emphasis in this monograph is upon the facts and their scientific explanation. Evaluations of the results are carefully avoided. In the more popular treatise stress is placed upon the meaning of the facts from the point of view of the practical worker who wishes to aid in framing a reasonable and effective public policy for the incorporation into American life of the numerous immigrant groups and of their immediate descendants. Of the ten chapters in the Macmillan publication, three are substantially the same in content as Chapters II., III. and IV. of this monograph. Chapter V., Statistical Appendix, however, is almost wholly omitted. This part contains all the source material and important derived tables that make the monograph of value to students who may desire to follow out some of the lines of investigation indicated.

I am deeply indebted to Professors A. A. Tenney and R. E. Chaddock for their invaluable aid while the manuscript was in preparation.

The printing of the study would have been impossible, had it not been for the generous aid of Professor Edwin R. A. Seligman in securing the major portion of the publication fund through contributions from Mrs. Sidney C. Borg, Messrs. D. M. Heyman, Fred M. Stein, Cyrus L. Sulzberger and Justice Irving Lehman. To these I wish to express my great and lasting obligation.

A final word of thanks is due to Professor F. H. Giddings; also to Professor Henry R. Seager for his kindness and courtesy in editing for the Studies a statistical monograph which presented peculiarly difficult problems of printing and publication.

JULIUS DRACHSLER.

New York City,
January 1st, 1921.

CONTENTS

INTERMARRIAGE IN NEW YORK CITY

A Statistical Study of the Amalgamation of European Peoples

CHAPTER I.

INTRODUCTION: THE PROBLEM

I. LACK OF SCIENTIFIC DATA

By common agreement among competent students of American social problems, the proper incorporation of the foreign-born and of their immediate descendants into the body politic is considered a question of basic national concern. But although there is much discussion of a controversial nature, both within the narrower circle of scholars and among the public at large, it is based upon comparatively scanty fundamental data. Unrelated, though frequently keen observations, alternate with generalizations that are superficial and often flippant, each based on more or less specious race theories.

On the biological aspects of amalgamation in the United States there is virtually no scientific information available. Little is known of the extent of the fusion, of the rate at which it is taking place, of the groups amalgamating quickly or slowly. Still less is known of the biologic effects in the actual cases of intermarriage, while the subtle interplay in mixed marriages of different types of mind and of culture has thus far almost completely eluded the observation of the scientific student. "Much remains to be done in the study of this subject," writes Professor

Boas[1], "and, considering our lack of knowledge of the most elementary facts that determine the outcome of this process, I feel it behooves us to be most cautious in our reasoning .. .. .." Little more that can stand the test of scientific criticism has been added to an understanding of the sociological phases of the problem.[2]

II. CHARACTER OF THE NEW IMMIGRATION

The turning point in the character of immigration is generally conceded to have been around 1882 which marks the beginning of a strong migratory movement of the Eastern and Southern European peoples as contrasted with the earlier movements of Northern and Northwestern European nationalities. The latter had come in comparatively small groups; they were ethnically related to each other, and they tended to scatter over a wide area instead of concentrating

[1] Franz Boas, *The Mind of Primitive Man.* Ch. X., Race Problems in the United States, p. 263.

[2] No exhaustive studies of the community life of the various immigrant groups are as yet available. The study of "Methods of Americanization" which is being conducted by the Carnegie Corporation of New York, is perhaps the most comprehensive effort thus far launched in this field of research. The results of the study have not yet been published. The most elaborate single analysis is contained in the *Jewish Communal Register for New York City,* 1917-18, a survey of the activities of the Jewish Community of Greater New York. Other, more or less authoritative sources are:

Reports of the Immigration Commission, Vol. I., pp. 494-497, Types of Immigration Communities; J. W. Jenks and W. J. Lauck, *The Immigration Problem,* Ch. V., Manufacturing and Mining Communities, pp. 72-79; Ch. VII., Immigrant Institutions; *Report of the Commission on Immigration to Massachusetts,* Ch. IX., Sec. 2, Organizations Among Immigrants for Self-Help; Emily G. Balch, *Our Slavic Fellow Citizens.* Ch. XVII., The Organized Life of Slavs in America; H. P. Fairchild, *Greek Immigration to the United States;* Grace Abbott, *The Immigrant and the Community;* Robert F. Foerster, *The Italian Emigration of Our Times;* Lord, Trenor and Barrows, *The Italian in America;* Thomas Burgess, *Greeks in America;* Enrico C. Sartorio, *Social and Religious Life of Italians in America;* Archibald McClure, *Leadership*

in the cities. The problem of assimilation thus virtually solved itself. Had the new settlers, who were ethnically different groups, come in small numbers or as detached individuals, their presence among the earlier comers would hardly have attracted much attention. As it was, however, the huge waves of immigration which flooded the shores of America began slowly to arouse the fears of the native population. The high water mark of the new immigration was reached in 1907 when almost 1,300,000 immigrants landed here.[3] During the year ending June 30, 1914, very nearly one and a quarter millions came, representing almost forty nationalities in Europe.

The outstanding features, then, of immigration during the 30 years before the European War were the steady rise, on the whole, in the volume of the incoming flow and the massing of the foreign-born in the large commercial and industrial centres. While the proportionate number of foreign-born whites in the United States increased only slightly in this period, the absolute number increased from a little over six and a half millions to thirteen and a half millions.[4] Still more significant was the growth of the foreign colonies, which doubled and trebled their numbers between 1890 and 1910.[5] This was especially marked among the peoples from Eastern and Southern Europe. A very considerable portion of the foreign-born, it was constantly pointed out, cannot speak English at all, and a still larger number have only a fragmentary knowledge of it.[6]

of the New America, Racial and Religious; H. B. Grose, *Aliens or Americans,* Ch. VII, Immigration and the National Character, The American of To-morrow; Wm. P. Shriver, *Immigrant Forces,* Ch. III., The New Communities.

[3] Report of the Commissioner General of Immigration, 1915, p. 122, Table XV.

[4] *13th Census,* 1910, Vol. I., Pop. Stat. p. 831, Table 32.

[5] *13th Census,* 1910, Vol. I., Pop. Stat. p. 854, Table 37.

[6] Basing its estimate upon the census of 1910, the Bureau of Education of the Department of the Interior gives for the United States

III. THE MOVEMENT FOR AMERICANIZATION

The growing seriousness of the problems arising from the presence of large numbers of unassimilated aliens had come to be recognized long before the outbreak of the Great War. Congestion, unsanitary housing, industrial exploitation, undue strain upon educational facilities for children and adults were increasing more rapidly than the number of effective social measures calculated to remedy them. While publicists and students of race problems had begun the discussion in a more or less tentative spirit

Foreign born whites, ten years of age or over, unable to speak English	2,953,011
(Foreign born whites, 21 years of age and over, unable to speak English, 2,565,612)	
Colored population, ten years of age and over, unable to speak English, (Negro, Indian, Chinese, Japanese, etc.)	138,196
Making a total, unable to speak English, of	3,091,207

From 1910 to 1919, according to the annual reports of the Commissioner General of Immigration, over 4,000,000 immigrants arrived from non-English speaking countries. Therefore, it has been estimated that there are at least 5,000,000 non-English speaking persons in the United States at present.

For detailed figures of foreign born whites, men and women 10 years of age and over, by States, unable to speak English, see *Circulars No. 30, 33, 34, Bureau of Education*, Department of the Interior; also Bulletin *Americanization* for June 1st, 1919, p. 16.

The inability to read and understand English not only handicaps the foreigner in his pursuit of a livelihood, but in some occupations places him in danger of his life. According to the director of the United States Bureau of Mines, the rate of accidents among the non-English speaking miners is not only greater in the great mining districts of the country, but the increased ratio is uniform in all districts. In his opinion, this demonstrates clearly that the inability to read warning signs, to comprehend fully the company's instructions and to understand their foremen, places an unnecessary hazard upon the foreign-born. In the Pennsylvania anthracite mines, for example, the figures show that 43% of the employees are English speaking and this number is charged with only 28.8% of the fatalities, whereas the other 36% sustained 71% of the fatalities. This is a comparative ratio of 669 to

of speculation,[7] and settlements and social centres were pointing the way towards a clearer and more sympathetic understanding of the life of the foreign-born, it was not until 1907 that a federal immigration commission was ap-

1268 against the non-English speaking. In the Pennsylvania bituminous mines the ratio is 771 to 1123 and in the West Virginia district 790 to 1424. The report is concluded by the statement: "Had the fatality and injury rate for the English speaking Americans been maintained throughout the three groups there would have been a saving of 716 fatalities and 900 very serious injuries, a strong argument for Americanization and education of the miner." Abstract of report by Van H. Manning, Director of the U. S. Bureau of Mines. Bulletin, *Americanization,* June 1st, 1919, p. 11.

Similarly, the value of English in curbing traffic accidents is coming to be stressed by transportation experts. They urge communities to stress to the foreign-born resident that a knowledge of the English language will help reduce the death list of 10,000 persons estimated to be the United States' annual toll to public carelessness, and ignorance of highway traffic. "Americanization committees," says W. P. Eno, chairman of the Advisory Committee of the Highway Transport Committee of the Council of National Defense, an international authority on traffic regulation, "should investigate their local conditions in this respect and should ask for the strictest enforcement of the English language test (for driver's license). Traffic offers an unlimited study of primary value upon which to base the lessons of the evening schools. It is a topic of as much universal appeal as the purchase of food or the employment office dialogue, for at some time during the day, practically every born foreign man or woman must use the streets." Bulletin, *Americanization,* June 1, 1919, p. 14.

[7] Among numerous articles the following may serve as illustrations:

a. G. Michaud, and F. H. Giddings, The Coming Race in America. *Century Magazine,* March, 1903, Vol. 65, pp. 683-692.

b. F. H. Giddings, The American People, *International Quarterly,* Vol. 7, Number 2, June, 1903.

c. M. Fishberg, Ethnic Factors in Immigration, *Proceedings, National Conference of Charities and Correction,* 1906, pp. 304-314.

d. Wm. Z. Ripley, The European Population of the U. S., *Huxley Memorial Lecture for* 1908. *The Journal of the Royal Anthropological Institute of Great Britain and Ireland,* Vol. XXXVIII, 1908.

e. A. Alleman, Immigration and the Future American Race, *Pop. Sci. Monthly,* December, 1909, Vol. 5, pp. 586-596.

pointed which, four years later, issued its comprehensive report of more than forty volumes.

But it was the war crisis (July, 1914 to November, 1918) that brought the question of the assimilation of the foreign-born to a head. Americanization activities multiplied rapidly.[8] The propaganda of the Bureau of Naturalization, the "America First" campaign of the U. S. Bureau of Education, the organization of the committee of One Hundred of the National Education Association, the organization of committees on Americanization by various trade associations and chambers of commerce and other similar efforts culminated in the conference on methods of Americanization in Washington, on May 12-15, 1919, called by the Secretary of the Interior.

As a result of the interchange of opinions and of experiences effected by the Conference, it became clear that if the problem of the proper incorporation of the foreign-born was to be adequately treated, future efforts must proceed along three important lines, namely, the establishment of more intimate and more sympathetic personal relations between the native-born population and the alien groups, stressing particularly the need and the value of the cultural contributions of the foreign-born to American life; the co-ordination of the manifold Americanization activities throughout the country to eliminate duplication of work and to save energy and initiative; the promotion of co-operation between the Federal and the State governments in the field of Americanization, definitely recognizing the national scope and character of the question. Steps have already been taken to secure Congressional legislation upon this subject.[9]

[8] For a brief account of the efforts made to arouse public interest in Americanization, see article by Howard C. Hill, "The Americanization Movement," *American Journal of Sociology*, May, 1919.

[9] As an illustration may be cited the Smith-Bankhead bill on Americanization (S. 5464—H. R. 15402) now before Congress.

IV. NEED FOR A NEW APPROACH

In the meantime nothing has impressed itself more definitely upon the mind of the critical student of the Americanization movement as a whole, than the more or less superficial character of the efforts made thus far and the urgent need of approaching the problem from a more secure basis than can be furnished by cursory observation and reflection. It would, of course, be unwise to discard altogether the results arrived at in these two ways, since it is through suggestions which they yield that valuable working hypotheses may be framed and an understanding obtained of the inner meaning of the problem. Nevertheless, it is hazardous to be guided solely by such findings in formulating public policies of assimilation. The basic facts sought, should, if possible, be measurable quantities. They should, among other things, throw light upon such vital questions as the degree of actual amalgamation or biologic fusion among the European peoples and their descendants in the United States, the groups among which the amalgamation is occurring and the social and economic conditions under which the fusion is proceeding.

While in a strictly scientific study the facts bearing upon these questions would have to be kept distinct from their interpretations or ethical evaluations, nevertheless the data gathered could serve as a much needed new approach to the discussion of the public policy to be followed in the proper incorporation of the immigrant groups.

V. AIM OF THIS STUDY

It is the aim of this study to make a beginning in this direction, by analyzing the situation as it presents itself in one of the large immigrant centers in the United States. The following monograph, accordingly, is devoted to setting forth some of the facts bearing upon the amalgamation of European peoples in New York City during a representative five-year period before the Great War (1908-1912).

CHAPTER II.

METHOD AND SCOPE

1. EARLIER METHODS OF STUDYING THE PROBLEM OF AMALGAMATION

A natural consequence of the lack of quantitative data bearing upon the amalgamation of peoples of different stocks is that statistical methods of treatment of the problem have not been fully developed. Whatever work has been done is either historical or observational in its content and method. Instances of group interaction in the past are selected, the general results noted from an analysis of historical records, and conclusions drawn that have more or less universal validity.[1] Or, the process of assimilation is carefully observed in the case of living social groups.[2]

In all research of this nature, definite limits are set by the authenticity of the historical evidence, by the small number of proper examples illustrating the process,

[1] A striking illustration of this type of work is that by Ludwig Gumplowicz, *Der Rassenkampf*; also Sarah E. Simons, Social Assimilation, *American Journal of Sociology*, Vol. 7, July-May, 1901-1902; Part II, V. Assimilation in the Ancient World; VI. Assimilation during the Middle Ages.

[2] Simons, Ibid., Part II, VII, Assimilation in the Western World (including Russia, Austria-Hungary, Germany, United States.) An ingenious method of study is employed in *The Polish Peasant in Europe and America, Monograph of an Immigrant Group*, by Wm. I. Thomas and Florian Znaniecki. Through an analysis of a series of peasant letters and autobiographical materials, light is thrown upon the organization of Polish peasant group-life and its modification in a new environment.

by the skill and social insight the student exhibits in the interpretation of the facts and by the validity of the theory of race fusion the writer happens to espouse.

With the development of statistical science, quantitative methods will doubtless come to supply the deficiencies in a substantial manner. It is even possible to conceive, without an undue stretch of the scientific imagination, that experimentation may be added as a further device for arriving at the social laws underlying the process of group interaction. The situation in the United States strongly suggests such a possibility. Here is to be found the requisite human material in great abundance and variety. Here group and class consciousness are, relatively speaking, less intense and less exclusive than perhaps in any other country. Consequently, while the biologic factors involved may possibly for a long time elude social control, the sociopsychic forces generated in the group contacts are certainly more amenable to conscious manipulation. At any rate, students are beginning to point out the unique opportunity America possesses in this respect.

II. GENERAL METHOD AND LIMITATIONS OF THIS STUDY

In this monograph the method followed is that of a statistical analysis of pertinent data contained in authentic marriage certificates. The general plan is to present the facts, as such, in the form of suitable statistical tables, to frame and test hypotheses to explain these facts, and to exclude from the discussion the ethical evaluation of the results themselves.

No attempt, however, is made to treat the subject exhaustively or to go into statistical refinements. Indeed, this could hardly have been possible or justifiable with the materials at hand and with the limitations under which the statistical analysis itself had to proceed. There was, first, the lack of certain important figures necessary for more detailed comparisons between the various ethnic groups and for calculating corrections. Thus the basic figures showing the number of marriageable men and women for each immigrant group separately and for each "generation"[3] (foreign-born of foreign parents, native-born of foreign parents and native-born of native parents) separately, are at present available only in the form of estimates and could therefore be used only to a limited degree in the comparisons between the broad "generation" groups. But even if the data lacking had been obtainable, it is doubtful if very much more accurate results would have been achieved, since, owing to the large number of cases involved, the significant facts stand out almost as clearly as they would if corrected figures could be calculated. Furthermore, it is clear that an adequate study of the problem of amalgamation would involve the gathering and the analysis of additional data on the situation in smaller cities and towns throughout the country, and possibly also in the rural sections; on the biologic aspects of ethnic fusion, such as the relative fecundity of mixed marriages,[4] the physical and mental vigor of the offspring; and on the sociological phases, such as the cultural effects of mixed marriages upon the home life, including the question of family desertion[5] and intermarriage and divorce.[6]

In view of these definite limitations, this monograph can

[3] The term "generation" as used in this study denotes not an age group, but a "nativity" and a "parentage" group; that is, it refers to the fact of the birth of a person in the United States or in a foreign country, whether of foreign born parents or of native born parents. Differences between persons of different "generations," then, do not mean differences of age, at all, but rather differences of traditions, social attitudes, outlooks, in short, differences of civilization and culture. The "first" generation (foreign-born of foreign parents or FBFP, the abbreviated form used in the statistical tables) would thus be the one furthest removed from what we think of as "American" life, the "second" generation (native-born of foreign parents or NBFP) would mark the transition period, the "third" generation (native-born of native parents, or NBNP) would very nearly represent the "Americanized" product.

[4] An interesting study of relative fecundity among amalgamating peoples is that of A. E. Jenks, Ethnic Census in Minneapolis, *American Journal of Sociology*, Vol. 17, July-May, 1911-12, pp. 776-782. "The

claim simply to present some tentative conclusions and partial generalizations. More specifically it attempts:

1. To ascertain some of the more significant facts and probable explanations of these facts, showing the *general trend* in the fusion of the various European peoples, as it is proceeding in a large centre like New York City.

2. To point out by way of these illustrations how fuller data could be treated to yield significant results.

3. To indicate the possibilities for some further statistical studies on the basis of some of the original source material presented in the Statistical Appendix of this monograph.

4. To set out briefly the larger bearings of such data as are brought together in this study, upon public policies of assimilation.

The first three topics are the subject of Chapter III. The fourth is treated in a summary fashion in Chapter IV.

III. INTERMARRIAGE RATIO AS INDEX OF ASSIMILATION

Before proceeding to a detailed discussion of the data presented in Chapter III, the following brief statement of the most important considerations of method and scope may serve as a useful introduction:

A study of the facts of intermarriage offers a reasonably

Irish blood tends to increase fecundity and Scandinavian blood tends to decrease fecundity of other peoples in amalgamation."

[5] Differences in nationality between husband and wife have been found to be a contributing cause to desertion. "The 138 cases in which there was a difference of nationality formed about 28% of the 499 for which information on this point was given. In the general population of the United States in 1900 only 8.5% was of mixed parentage and for New York City the proportion was less than 13% . . . A difference in nationality was more than twice as frequent among the cases of desertion as among the general population of the city where it is most common." *Family Desertion,* Lillian Brandt, pp. 18-19, a report published by The Charity Organization Society of New York, 1905.

[6] For the proportion of divorce in marriages between Jews and non-Jews, see Maurice Fishbers, *The Jews,* p. 217.

secure base from which to begin a scientific study of the whole problem of assimilation. Several reasons tend to confirm this view. Intermarriage, as such, is perhaps the severest test of group cohesion. Individuals who freely pass in marriage from one ethnic circle into another are not under the spell of an intense cultural or racial consciousness. Consequently, the greater the number of mixed marriages the weaker, broadly speaking, the group solidarity. Moreover, such a test as this is quantative. Statistics of intermarriage furnish concrete and measurable materials in a field where such data are as urgently needed as they are hard to secure. The intermarriage ratio, therefore, obtained on the basis of facts collected from authentic marriage certificates, can be used as a good index of assimilation.

It may be urged, however, that the ratio of intermarriage is not the only test of assimilation, as is proved by the mental and social assimilation of individuals and of groups, without actual amalgamation; that a more accurate test of group cohesion would perhaps be affiliation with specific and characteristic communal activities of the immigrant groups. Were this test applied, the lack of cohesion and disintegration of group life among the immigrant peoples would be found to be far greater and more wide-spread than the ratios of intermarriage seem to indicate. Thus, while the proportion of intermarriage among the Jews is very low,[7] the ratio of the unsynagogued (that is, those upon whom the synagogue, the characteristic Jewish social institution, has a much less vital hold than in the past) is rather high.[8] To cite this instance, however, is to show that the exception proves the rule. Unless there exists a strong racial self-consciousness, which tends to bar biological

[7] See Table IVa, p. 43.

[8] *Jewish Communal Register*, 1917-18. Affiliation with the Synagogue, by Prof. M. M. Kaplan, p. 117. Out of 900,000 Jews in New York City only about 415,000 are synagogue Jews, and out of a seating capacity of 217,725 there are only 39,260 seats in synagogues where English sermons are preached.

fusion with other religious and cultural groups, there is comparatively little to prevent amalgamation, once superficial differences of habit-life have been swept away in the course of living and working together. While, therefore, the proportion of intermarriage might be taken to indicate the *minimum* measure of group solidarity, it is evident that the higher the proportion of intermarriage, the lower is the degree of cohesion, or, to put it differently, the higher the proportion of intermarriage, the higher is the degree of assimilation with other groups. If the ratio of intermarriage among persons of the second generation (native-born of foreign parents) is found to be considerably higher than that among the first generation, it is certain that lack of affiliation with immigrant communal life is correspondingly high and even higher. To argue from facts of intermarriage of ethnic groups, then, is to err by *under-estimating* rather than *over-estimating* the extent of assimilation.

IV. SELECTION OF AMERICAN COMMUNITY FOR STUDY

Coming now to the question of selecting an American community for study, it would seem that of all American cities, Greater New York is more admirably fitted for such an inquiry than perhaps any other community that might be chosen. Here are gathered together nationalities and races from all lands and all climes. Here immigrant colonies flourish. Here opportunity for self-sufficient communal life is as complete as is possible away from the native soil. Yet here there is mobility and contact, subtle temptation of all kinds to break with the old tradition and blend with the attractive stranger. In this, New York City is typical of all other large American cities that have received their share of the immigration of the last twenty-five or thirty years.[9]

[9] Of the foreign-born whites in the United States in 1910 no less than 72.2% were in urban communities (cities of 2500 and above), 56.1% were in cities of 25,000 and more. *U. S. Census*, 1910, Pop. Stat. Vol. I, p. 172. Table 32. Of fifty cities of 100,000 inhabitants or more

To be representative of the country as a whole the intermarriage statistics gathered for such a community as New York would, of course, have to be supplemented by figures for smaller towns and cities and for rural districts. But here again, the ratio for the larger centre would be, so to speak, the lower limit, or the minimum ratio. If fusion goes on in the bigger city, then, *a fortiori*, it will go on in the smaller place. All that is known of community life in minor centres and in rural districts tends to confirm this view. The more intimate contact with the much smaller native population, the heightened economic ability to marry due to a less severe competition in earning a living, the lack of stimuli for a group consciousness, (such as a large massing of the foreign-born, the presence of intensely nationalistic leaders, the existence of communal institutions, e.g., the foreign language press, theatre and special social welfare agencies meeting the needs of the immigrants apart from the general community) all these strongly suggest such an opinion, until evidence is presented to the contrary.

V. SOURCE OF DATA

The figures offered in this monograph were gathered from original marriage certificates in the files of the office of the City Clerk of New York City. Only records for the

in 1910, thirty had a foreign-born white population amounting to more than 25% of their total population. N. Y. City had a foreign-born white population of 40.4%. Only two other cities, Fall River, Mass. (42.6%) and Lowell, Mass. (40.9%) had a higher percentage than Greater New York. J. W. Jenks and W. J. Lauck, *The Immigration Problem*, p. 527, Table 27.

The presence of a rather small proportion of persons of colored races (black, yellow, red) in New York City adds rather than detracts from the propriety of the choice of that city, as this study is devoted primarily to an analysis of amalgamation among European peoples. In 1910 the negro population of New York City was 91,709 or 1.9% of the total. Indians, Chinese, Japanese and all others together numbered 6,012. *U. S. Census*, 1910. Vol. I, Pop. Stat., p. 178. Table 37.

Boroughs of Manhattan and Bronx were available for inspection. This enforced delimitation of territory, does not however affect the results materially, as the population of these two boroughs differs in no fundamental respect from the inhabitants of the excluded three Boroughs of Brooklyn, Richmond and Queens.[10].

VI. NUMBER OF RECORDS ANALYZED

The total number of marriage licenses issued during the five years (1908-1912), covering the period studied, was 171,356 distributed as follows:

Year	Number of Licenses Issued
1908	29,491
1909	31,597
1910	34,657
1911	36,621
1912	38,990
TOTAL	171,356

Of this total, 101,854 or 59.4% were selected for this inquiry. From this number, however, were excluded all marriages where either the bride or the groom was born in the United States of native-born parents (NBNP).

This was necessary, since the original nationality in such cases could not be determined, and "American" nationality, as such, was a doubtful term. Jews and Negroes of the third generation (native born of native parents) were not excluded because, in the one case, religion and race, in the other, color (race), was a clear enough distinction marking

[10] Out of a total population of 4,766,883 for New York City in 1910, the Boroughs of Manhattan and Bronx had 2,762,522 or 57.9%. The proportions of foreign-born in the various Boroughs were: Manhattan, 47.9%; Bronx, 34.7%; Brooklyn, 35.2%; Queens, 27.9%; Richmond, 28.4%. *U. S. Census,* 1910. Pop. Stat., Vol. I.

the groups as separate. For the immediate purposes of the study, then, only 79,704 marriages or couples were considered.

This substantial portion of the total number of certificates issued (59.4%) was selected by a broad sampling process as indicated below, and is thus sufficiently representative.

VII. METHOD OF SELECTION

The selection of the five year period (1908-1912) was guided by three considerations. The first was the lack of complete data before 1908. Beginning with that year the contract form of marriage record, with hardly any information except the names and addresses of the contracting parties, was replaced by a rather elaborate questionnaire form. Moreover, the census year, 1910, appeared to be a useful pivotal year for purposes of comparison in dealing with the figures gathered for the two years previous to and the two years succeeding the taking of the Federal census. The fact, also, that abnormal social influences (such as arose out of the Great War which opened in August, 1914), were not operative as yet in the lives of the foreign-born, marked the period as acceptable for study.

The records selected (101,854) were spread over the five year period in such a way that approximately 20,000 cases fell within each year. These were further distributed about evenly over every month of every year, and over the beginning, middle and end of each month of the year. This precaution was necessary in order to take account of the fluctuation in the number of marriages during the more or less "popular" and "unpopular" parts of the year. Thus during the early summer months (particularly May and June) and the later months of the fall (such as October and November) a larger number of marriage certificates is issued than during the other months. Otherwise the records were examined as they appeared serially in the record books.

Each marriage certificate was carefully examined and the pertinent facts summarized on individual record cards.

VIII. KINDS OF DATA GATHERED

The following kinds of data were taken from the marriage certificates:

1. Country of birth of Groom
2. Country of birth of Bride
3. Country of birth of Groom's father
4. Country of birth of Groom's mother
5. Country of birth of Bride's father
6. Country of birth of Bride's mother
7. Occupation of Groom (whenever given)
8. Occupation of Bride (whenever given)
9. Generation of Groom[11] (FBFP, 1st generation)
(NBFP, 2nd generation)
(NBNP, 3rd generation)
10. Generation of Bride[11] (FBFP, 1st generation)
(NBFP, 2nd generation)
(NBNP, 3rd generation)
11. Color of Groom
12. Color of Bride.

IX. STATISTICAL TABLES

The facts were then classified in various ways, to yield the following statistical tables which form the basis of the discussion in Chapter III:

Group A: Tables containing facts on intermarriage, according to generation,* among ethnic groups in New York City.

Table I—Intermarriage between persons of different generations. (Men.)

[11] See p. 16, Note 3.

* For the explanation of the term "generation" as used in this monograph, see p. 16, Note 3.

Table II—Intermarriage between persons of different generations. (Women.)

Table III—Proportion of intermarriage according to sex and generation.

Group B: Tables containing proportion of intermarriage among the various nationalities represented in this study.

Table IV (a)—Proportions of intermarriage arranged in order of magnitude, in five classes. (Class I-Class V), for men and women of the 1st, 2nd and 3rd generations considered together as a group.

Tables IV (b)—IV (i) Proportions of intermarriage arranged in order of magnitude, in five classes (Class I-Class V) for men and women separately and for each generation separately.

Table V—Summary Table showing proportions of intermarriage among the nationalities studied (nationalities arranged alphabetically).

Table VI—Number of intermarriages for each nationality separately (showing nationalities intermarried with and generations of persons intermarrying).

Series I-91: One table for the men of each of the nationalities considered in the study.

Series I-88: One table for the women of each of the nationalities considered in the study.

Table VII—Classification of nationalities by percentage of increase in intermarriage of 2nd generation over 1st generation.

Group C: Tables containing facts on number of nationalities intermarried with and nationalities selected in intermarriage.

Table VIII—Number of distinct nationalities with which persons of various immigrant groups intermarried.

Table IX—Nationalities selected in intermarriage by persons of 2nd generation.

Group D: Tables containing facts on the relations between occupation, cultural level and intermarriage.

Table X—Proportion of intermarriage according to occupation groups.

Table XI—Proportion of intermarriage according to occupation and culture level.

Table XII—Proportion of intermarriage according to occupation and generation (men and women).

Table XIII—Proportion of intermarriage among men according to occupation and generation.

Group E: Miscellaneous Tables:

Table XIV—Proportion of marriageable persons among various immigrant groups (1910-1917), upon their entrance to the United States.

Table XV—Proportion of sexes in the first and second generations among various nationalities in N. Y. City (1910) according to generation.

Table XVI—Proportion of marriageable persons in N. Y. City (1910) according to generation.

Table XVII—Proportion of marriageable persons in Manhattan and Bronx Boroughs, in New York City (1910), according to generation.

X. SOURCES OF ERROR

In the gathering and the treatment of the data several sources of error had to be kept in mind. There was first, the possibility of error arising out of a misjudgment of the nationality of either the groom or the bride or both. In the cases of natives of such countries as England, Scotland, Ireland, Germany, Sweden, Norway, Denmark and others with a relatively homogeneous population, the facts as given in the marriage certificate (country of birth of bride and of groom, and country of birth of parents of both) were sufficiently clear to make the proper judgment. However, for countries like Austria-Hungary and Russia, as they were before the Great War, the persons belonging to the various constituent populations had to be separated as carefully as possible. The nationalities in the former Austro-Hungarian Monarchy were found to fall into the following groups:

Austria (Bohemian)
Austria (German)
Austria (Polish)
Austria (Jewish)
Hungary (Slovak)
Hungary (German)
Hungary (Hungarian)
Hungary (Jewish)

The marriage records contained sufficient information to make the classification in these cases fairly reliable. These items were taken into consideration:

1. Geographic section of the country of birth of both persons who married and his or her parents. (The various nationalities in these countries are concentrated in certain well-defined areas).
2. Name of groom and of bride (distinctive Bohemian or German or Jewish or Slovak or Hungarian or Polish name).

3. Names of witnesses to the marriage ceremony.
4. Name of the priest or clergyman officiating. In quite a number of cases the clergyman was well-known in New York City as belonging to a definite religious sect and a definite nationality.

Wherever there was doubt, the record was omitted.

For both Austria-Hungary and Russia, the Jews were classified under the heads: Austria (Jew), Hungary (Jew) and Russia (Jew). In a similar manner, the Jews of all other countries were indicated separately, as Rumanian Jews, German Jews, French Jews, English Jews, American Jews, and so on. Of course, in the records of intermarriages between Jews and non-Jews even greater care had to be exercised to include only genuine intermarriages. Here the determining facts were:

1. Country of birth of groom and bride.
2. Country of birth of parents of groom and bride.
3. Name of groom and bride.
4. Names of witnesses.
5. Name of officiating clergyman.

Only those cases were recorded where there was absolutely no doubt as to the intermarriage. This naturally would make the intermarriage ratio lower than it probably is in actuality; for, numerous Jews and Jewesses who intermarry drop their original Jewish names and adopt non-Jewish names. Moreover, in intermarriages between Jews and non-Jews it is very frequent not to have a clergyman of either faith perform the ceremony, thus accentuating the lack of religious affiliation of the parties to the marriage.

Still another source of error that must be noted, is one arising out of the definition of what constitutes an intermarriage. Two interpretations are possible, a strict and a liberal one. According to the first, an inter-marriage is a marriage between two persons of distinct national, religious or racial descent (the nationality of the father being taken as the nationality of the child). A marriage between an Italian man born in Italy of Italian parents or born in the United States of Italian parents, and an English woman born in England of English parents or born in the United States of English parents would be a case in point. Another illustration of this type of marriage (somewhat less strict) is that between a man born in Scotland whose father was Scotch and whose mother was French, and a woman born in Sweden, whose father was Swedish and whose mother was German. According to this definition, cases in which the mothers of both bride and groom were of the same nationalities or were born in the United States would be excluded.

A more liberal definition, however, might be framed. This would include all cases where either the fathers or the mothers of the parties to the inter-marriage were of the same nationality. An illustration of this type of marriage would be the case of the Irish groom, whose father was Irish and whose mother was Italian, and the bride whose father was German and whose mother was Italian. Here the fathers are of different nationalities but the mothers are of the same nationalities.

In this study the *broader* definition was followed: but since the proportion of cases that would have to be excluded according to a strict interpretation of intermarriage was found to be only 3.03%, the results can hardly be appreciably affected by their inclusion.

One other source of error that could not have been avoided must be pointed out. The original marriage records give the age of the person marrying, but (for the foreign-born) give neither the year of arrival in the United States nor the length of residence in this country. It is thus impossible to tell how old the foreign-born man or woman was at the time of arrival. The person may have been less than a year old or may have been 14 years of age or 18 years or 25 years. And yet, in each of these cases, the person is considered as of the "first generation" with all that this term implies.[12]

It can thus plausibly be argued that the "first generation" group considered in this study may in reality not be a group consisting of adult foreigners upon whom the old world culture had left an unmistakeable impress, and who are therefore quite distinct from the native-born "second generation" as social types. The "first generation" cannot then be contrasted with the "second generation", for, the "first generation" may include a large proportion of foreign-born who came here at a very early age, grew up in a new-world environment and are practically, if not completely, the same in behavior, in outlook, in sentiment as the true "second generation". In other words, the "first generation" group considered here may be a sort of "specious" "second generation" group, and much of the reasoning about it as a "first generation" group would really not be applicable.

It must be admitted that theoretically there is much force in the objection, and that this criticism cannot be fully met, since the necessary data are lacking in the marriage records themselves. In spite of this difficulty, however, the figures are not by any means seriously invalidated. Reasoning from an inspection of the actual results obtained, on the assumption that the two groups are distinct "generation" groups, it may be said that the differences between the intermarriage ratios of the two groups are obviously so striking that there must be a great qualitative distinction between the groups considered. If the proportion of intermarriage for the "first generation" as a group is 11 per 100 and the proportion for the "second generation" is 31 per hundred (with a wider range by far, for specific nationalities) then, *a priori*, the view would seem plausible that the assumed "first generation" is most probably composed of social types quite different from those comprising the "second generation" group. Of course, as all *a priori*

[12] For a definition of "generation" as used here, see Chapter II, p. 16, Note 3.

arguments, this has its definite limitations and ought to be checked if possible by a recourse to an analysis of the facts themselves. These, however, are not available at present.

XI. STATISTICAL REFINEMENTS OMITTED

As was pointed out before, the figures gathered here have not been and could not be treated according to refined statistical methods, primarily because of the lack of certain basic figures in accurate enough form. An exact analysis of group cohesion in each of the immigrant groups involved and therefore significant comparison, could not be undertaken. Moreover, the number of marriages recorded in some of the groups is too small to yield significant proportions in themselves. Only results derived from the mass figures are consequently of real meaning. But this is all that is needed to bring to light the *main tendencies* in the process of fusion as it is at present proceeding in large American cities. It is open to serious doubt whether further refinements would substantially alter the conclusions reached.

CHAPTER III.

Results

The aim of this chapter, as stated above, is to present the most significant facts and their probable explanations, derived from the data compiled in Tables I-XVII (see Chapter II, pp. 23-25), to indicate how these analyses could serve for further researches along the same lines, and finally to point out how some of the source material can be utilized for more detailed studies.

I. INTERMARRIAGE WITHIN GENERATIONS

Viewing the phenomenon of amalgamation in the broadest way, namely, that of fusion among persons of different generations, (for a definition of "generation" see Chapter II, p. 16, Note 3) the first striking fact that appears is, that almost three-fourths of the intermarriages, (74.0%) both among men and among women take place between persons of the same generations. That is, members of the first generation tend to intermarry with members of the first, members the second generation with members of the second.[1] Upon reflection this would seem to be the natural result. Differences between generations are primarily differences in stage of assimilation.

Immigrants of the first generation belonging to different national groups have more in common with one another than they have with persons of the second generation. But it is a sort of negative community of interest. The foreign-born man and woman both do not yet speak the language of the country well enough; both have not yet acquired the

[1] The reason for omitting the third generation is given in the Explanatory Note, Table I, p. 33.

new habits of life, and still hark back in their thoughts and actions to the European environment. Both are in the first stages of a transition and both feel more at ease among persons of the first generation, (even though these be of a different nationality), than among persons of the second generation, who by their superior knowledge of the strange land and by a subtly condescending manner make the foreigners feel rather apart from the new currents of life. At any rate, this would seem a plausible explanation of the fact.

That persons of the second generation, though of different national descent, should group together in marriage, is still more easily understood. The irresistible levelling influences of American life have stamped persons of the second generation as unmistakeably alike, though largely only outwardly alike. They speak the same tongue, study in the same schools, dress, act, and think alike. Another fact tending to confirm this view is, that the proportion of intermarriage between persons of different generations decreases as the interval between the generations increases. This holds for both men and women. Out of almost 11,000 intermarriages (10,835) practically one-half (47.7%) were intermarriages between persons of the first generation. About three and a half times as many intermarriages occurred between *first* generation *men* and *first* generation *women,* as between *first* generation *men* and *second* generation *women* (47.7% and 13.8% respectively) and about two and a half times as many between *second* generation *men* and *second* generation *women,* as between *second* generation *men* and *first* generation *women* (26.3% and 9.4% respectively.)[2]

The figures for the women are similar. Intermarriages between *first* generation *women* and *first* generation *men* were five times as frequent as those between *first* generation *women* and *second* generation *men* (47.7% and 9.4% respectively) while about twice as many intermarriages

[2] See Table I, p. 33

TABLE I

INTERMARRIAGE BETWEEN PERSONS OF DIFFERENT GENERATIONS

(1908-1912)

MEN

Explanatory Note:

1) FB FP=Foreign born of foreign parents; NB FP=Native born of foreign parents; NB NP=Native born of native parents.

2) For definition of the term "generation" see Chapter II, p. 16.

*Figures for third generation here include only Jews and Negroes and other NB NP intermarrying with them. All other NB NP (3rd generation) are excluded as uncertain since the original nationality in such cases could not be determined from the records, and "American" nationality as such, was a doubtful term. Therefore, 3rd generation figures here are not to be compared with figures for 1st and 2nd generations.

Intermarriages between Generations	1st, 2nd and 3rd Generation Men with 1st, 2nd and 3rd Generation Women	1st Gener. (FB FP) Men with 1st Gener. (FB FP) Women	1st Gener. (FB FP) Men with 2nd Gener. (NB FP) Women	1st Gener. (FB FP) Men with *3rd Gener. (NB NP) Women	2nd Gener. (NB FP) Men with 2nd Gener. (NB FP) Women	2nd Gener. (NB FP) Men with 1st Gener. (FB FP) Women	2nd Gener. (NB FP) Men with *3rd Gener. (NB NP) Women	*3rd Gener. (NB NP) Men with *3rd Gener. (NB NP) Women	*3rd Gener. (NB NP) Men with 1st Gener. (FB FP) Women	*3rd Gener. (NB NP) Men with 2nd Gener. (NB FP) Women
Number of intermarriages.............	10835	5170	1497	47	2847	1018	83	45	61	67
Per cent. total number of intermarriages..	100.0	47.7	13.8	.4	26.3	9.4	.8	.4	.6	.6

TABLE II

INTERMARRIAGE BETWEEN PERSONS OF DIFFERENT GENERATIONS

(1908-1912)

WOMEN

Explanatory Note:

See Table I, p. 33.

Intermarriages between Generations	1st, 2nd and 3rd Generation Women with 1st, 2nd and 3rd Generation Men	1st Gener. (FB FP) Women with 1st Gener. (FB FP) Men	1st Gener. (FB FP) Women with 2nd Gener. (NB FP) Men	1st Gener. (FB FP) Women with *3rd Gener. (NB NP) Men	2nd Gener. (NB FP) Women with 2nd Gener. (NB FP) Men	2nd Gener. (NB FP) Women with 1st Gener. (FB FP) Men	2nd Gener. (NB FP) Women with *3rd Gener. (NB NP) Men	*3rd Gener. (NB NP) Women with *3rd Gener. (NB NP) Men	*3rd Gener. (NB NP) Women with 2nd Gener. (NB FP) Men	*3rd Gener. (NB NP) Women with 1st Gener. (FB FP) Men
Number of intermarriages.............	10835	5170	1018	61	2847	1497	67	45	83	47
Per cent. of total number of intermarriages	100.0	47.7	9.4	.6	26.3	13.8	.6	.4	.8	.4

occurred between *second* generation *women* and *second* generation *men* as between *second* generation *women* and *first* generation *men* (26.3% and 13.8% respectively.)[3]

That this disparity in the proportions of intermarriage is not due to a disparity in the ratios of marriageable persons in the first and second generation, is evident, when it is found that the proportions of marriageable *men* of the *first generation* to marriageable *women* of the *first generation* (1. 29:1) is almost the same as the proportion of marriageable *men* of the *first generation* to marriageable *women* of the *second generation* (1. 22:1) and vice versa, (.77:1 and .82:1).[4] The powerful forces thus at work are undoubtedly the expression of sympathy and conform to the law that "the degree of sympathy decreases as the generality of resemblance increases."[5]

But while the influences of cohesion undoubtedly make themselves felt within the generation groups in an unmistakeable fashion, the forces of disruption are relentlessly undermining the solidarity of the immigrant communities. It comes somewhat as a surprise that out of every 100 marriages in New York City as many as 14 are intermarriages (13.59).[6]

One would expect that with the great massing of foreign-born in separate communities and the consequent accentuation of group relationships, the ratio would be much less.

II. INCREASE IN PROPORTION OF INTERMARRIAGE IN SECOND GENERATION

But this figure gives no hint of the wide gap between the intermarriage ratios of the first and of the second generations. Whereas among persons of the first generation

[3] See Table II, p. 33

[4] See Statistical Appendix, Table XVI, p. 211.

[5] F. H. Giddings, *Inductive Sociology*, p. 108.

[6] See Table III, p. 35

who marry, about 11 per 100 seek mates outside of their own group, (10.39% for men and 10.10% for women) among those of the second generation the proportion jumps to about 32 per 100 (32.40% for the men and 30.12% for the women.) In other words, there is an increase of approximately 300%, (311.8% for men and 298.2% for women.)[7] The slight difference between the men and the women might perhaps adequately be accounted for by the relatively greater mobility and aggressiveness of the men, and the greater conservatism of the women. But the striking increase for both, in the second generation calls for a more detailed explanation.

TABLE III
PROPORTION OF INTERMARRIAGE ACCORDING TO SEX AND GENERATION
(1908-1912)

*Explanatory Note: See Table I, p. 33.

	Men				Women			
	Total	1st Gener. (FB FP)	2nd Gener. (NB FP)	*3rd Gener. (NB NP)	Total	1st Gener. (FB FP)	2nd Gener. (NB FP)	*3rd Gener. (NB NP)
Per cent. of intermarriage	13.59	10.39	32.40	5.87	13.59	10.10	30.12	5.35
Number of marriages....	79704	64577	12184	2943	79704	61823	14611	3270
Number of intermarriages	10835	6714	3948	173	10835	6249	4411	175

[7] See Table III, p. 35.

If these proportions of intermarriage are applied to the total number of married persons (15 yrs. of age and over) in New York City in 1910, (*U. S. Census Abstract. With Supplement for New York*, p. 604, Table 16) the following figures are obtained:

a. Number of married foreign-born white males (first generation) —575,460; number of males who intermarried (11%)—63,190;

b. No. of married foreign-born white females (first generation)— 521,855; number of females who intermarried (10%)—52,185;

III. HYPOTHESIS I. DISPARITY IN SEX RATIOS AMONG MARRIAGEABLE PERSONS

What, then are the possible hypotheses by which this basically important fact may be explained and which one of the hypotheses is most probable? It might be urged, first, particularly in reference to the men, that not having enough women of their own group in the second generation, they are compelled to seek wives among other groups. In other words the disparity in the proportions of marriageable

Or approximately 115,375 *foreign-born white persons (first generation) who intermarried.*

c. Number of married native white males of foreign or mixed parentage (second generation)—185,301; number of males who intermarried (33%)—61,769;

d. Number of married native white females of foreign or mixed parentage (second generation)—216,223; number of females who intermarried (31%)—67,029;

Or approximately 128,798 *native white persons of foreign or mixed parentage (second generation) who intermarried.*

The *total number* of persons (first and second generations) who intermarried was approximately 244,173.

Treating the figures for the United States in a similar way (the intermarriage ratios for N. Y. City being assumed to be the *minimum* ratios) the results are:

a. Number of married foreign-born white males (first generation) —4,432,298; number of males who intermarried (11%)—487,552;

b. Number of married foreign-born white females (first generation)—3,624,215; number of females who intermarried (10%)—362,421;

Or approximately 849,973 *foreign-born white persons (first generation) who intermarried.*

c. Number of married native white males of foreign or mixed parentage (second generation)—2,677,885; number of males who intermarried (33%)—883,702.

d. Number of married native white females of foreign or mixed parentage (second generation)—3,008,927; number of females who intermarried (31%)—932,767;

Or approximately 1,816,469 *native white persons of foreign or mixed parentage (second generation) who intermarried.*

The *total number* of persons (first and second generations) then, who intermarried was approximately 2,666,442. (*U. S. Census,* Vol. I, p. 518, Table 14.)

persons might account for the increased proportion of intermarriage. This is hardly tenable in the light of facts. While there is a preponderance of marriageable men over marriageable women in the *first* generation, the discrepancy very largely disappears in the second generation, which shows the normal, approximately equal, distribution of the sexes.[8] The marriageable sex ratio factor, then, might explain intermarriage among men of the first generation, but must be ruled out as an explanation for the second generation. In cases of women it would seem inapplicable even for the first generation. For, with a preponderance of men over women, there would be no reason for women to leave their group in search of husbands, if the factor of sex ratio were the only one operating to determine choice.[9]

[8] Since figures of the proportion of marriageable persons for each nationality separately are not obtainable at present, it must suffice to establish the fact of the general preponderance in the first generation of marriageable men over women and the definite approach to an equality of sex ratios among the marriageable in the second generation. This is clearly brought out by Tables XIV-XVII, Statistical Appendix, pp. 210-212.

[9] There appear to be exceptions to this, where, in spite of the preponderance of marriageable men over women, the proportion of intermarriage among the women is higher. This would seem to be the case for the Austrian Poles, Slovaks, Irish, Bohemians, Finns, French, Norwegians and the Swedes. (See Statistical Appendix, Table V.) If it were solely and exclusively the factor of the marriageable sex ratio that was operating in the first generation to determine choice, then in those groups where there is a preponderance of men over women, there ought to be no intermarriage whatsoever on the part of the women. The fact, however, that they do intermarry at all, indicates either that other forces are at work, or that the presence of a surplus of men of other nationalities in search of wives (in addition to the men of their own nationality) acts as an indirect compulsion or attraction to the women to leave their own groups.

In the cases of those groups where the women not only intermarry but intermarry more frequently than the men, in spite of the preponderance of men over women, the explanation may be that a certain percentage of the eligible men do not marry at all, either because they are not in a position economically or because they prefer not to *inter-*

III. HYPOTHESIS 2. RISE IN ECONOMIC STATUS

As it is, possibly another influence might urge men and women of the *second* generation to intermarry more frequently than men and women of the *first* generation. The argument may run somewhat as follows: With higher economic status generally goes greater mobility. With greater mobility comes a wider circle of contacts, and inevitably a wider field of choice. Now, since persons of the second generation are generally to be found in the higher economic classes, owing to their better acquaintance with the economic life of the country, they would thus be freed from the shackles of the lower economic existence and be permitted to move about, with greater probability of selecting a mate from among the people of other social groups with whom they come into contact.

If, in addition, it be kept in mind that the economic ability to marry is probably higher in the second generation than in the first, a reasonable explanation might be found for the unusual increase in the ratio of intermarriage.

But, it may be pointed out in reply, that *a priori*, this hypothesis also, appears rather improbable. In the first place, while it is true that lower income might act as a retarding cause of marriage, it does not actually seem to do so in the lower economic classes. On the other hand, with increase of income, other subtle social causes would seem to operate to reduce the frequency of marriage. Whatever

marry and thus do not marry at all. This would tend to leave free an equal proportion of women. These again would be absorbed into the groups where the proportion of intermarrying men is higher than the proportion of intermarrying women. But since it is quite probable that even in the first generation other factors, besides that of the sex ratio among the marriageable are operative, these explanations are undoubtedly incomplete.

In any event, the proof or disproof of these conjectures, must wait upon the gathering of more complete data, among other things the distribution of the specific immigrant groups according to sex and marital condition.

decrease in marriages may occur in the first generation, is likely to be offset by a corresponding decrease in the second generation.

Such reasoning as this, however, is hardly sufficient to refute the proposed explanation. If it could be shown from actual records of intermarriages, that among intermarrying persons of the second generation there is a larger proportion of individuals who belong to the higher economic classes, than there is among intermarrying persons of the first generation, it could be fairly asserted that increased income *does* bring about an increased proportion of intermarriage.

Applying this test, it appears from a comparative study of the occupations of intermarrying persons of the first and second generations that, while there is an increase in the proportion of individuals of the second generation within the higher economic groups (and a corresponding decrease in the lower groups) the increase is hardly large enough to account for the jump in the ratio of intermarriage.[10]

[10] This is brought out in Table XII, p. 65, by a broad grouping of occupations of intermarrying persons into:

(a) Highest group (comprising persons in professional service) *1st generation*: 9.4% for men; 11.3% for women; *2nd generation*: 9.4% for men; 9.3% for women.

(b) Middle group (comprising persons in commerce and trade, and manufacturing and mechanical pursuits) *1st generation*: 54.2% for men, 34.1% for women; *2nd generation*: 63.0% for men, 66.4% for women.

(c) Lower group (comprising persons in personal and domestic service and the lower grades of public service) *1st generation*: 22.8% for men, 52.7% for women; *2nd generation*: 8.8% for men, 19.4% for women.

(d) Low group (comprising persons in agriculture and transportation and navigation) *1st generation*: 4.9% for men, 0% for women; *2nd generation*: 2.5% for men, 0% for women.

(e) Lowest group (comprising unskilled workers) *1st generation*: 8.7% for men, 1.9% for women; *2nd generation*: 16.3% for men, 4.9% for women.

For similar results see also Table XIII, giving comparative proportions of intermarriage for 5932 men (3400 of the 1st generation and

(The average increase, it will be remembered, is about 300%; but the full range of increase in the ratios of intermarriage is for men, from 103% to 1446.1%; for women, from 112.9% to 1294.1%.).[11]

It should be noted, however, that the economic factor seems to be more effectively at work among women than among men. The freer and more wide-spread participation of women of the second generation in the commercial and industrial life of the country doubtless creates a greater contrast between them and women of the first generation, than is to be found in this respect among the men, who are not so restricted in their economic activities. As the sphere of women in the economic world widens, this factor will grow increasingly stronger, particularly as sex propinquity in modern industry seems definitely to affect matings.[12]

2532 of the 2nd generation,) classified according to occupation groups.

The marked decrease for the second generation in the personal and domestic service group is due undoubtedly to the fact that these occupations are less frequently entered by "Americans" of the 2nd generation, while the unexpected increase in the unskilled groups indicates no doubt the prevalent lack of vocational training among young persons of the second generation, thus compelling many to enter "blind alley" occupations of which there is an abundance in a great city like New York. For a comparative study of occupations of the first and second generations of immigrants in the United States, tending to bear out this view see *Reports of the Immigration Commission of* 1911, Vol. 28, particularly pp. 5-105.

Note: No comprehensive statistics have thus far been compiled on the distribution of occupation groups according to incomes. The classification used in Tables XII and XIII, however, is in substantial agreement with the facts gathered by Frank H. Streightoff, in Chap. VI of "The Distribution of Incomes in the United States," *Columbia University Studies in History, Economics and Public Law,* Vol. 52, 1912. See especially Tables XXIV-XXXVI, pp. 111-139.

[11] See Statistical Appendix, Table V, opp. p. 100.

[12] For a study of "Occupational Propinquity as a Factor in Marriage Selection" see article by Donald M. Marvin, in *Quarterly Publications of the American Statistical Association,* Vol. XVI, Sept., 1918, pp. 138-150.

III. HYPOTHESIS 3. WEAKENING OF GROUP SOLIDARITY

Now if neither disparity in the ratio of marriageable persons nor rise in economic status is an adequate explanation of the unusual increase in the proportion of intermarriage in the second generation, the only hypothesis left is to ascribe it to the weakening or destruction of the attitude of group solidarity. Once the subtle and numberless bonds that tie the individual to his traditional group are snapped, he is set adrift in a vast sea upon which float countless similar "kin-wrecked" folk. Choice of mates is then determined largely, if not wholly, by two factors: propinquity and physical attraction. The same forces that strengthen or weaken immigrant community life are the forces that fortify or undermine this attitude of attachment to the group. The most important of these are:

Forces Tending to Strengthen Immigrant Community Life.	*Forces Tending to Undermine Immigrant Community Life.*
1. Geographic massing of immigrant population.	1. Dispersion of immigrant population.
2. Stimulus by intensely nationalistic leaders, aided by crises in the fortunes of either the group in America or of the parent-group in the home-land.	2. Absence of intensely nationalistic leaders and normal condition in home-land.
3. Presence of numerous type of communal organizations ministering to the economic, educational and moral needs of the immigrants.	3. Paucity or absence of communal organizations.
4. Personal affiliation with communal enterprises.	4. Lack of personal affiliation with communal enterprises.
5. Transmission through systematic education of the cultural heritage of the group to the growing youth.	5. Indifference and neglect on the part of the older generation in regard to transmission of cultural heritage to the younger generation.
6. Conscious attempts by the thinkers of the group to formulate a theory of group-adjustment to American life.	6. Lack of critical thought within the group upon future relations to the new environment.

But after reflecting upon the nature of these forces and their influence upon the "second generation" the well-informed student of immigrant community life might point out that it is hardly accurate to speak of them as *undermining* or *fortifying* the attitude of group loyalty. For, in reality the "second generation" have no group attitude or loyalty that can be undermined or fortified. The whole trend of immigrant communal life in America has rather been to prevent the formation of any attitude of group attachment on the part of the younger generation. This criticism is not wholly beside the point, especially when it is remembered that the common characteristics of the "diluted" second generation are reputed to be on the one hand, a lack of knowledge and appreciation of the cultural heritage of their group and on the other hand, a lack of affiliation with specifically communal undertakings. Nor have most of the immigrant groups devised adequate educational methods to impart an understanding of their cultural background to their children.[18] In the main, however, the inevitable conclusion would seem to be that the increased proportion of intermarriage in the second generation must be attributed almost wholly to the weakening of the sentiment of group solidarity.

The relative efficacy, then, of the three factors in bringing about intermarriage may be summarized as follows: In the first generation the factor of disparity in the sex ratios among marriageable persons is strongest, the economic factor next (particularly for women) and the group consciousness factor third. In the second generation the order is reversed, the factor of group consciousness or rather the lack of it.

[18] Even in such a highly self-conscious group as the Jews, religious and cultural education of the youth is in a relatively backward state. Of the 275,000 Jewish school children in N. Y. City in 1917, the total number receiving some form of Jewish education was 65,400. This is less than 24% of the estimated number of Jewish children of elementary school age. See A. M. Dushkin, *Jewish Education in N. Y. City*, Part II, Ch. 1, The Extent of Jewish Education in N. Y. City, pp. 156-157.

being most prominent, the economic factor being second, and the sex ratio factor playing the smallest role.

IV. GROUPING OF NATIONALITIES ACCORDING TO RATIO OF INTERMARRIAGE

The facts presented thus far have had reference mainly to the relation between intermarriage and generation, irrespective of national descent. Equally characteristic results are obtained when the various nationalities are grouped according to the magnitude of their ratios of intermarriage. Beginning in Class I with nationalities that intermarry least frequently and ending in Class V with those that fuse most readily, the array appears as follows:[14]

Table IVa

Classification of Nationalities according to Proportion of Intermarriage. (Men and Women of the 1st, 2nd and 3rd generations)*

(1908-1912)

Class I

(0 to 4.99 intermarriages per 100 marriages)

Nationality	*No. of Intermarriages per* 100 *Marriages*
Roumania (Jew)	.45
British West Indies (Colored)	.48
Russia (Jew)	.62
Turkey (Jew)	.80
Colored (combined groups)	.93
Austria (Jew)	.99
United States (colored)	1.08
Jewish (combined groups)	1.17
Dutch West Indies (Colored)	1.44
Hungary (Jew)	2.24
England (Jew)	3.47
Holland (Jew)	4.00
United States (Jew)	4.26
Syria	4.63

[14] For the number of cases upon which the computation of the proportions of intermarriage is based, see Statistical Appendix, Table V, opp. p. 100.

* The following groups, represented by less than 50 marriage cer-

Class II

(5 to 9.99 intermarriages per 100 marriages)

Nationality	*No. of Intermarriages per 100 Marriages*
Germany (Jew)	5.16
Italy (not located)	5.58
Italy (South)	5.83
France (Jew)	6.54
Italy (combined groups)	6.76
Hungary (Hungarian)	8.59
Armenia	9.63

Class III

(10 to 24.99 intermarriages per 100 marriages)

Nationality	*No. of Intermarriages per 100 Marriages*
Turkey	13.15
Austria (Polish)	13.56
Hungary (Slovak)	14.09
Italy (North)	16.73
Finland	16.82
Russia (Polish)	20.25
Ireland	21.59
Germany (not located)	21.68
Greece	22.14
Hungary (German)	24.41

Class IV

(25 to 49.99 intermarriages per 100 marriages)

Nationality	*No. of Intermarriages per 100 Marriages*
Austria (Bohemian)	25.15
Sweden	31.04
Spain	33.11
Germany (combined groups)	33.34
Norway	39.14
British West Indies (English)	39.86
Denmark	47.42
France	49.55

tificates, have been omitted in this classification: Cuba (colored), Canada (colored), Roumania, Austria (Italian), China, Switzerland (Italian), Mexico (Spanish), Serbia.

Class V

(50 to 100 intermarriages per 100 marriages.)

Nationality	*No. of Intermarriages per 100 Marriages*
Porto Rico (Spanish)	50.76
Germany (North)	53.05
Germany (South)	55.98
Wales	59.44
Belgium	59.63
Austria (German)	59.71
Scotland	59.79
Holland	62.58
England	62.70
Switzerland (German)	66.32
Japan	72.41
Cuba (Spanish)	73.73
Canada (French)	75.60
Canada (English)	79.85
Switzerland (French)	82.08
Portugal	88.23

Even a casual inspection of this table reveals at once distinct groupings at either end of the scale. Jews and Negroes are at the lowest point, while the Northern, Northwestern and Central European peoples tend to gather near the highest point. The Italians and the Irish, together with the Poles (Russian and Austrian), the Slovaks, the Greeks and the Finns, occupy the middle-ground. This distribution with slight modifications was found to hold for both men and women, and for both the first and the second generations.[15]

In an exhaustive treatment of the problems of amalgamation each one of the ethnic groups in the five classes shown in Table IVa would be taken up for discussion separately. This is not feasible here because of the limitations of cost and space.

The discussion which follows is therefore offered largely for purposes of illustration of type facts and explanations.

[15] See Statistical Appendix, Tables IVb-IVi, pp. 93-100.

The Jews and the Negroes are selected to represent the low ratio groups, the Italians and the Irish the middle ratio groups, while the Northern and N. W. European peoples are made to serve as representatives of the high ratio group. These ethnic stocks are chosen partly because they are large and important constituents in the population of the United States and partly because it is easier to frame an explanation as to why their intermarriage ratio is what it is, owing to the general knowledge we possess of the life of these groups and their attitude towards amalgamation.

V. INTERMARRIAGE BETWEEN JEWS AND NON-JEWS

The explanation for the small proportion of intermarriage among the Jews is not far to seek.[16] From the earliest period in their history the leaders of the people, feeling almost instinctively the danger of extinction of a minority group, have steadfastly set their faces against fusion with non-Jews.[17] The strict prohibition of Ezra and Nehemiah (about 400 B. C.) was supplemented on the Christian side by the various edicts of the Church, beginning with that enacted by the Eastern Church at the Council of Chalcedon

[16] For an excellent discussion of intermarriage among the Jews both historically and statistically treated, see Arthur Ruppin, *The Jews of Today*, Ch. X, Intermarriage, and Maurice Fishberg, *The Jews—A Study of Race and Environment*, Ch. VIII, Proselytism and Intermarriage Among Jews; Ch. IX, Mixed Marriages in Modern Times. A readable account of the arguments against intermarriage from the Jewish point of view is that of Dr. David De Sola Pool on "Intermarriage," *The Hebrew Standard*, Vol. LXXIII, No. 6, February 7, 1919.

[17] The prohibition against intermarriage is expressed in Deuteronomy, VII, 1-4, as follows: "When the Lord thy God shall bring thee into the land whither thou goest to possess it, and shall cast out many nations before thee . . thou shalt make no covenant with them . . . neither shalt thou make marriages with them; thy daughter thou shalt not give unto his son, nor his daughter thou shalt take unto thy son. For He will turn away thy son from following me that they may serve other gods; so will the anger of the Lord be kindled against thee and He will destroy thee quickly."

in 388 A. D. and followed by those of the Councils of Orleans (A. D. 538), Toledo (A. D. 689) and Rome (A. D. 743)[18] enjoining Christians from marrying Jews. It was not until the latter part of the eighteenth and the opening years of the nineteenth centuries when religious and social ostracism of the Jews began to slacken in its rigor, that intermarriage became a pronounced factor. All careful students of the problem[19] agree that with the emancipation has come an increasing tendency to amalgamate with the peoples among whom the Jews happened to live. This holds especially of the Western European countries. Ruppin, reviewing all available facts bearing upon intermarriage of Jews and Christians, groups the various countries into four classes:

1—Those where mixed marriages are less than 2%, as in Galicia, Bukovina, Rumania and the Jewish immigrant areas of England, France and the United States.

2—Those where the proportion of mixed marriages ranges from 2% to 10%, namely, Catholic Germany,* Hungary (excluding Budapest) and Bohemia.

3—Those where intermarriage goes on to the extent of from 10% to 30% of Jewish marriages, as in Protestant Germany,* Holland, Austria (Vienna and Budapest).

[18] B. Feldman, *Year Book of the Central Conference of American Rabbis*, 1910, pp. 217-307. "Intermarriage Historically Considered."

[19] Among them particularly Ruppin, Zollschan and Fishberg.

* Figures of 1911 (three years before the Great War) present a striking contrast when compared with figures for 1915 (one year after the opening of the War.) Of 4449 Jewish men who married within the German Empire in 1911, 635 or 14.2% married non-Jewish women. The latter included 471 Protestants, 117 Roman Catholics and 47 of other denominations. Of 4267 Jewish women who married in the same year, 453 or 10.6% married non-Jewish men (302 Protestants, 111 Roman Catholics and 40 of other denominations.)

The 1915 figures are as follows: Of 1842 Jewish men, 744 or 40.3% married non-Jewish women (542 Protestants, 159 Roman Catholics and 43 of other denominations.) Of 1497 Jewish women, 399 or 26.6% married non-Jewish men (287 Protestants, 82 Roman Catholics and 30 of other denominations.)

4—Those where one-third of Jewish marriages are mixed marriages (Denmark, Australia, Italy and the older Jewish communities in England and France and the United States). The general and inescapable conclusion at which Ruppin arrives is: "The more Jews and Christians mix with one another in economic and social life, the more likely is it that they will intermarry with one another[20] . . . The increasing spread of intermarriage is indeed not likely to be hindered by any race theories,[21] so long as the social differences between Christians and Jews are wiped out and the path to intermarriage made smooth."[22] In the face of this rapid process of disintegration it is not surprising that strong counter-currents against complete amalgamation should have been created within the Jewish group as such. Apart from the argument of inexpediency or impracticability of mixed marriages[23] (growing out of the incompatibility of traditional and cultural backgrounds in the family life) the more fundamental objection raised by many modern spokesmen of the Jewish people is that assimilation is a

This means an increase in the proportion of intermarriage of 283.8% for the men and of 250.9% for the women. What the causes of this unusual increase have been is difficult to conjecture. (For tables from which the figures above have been compiled see *Statistisches Jahrbuch für das Deutsche Reich,* 1913, p. 23, Table 5, and 1918, p. 7, Table 5.)

[20] Ruppin, op. cit., p. 170 and p. 171.

[21] Such as Dühring's notion that Jewish blood destroys the pure Aryan race and that there is a physiological antipathy between the Semite and the Aryan. Eugene Dühring, *Die Judenfrage als Frage der Rassenschädlichkeit.* Also Eduard von Hartmann, *Das Judenthum in Gegenwart and Zukunft,* pp. 6-8.

It is noteworthy that among the Jewish people arguments against intermarriage rarely, if ever, are of the biological variety. With them the problem has been and is still primarily one of the integrity of Jewish home life, and therefore of the social solidarity of the Jewish people.

[22] Ruppin, op. cit. p. 170 and p. 171.

[23] Fishberg's conclusion is: "Mixed marriages are thus three to four times more likely to be dissolved than pure marriages." Op. cit. p. 217.

constant menace to the integrity of the group. Only a strong nationalist movement looking ultimately to the establishment of a home-land in Palestine can save them from final disappearance. The growing Zionist movement which embodies this aspiration, draws its vigor as much from this deep-seated dread of extinction as it does from the romantic idealism of the re-birth of a dead nationality.[24]

For New York City, where one-half of the total Jewish population of the United States is concentrated, the intermarriage ratio, according to the data gathered for this study, is less than 2% (1.17). It varies, however, with the particular country of origin and consequently the degree of assimilation of the section of Jewry considered. Thus,[25] while among Rumanian Jews the proportion is .45% and among Russian Jews .62%, it rises to 4.26% among native born Jews of native parents; to 5.16% among German Jews and to 6.54% among French Jews. The English Jews, with 3.47% seem to hold the middle ground. In the smaller cities and rural districts the extent of intermarriage is far greater, although exact figures are not available.[26]

VI. MISCEGENATION AMONG NEGROES

Just as difference of religion explains adequately the low proportion of intermarriage betweens Jews and non-Jews, so difference of color accounts for the small proportion of fusion between negro and white. There can be no doubt that the amalgamation of the two races, especially in the

[24] The Balfour Declaration of November 2nd, 1917, favoring the establishment of a Jewish home-land in Palestine, has given the modern Zionist movement a concrete basis such as it has not had since its rise in the latter part of the 19th century.

[25] See Table IVa, p. 43.

[26] Fishberg quotes the estimate of the director of circuit preaching of the Central Conference of American Rabbis, as 5% in the northern parts of the United States and 20% to 50%, most probably 33% in the South. Fishberg, op. cit., pp. 203-204.

southern states, is going on, and that there is already a considerable mulatto population.[27] In the North, however, in spite of the absence of laws against miscegenation, the proportion seems to be negligible and perhaps also on the decline.[28] In New York City, for a period of five years (1908-1912) the ratio was 1.08%.

For colored men it was 1.78%, for colored women, .44%. In other words, the men intermarry about four times as frequently as the women.[29] As the question stands now, it is, in the opinion of an acknowledged negro leader, "of little practical importance. For, in practice, the matter works itself out; the average white person does not marry a negro, and the average negro, despite his theory, himself marries one of his race, and frowns darkly on his fellows unless they do likewise. In those very circles of negroes who have a large infusion of white blood, where the freedom of marriage is most strenuously advocated, white wives have always been treated with a disdain bordering on insult,

[27] F. Boas. *The Mind of Primitive Man,* Ch. X, Race Problems in the United States, pp. 275-276.

[28] Ray Stannard Baker, *Following the Color Line,* p. 172: "Altho the Negro population of Boston has been steadily increasing, the number of marriages between the races, which remained about stationary from 1875 to 1890, has since 1900 been rapidly decreasing. Here are the exact figures as given by the Registry Department:

Racial Intermarriages in Boston

Year	Groom Colored Bride White	Groom White Bride Colored	Total Mixed Marriages
1900	32	3	35
1901	30	1	31
1902	25	4	29
1903	27	2	29
1904	27	1	28
1905	17	2	19

For further evidence tending to show the decline in racial intermarriages, see Frederick L. Hoffman, *Race Traits and Tendencies of the American Negro,* pp. 198-200.

[29] See Statistical Appendix, Table V, opp. p. 100.

and white husbands never received on any terms of social recognition."[80]

VII. AMALGAMATION AMONG NORTHERN AND NORTHWESTERN EUROPEAN PEOPLES

It would be only reasonable to expect that among groups where barriers of religion and color are not marked, fusion would proceed rather rapidly. This expectation appears to be borne out by the fact that the highest proportion of intermarriage is found among the Northern, Northwestern and some of the Central European nationalities.[81] Here, except for the possible prejudice between Protestant and Catholic, no serious obstacles exist in the way of amalgamation.

Besides, the longer period of residence in the United States of these older immigrant groups has undoubtedly further predisposed them to the assimilating process.

But upon a closer examination of the figures, another and perhaps simpler explanation of the high proportion of intermarriage suggests itself.

Arranging the various nationalities in language groups, or what are broadly speaking cultural groups,[82] the Teutonic peoples were found to fuse most with Teutonic groups,

[80] W. E. B. Du Bois, *The Philadelphia Negro, A Social Study*, Publications of the University of Pennsylvania Series in Political Economy and Public Law, No. 14, p. 359.

[81] See Table IVa, pp. 43-45.

[82] For the scheme of classification of language groups used, see article in *National Geographic Magazine*, Dec., 1918, by Edwin H. Grosvenor, "The Races of Europe." The number of nationalities represented in the various language groups in this study was as follows: Teutonic, 12; Slavic, 6; Greco-Latin, 13; Celtic, 2; Finno-Ugrian, 2; Syro-Arabic, 2; Iranian, 2; Turkish, 1. There are also included two racial groups, black (Negro) and yellow, the latter represented by 2 groups, the Chinese and Japanese, while the former were represented by British West Indian, Canadian, Cuban and Dutch West Indian negroes.

apparently because there is a considerable assortment of Teutonic language groups present in the population. In other words, while the Northern and Northwestern European peoples show a high ratio of intermarriage, this occurs predominantly within the same language or cultural group. In practically every case where a Teutonic nationality intermarried with other groups, almost one-half of the number of nationalities intermarried with, was found to fall within the Teutonic group. This was clearly not so in the other language groups, apparently because there is a much smaller representation of similar language classes present in the population. Three general factors, then, might be cited in explanation of the relatively high degree of amalgamation of the Northern and Northwestern European immigrant: lack of racial and religious barriers, comparatively long period of settlement in the United States, and the presence of a fairly numerous variety of similar language or cultural groups in the population. Exactly what share is contributed to the production of the amalgamating process by each of these factors, is extremely difficult to calculate and because of incomplete data about the immigrant population hardly possible.

VIII. FUSION AMONG IRISH AND ITALIANS

With some modifications, the explanation for the Teutonic groups would hold for the Italians and the Irish, who occupy the middle position in the series. A shorter period of residence in America, together with a constant shifting, characteristic of much of the migratory Italian population, as also a somewhat lower social prestige among the immigrant groups, would go far to explain the low position of the Italians in the scale; while strong religious preferences among the Irish may have tended to keep their ratio of intermarriage lower than their period of residence and their traditional sociability would lead one to expect.

IX. INCREASE OF PROPORTION OF INTERMARRIAGE OF SECOND GENERATION OVER FIRST

Closely connected with the characteristic groupings of the nationalities according to ratio of intermarriage, are the further facts of the increase of proportion of intermarriage of the second generation over the first. The general statement is easily borne out that the lower the ratio of intermarriage in the first generation, the greater the ratio in the second and therefore the greater the relative increase.[33] If the nationalities are grouped according to proportions of increase, the Jews, who have the lowest ratio for the first generation are found in the higher increase groups, while the Northern, Northwestern and some of the Central European peoples fall into the lower increase groups. This holds also for the Italians and for the Irish.

For the Jews as a combined group, the ratio for the first generation is .64%, for the second generation, 4.51% —an increase of a little over 700% (704.6%). In other words, in the second generation, Jews intermarry about seven times as frequently as in the first. It must, however, be added that while the proportional increase is very great, the absolute number of intermarriages is comparatively insignificant.[34] Among Jewish men the increase is far greater than among Jewish women.[35] The country of origin too, indicating as it does, the stage of assimilation and the length of residence in the United States, produces differences in the proportion of intermarriage and in the increases. Thus, among Russian Jews, comparatively recent arrivals, the ratios are: .36% for the first generation (men, .26%; women, .47%); 3.40% for the second generation (men, 3.76%; women, 3.14)%. The average increase here is 944.4%. Among the German Jews, however, an older and

[33] See Statistical Appendix, Table VII, p. 208.

[34] See Statistical Appendix, Table V, opp. p. 100.

[35] Men: 1st generation, .50%; 2nd generation, 5.67%—increase of 1134%. Women: 1st generation, .78%; 2nd generation, 3.58%—increase of 458.9%.

more assimilated section of Jewry, the amalgamating process has already reached a higher level and therefore the break between the first and the second generation is much less marked. The figures here show that in the first generation the number of mixed marriages per 100 marriages is 3.74 (men, 8.85; women, 2.96). The increase of the second generation over the first, then, amounts to only 160.9% as compared with 944.4% among the Russian Jews.

For the Germans, Dutch, English, Canadians (English and French), Swiss, Welsh, Scotch, Danes, Norwegians, Swedes, Bohemians, Poles (Austrian and Russian), with a higher proportion of intermarriage, the percent of increase is between 100% and 300%.

For the Irish as a group, it is somewhat over 200% (233.7%), the men showing a higher increase than the women[36] because the proportion of intermarriage among them in the first generation is lower than among the women.

The Italians, standing midway between the Irish and the Jews, show increases of 300% to 700%,[37] the average increase for the group as a whole being 330.6%.

One reason why in the groups showing high proportions of intermarriage, the percentage of increase is lower than that for the low-proportioned groups, is undoubtedly the range within which the increase can take place. Where the ratio of intermarriage is high to begin with (*i. e.*, in the first generation) the range is already narrowed and the possible proportionate increase limited. Where the initial ratio of intermarriage is low, there is a much wider interval between it and the maximum point and therefore a wider range for any possible increase. The mere fact, however, of the wider range does not of itself produce the larger increase. It only makes increase *possible*, should forces be at work tending to create the increase. There

[36] Men: 1st generation, 9.61%; 2nd generation, 29.85%; increase of 310.6%. Women: 1st generation, 18.66%; 2nd generation, 38.31%; increase of 205.3%.

[37] See Statistical Appendix, Table V, opp. p. 100.

is thus an added significance in the striking rise in proportion of intermarriage in such groups as the Jews and the Italians. The forces of disruption among them are relatively more powerful than among the other groups where these forces have already accomplished much of their work. The suddenness and magnitude of the break between first and second generations are greater, and the corresponding strain upon group solidarity, with its accompaniment of a heightened group consciousness, more intense. If, in addition, it be remembered that the intermarriage index is only a *minimum index* of group disintegration, the full meaning of the large increase becomes vividly clear.

X. NUMBER OF NATIONALITIES INTERMARRIED WITH IN SECOND GENERATION

The process of fusion characterized thus far, naturally implies amalgamation with numerous distinct national groups. With a large increase in the proportion of intermarriage, such as is the distinguishing feature of the second generation, the simple deduction might be made that the number of nationalities with which each group intermarries in the second generation, would also correspondingly increase. This, however, is far from being the case. On the contrary, there is a definite reduction in the number of nationalities intermarried with. A curious process of narrowing down seems to take place. Whereas in the first generation the average number of distinct nationalities with which persons of a group intermarry is 12 (both for the men and for the women) this is cut in half for the second generation (6 for both men and women) as shown by the following table:

*TABLE VIII

NUMBER OF DISTINCT NATIONALITIES WITH WHICH PERSONS OF VARIOUS IMMIGRANT GROUPS INTERMARRIED

Nationalities Intermarrying	No. of Distinct Nationalities with which 1st Gen. Men Intermarried	No. of Distinct Nationalities with which 2nd Gen. Men Intermarried	No. of Distinct Nationalities with which 1st Gen. Women Intermarried	No. of Distinct Nationalities with which 2nd Gen. Women Intermarried
1. Armenia	8	1	0	0
2. Austria (Boh.)	6	7	20	9
3. Austria (Ger.)	21	9	24	12
4. Austria (Ital.)	6	0	3	0
5. Austria (Pol.)	12	9	23	13
6. Belgium	15	5	17	6
7. British W. I. (Colored)	5	0	1	0
8. British W. I. (English)	11	0	0	0
9. Canada (Col.)	1	0	0	0
10. Canada (Eng.)	18	17	17	18
11. Canada (Fr.)	9	8	8	7
12. China	7	1	0	0
13. Cuba (Col.)	1	0	1	0
14. Cuba (Span.)	12	5	10	5
15. Denmark	19	11	17	10
16. Dutch W. I. (Col.)	0	0	1	1
17. England	27	21	30	21
18. Finland	12	1	15	3
19. France	21	15	33	18
20. Germany (not located)	27	28	29	29
21. Germany (North)	22	6	24	9
22. Germany (South)	23	7	26	11
23. Greece	21	1	4	0
24. Holland	19	10	14	7
25. Hungary (Ger.)	13	2	13	4
26. Hungary (Hung.)	7	0	11	2
27. Hungary (Slovak)	11	4	32	11
28. Ireland	25	27	46	36
29. Italy (not located)	26	20	17	18
30. Italy (North	17	3	10	1
31. Italy (South)	22	3	12	3
32. Japan	12	0	0	0
33. Mexico (Span.)	9	1	0	0
34. Norway	16	9	22	10
35. Porto Rico (Span.)	14	1	5	0
36. Portugal	6	3	0	0
37. Roumania	4	0	0	0
38. Russia (Pol.)	12	5	13	5
39. Serbia	5	0	0	0
40. Scotland	20	13	23	17
41. Spain	18	6	13	5
42. Sweden	19	12	30	13
43. Switzerland (Ger.)	18	11	25	12
44. Switzerland (Fr.)	7	0	8	2
45. Switzerland (Ital.)	3	1	3	0
46. Syria	4	0	3	0
47. Turkey	14	2	2	0
48. Wales	8	3	5	7
49. Austria (Jew)	9	6	10	7
50. England (Jew)	3	2	3	2
51. France (Jew)	0	4	1	0
52. Germany (Jew)	9	13	5	6
53. Holland (Jew)	2	2	0	0
54. Hungary (Jew)	9	4	20	5
55. Roumania (Jew)	3	0	2	2
56. Russia (Jew)	18	9	10	13
57. Turkey (Jew)	2	0	1	0
Average No. of Nationalities Intermarried with.	12	6	12	6

*Tables IVb-IVi, V, VI, VII, will be found in Statistical Appendix, pp. 93 to 200. Only Tables I, II, III, IVa, VIII, IX, X, XI, XII have been inserted into the body of the text for purposes of more convenient reference in following the argument at various successive points.

XI. APPARENT CHOICE OF NATIONALITIES IN SECOND GENERATION

If now the question be raised which nationalities it is that are thus apparently selected or preferred in intermarriage, the inquiry reveals that it is primarily the Northern and Northwestern European peoples. Of the thirteen nationalities selected most often, nine are Northern and Northwestern European groups. Whether or not this selection had the character of conscious choice is extremely difficult to determine.

The inclusion in the list of Germans, Irish, Italians and Jews, suggests that since these peoples are the most numerous in the population of New York City, it was perhaps the presence in larger numbers of representatives of the selected nationalities that mainly determined the frequency of the choice.[88] If to these four groups be added the other nationalities selected, the preferred groups together are found to have been almost 60% of the total population of the city.[89] But it would be hazardous to try to apportion an exact share of influence to this factor of population because no reliable data on the proportion of marriageable persons of both sexes in these individual groups are available. Thus the important question as to whether this apparent selection of a smaller number of nationalities with which to intermarry is due to genuine, conscious preference or is rather an enforced choice, must remain unanswered for the present. However, it is not an unreasonable hypothesis to state that in addition to the population factor, the higher social prestige of the Anglo-Saxon groups, due to longer residence and economic stability may also to a certain extent, have been an attractive force determining

[88] These four nationalities and their native born descendants constituted 50.8% of the total population of N. Y. City in 1910 (2,422,418 out of 4,766,883).

[89] 57.1% (2,722,547 out of 4,766,883). This excludes the Austrian Poles for whom no separate figures are given.

choice. Whatever the full explanation, the fact remains that persons of the second generation who intermarry, marry into a narrower circle of national groups than those of the first generation, that this circle is predominantly North-European and that it is this group of nationalities that is being diluted more than any other.

TABLE IX

NATIONALITIES SELECTED IN INTERMARRIAGE BY PERSONS OF THE SECOND GENERATION (NBFP)

(This table is based upon selections made by men of 36 different nationalities and women of 29 different nationalities)

*Nationalities most often selected

Nationality Selected	Number of times selected nationality occurs in intermarriages of persons of the second generation: Men of 36 nationalities selecting Women of a different group	Women of 29 nationalities selecting Men of a different group
Germany	Selected by Men of 26* out of 36 nationalities	Selected by Women of 26* out of 29 nationalities
Ireland	" " " 26* " " "	" " " 25* " " "
England	" " " 18* " " "	" " " 20* " " "
Austria (Pol.)	" " " 16* " " "	" " " 10* " " "
Scotland	" " " 16* " " "	" " " 17* " " "
France	" " " 14* " " "	" " " 14* " " "
Italy	" " " 14* " " "	" " " 20* " " "
Canada (Engl.)	" " " 13* " " "	" " " 11* " " "
Sweden	" " " 12* " " "	" " " 13* " " "
Denmark	" " " 11* " " "	" " " 9* " " "
Jewish	" " " 11* " " "	" " " 15* " " "
Norway	" " " 11* " " "	" " " 8 " " "
Austria (Ger.)	" " " 9 " " "	" " " 7 " " "
Switzerland (Ger.)	" " " 9 " " "	" " " 3 " " "
Holland	" " " 8 " " "	" " " 10* " " "
Hungary (Slovak)	" " " 8 " " "	" " " 6 " " "
Canada (Fr.)	" " " 7 " " "	" " " 7 " " "
Finland	" " " 7 " " "	" " " 4 " " "
Austria (Boh.)	" " " 6 " " "	" " " 7 " " "
Cuba (Span.)	" " " 6 " " "	" " " 4 " " "
U. S. (Col.)	" " " 6 " " "	" " " 6 " " "
Belgium	" " " 5 " " "	" " " 5 " " "
Russia (Pol.)	" " " 5 " " "	" " " 7 " " "
Hungary (Ger.)	" " " 4 " " "	" " " 3 " " "
Hungary (Hung.)	" " " 4 " " "	" " " 1 " " "
Wales	" " " 4 " " "	" " " 3 " " "
Portugal	" " " 3 " " "	" " " 2 " " "
Spain	" " " 3 " " "	" " " 6 " " "
B. W. I. (Col.)	" " " 2 " " "	" " " – " " "
Switzerland (Fr.)	" " " 2 " " "	" " " 1 " " "
Argentine	" " " 1 " " "	" " " – " " "
B. W. I. (Engl.)	" " " 1 " " "	" " " 6 " " "
Chile	" " " 1 " " "	" " " – " " "
United States	" " " 1 " " "	" " " 1 " " "
Greece	–	" " " 9 " " "
Porto Rico (Span.)	–	" " " 5 " " "
Armenia	–	" " " 3 " " "
Japan	–	" " " 3 " " "
China	–	" " " 2 " " "
Mexico (Span.)	–	" " " 2 " " "
Switzerland	–	" " " 2 " " "
Turkey	–	" " " 2 " " "
Australia (Engl.)	–	" " " 1 " " "
India	–	" " " 1 " " "
Peru	–	" " " 1 " " "
Roumania	–	" " " 1 " " "
Serbia	–	" " " 1 " " "
Syria	1	" " " 1 " " "

XII. OCCUPATION AND INTERMARRIAGE

Upon two other problems do the facts recorded in the marriage certificates throw some light. The question may be asked: Under what economic and social conditions is the amalgamation proceeding? Are these conditions, on the whole, favorable or unfavorable? Closely related to this is the second question: On what cultural levels do the intermarriages take place? Is it the intellectuals that fuse most often, or is it the untutored? Or is it both, as is frequently asserted from general observation; or do the facts reveal the opposite state of affairs?

The answers cannot be brought out by direct evidence, except by the indirect testimony gathered from the occupations of the persons intermarrying. Considering persons employed in professional service, in commerce, in manufacturing and in mechanical pursuits as belonging to the higher economic classes,[40] it is found that over two-thirds of the intermarriages among men (67.3%) and a little less than 60% (59.2%) among women fall within these groups. The economic plane, then, upon which the fusion is taking place is rather high.

[40] For a classification of occupations into economic groups, see Table XII, p. 65, and note 10, p. 39.

[41] The total number of intermarriages upon which this table and Tables XI and XII are based is only 3698, because out of the total number of intermarriages studied (10,835) only 3698 marriage certificates recorded the occupation of *both bride and groom*. There were 3400 additional records where the occupation of the *groom alone* was given. These figures were utilized as supplementary data (See Table XIII). Thus, there were 7098 marriage certificates out of 10,835 in which the occupation of both bride and groom, or of groom alone was recorded, and 3737 certificates in which the description of the occupation was so indefinite that the item had to be omitted.

TABLE X
PROPORTION OF INTERMARRIAGE ACCORDING TO OCCUPATION GROUPS [41]
1908-1912

OCCUPATION GROUP	MEN		WOMEN																	
	Total No. of Intermarriages	% of Grand Total	Professional Service	% of Total No. of Intermarriages	Commerce and Trade	% of Total No. of Intermarriages	Manufacturing and Mechanical Pursuits	% of Total No. of Intermarriages	Personal Domestic Service	% of Total No. of Intermarriages	Public Service (lower grades)	% of Total No. of Intermarriages	Agriculture (including Horticulture)	% of Total No. of Intermarriages	Transportation	% of Total No. of Intermarriages	Navigation	% of Total No. of Intermarriages	Unskilled	% of Total No. of Intermarriages
Professional service	350	9.5	146	41.7	55	15.7	72	20.6	74	21.1	....	....	....	....	....	....	....	....	3	.9
Commerce and trade	777	21.0	88	11.3	236	30.4	229	29.5	210	27.0	....	....	....	....	....	....	....	....	14	1.8
Manufacturing and mechanical pursuits	1362	36.8	85	6.3	229	16.8	514	37.7	498	36.6	....	....	....	....	....	....	....	....	36	2.6
Personal and domestic service	491	13.3	27	5.5	51	10.4	115	23.4	281	57.2	....	....	....	....	....	....	....	....	17	3.5
Public service (lower grades)	128	3.5	3	2.4	26	20.3	41	32.1	54	42.1	....	....	....	....	....	....	....	....	4	3.1
Agriculture (incl. horticulture)	64	1.7	6	9.4	4	6.3	7	10.9	47	73.4	....	....	....	....	....	....	....	....	....	....
Transportation	40	1.1	4	10.	9	22.5	13	32.5	14	35.	....	....	....	....	....	....	....	....	....	....
Navigation	40	1.1	4	10.	4	10.	14	35.	17	42.5	....	....	....	....	....	....	....	....	1	2.5
Unskilled	446	12.0	19	4.2	66	14.8	124	27.8	193	43.3	....	....	....	....	....	....	....	....	44	9.8
Grand Total	**3698**	....	**382**	....	**680**	....	**1129**	....	**1388**	....	....	....	....	....	....	....	....	....	**119**	....
Per Cent. of Grand Total	**100.0**	....	**10.3**	....	**18.4**	....	**30.5**	....	**37.6**	....	....	....	....	....	....	....	....	....	**3.2**	....

XIII. CULTURE LEVEL AND INTERMARRIAGE

Turning to the second question: if by "culture" is meant something practically synonymous with "education" and particularly education in the broad subjects of literature, the arts and the natural and social sciences, then it is possible on the basis of occupation to classify the intermarrying persons broadly according to "culture groups". The highest "culture group" would then be represented by persons in professional service, the lowest by those in unskilled work. Persons in commerce and trade, manufacturing and mechanical pursuits and personal and domestic service would constitute the middle or mediocre "culture group". Below this group (though here some exception might be taken) would be those in the lower grades of public service, agriculture, transportation and navigation.[42] The assumption underlying such a classification is that the lower the income, the lower the "culture level", because the less has been the opportunity to acquire a broad education. At the same time, it must be clearly understood that lack of "culture" in this sense does not, of course, imply lack of native capacity. The two may, and often do, exist entirely independently of each other.

Looked at in this light the striking fact emerges that the large majority of intermarrying persons come from neither the highest nor the lowest "culture groups". It is rather on the level of the mediocre cultural plane that the greatest amount of amalgamation is to be found. Of nearly 3,700 who intermarried, 9.5% were in professional service, the highest "culture group"; 12% were unskilled workers, the lowest "culture group". Those in commerce and trade, manufacturing and mechanical pursuits, and personal and domestic service together made up 71.1% of the total number of intermarriages. In other words, almost three-fourths of the mixed marriages were in the mediocre culture groups. For the women this holds even more clearly. In

[42] See Table XII, p. 65.

the highest group the proportion was 10.3%, in the lowest 3.2%, in the middle groups 86.5%.

It may be presumed that in the higher group it is a high degree of cultural self-consciousness that prevents fusion, in the lower group it is strong prejudices. In the middle groups where neither one nor the other is pronounced, and where constant contact in daily work levels differences, the amalgamation proceeds most easily and most rapidly.

TABLE XI

PROPORTION OF INTERMARRIAGE ACCORDING TO OCCUPATION AND CULTURE LEVEL

MEN				WOMEN								
				CULTURE LEVEL								
				High	Mediocre			Low				Very Low
Culture Level	Occupation Group	Total No. of Intermarriages	% of grand total	Professional Service	Commerce & Trade	Mfg. & Mechanical Pursuits	Personal & Domestic Service	Public Service	Agriculture (including Horticulture)	Transportation	Naviagation	Unskilled
High	Professional service	350	9.5	116	55	72	74	....	....	....	....	3
Medi-ocre	Commerce and trade	777	21.0	88	236	229	210	....	....	....	....	14
	Manufacturing and mechanical pursuits	1362	36.8	85	229	514	498	....	....	....	....	36
	Personal and domestic service	491	13.3	27	51	115	281	....	....	....	....	17
Low	Public service (lower grades)	128	3.5	3	26	41	54	....	....	....	....	4
	Agriculture (including horticulture)	64	1.7	6	4	7	47	....	....	....	....	....
	Transportation	40	1.1	4	9	13	14	....	....	....	....	....
	Navigation	40	1.1	4	4	14	17	....	....	....	....	1
Very low	Unskilled	446	12.0	19	66	124	193	....	....	....	....	44
	Grand Total	**3698**	....	**382**	**680**	**1129**	**1388**	....	....	....	....	**119**
	Per Cent. of Grand Total	....	100.	10.3	18.4	30.5	37.6	....	....	....	....	3.2

TABLE XII
PROPORTION OF INTERMARRIAGE ACCORDING TO OCCUPATION AND GENERATION

OCCUPATION GROUP	Total No. of Intermarriages		1st GENERATION (FB FP)				2nd GENERATION (NB FP)				3rd GENERATION (NB NP) (% of Grand Total not computed, as 3rd generation figures include only Jews and Negroes and other NB NP who intermarried with them, and are therefore not comparable with figures for 1st and 2nd generations.)	
	Men	Women	Men	% Grand Total	Women	% Grand Total	Men	% Grand Total	Women	% Grand Total	Men	Women
Professional service	350	382	198	9.4	226	11.3	148	9.4	151	9.3	4	5
Commerce and trade	777	680	381	18.1	169	8.4	395	25.1	503	30.3	1	8
Manufacturing and mechanical pursuits	1362	1126	760	36.1	518	25.7	596	37.9	601	36.1	6	7
Personal and domestic service	491	1388	419	19.9	1061	52.7	71	4.5	324	19.4	1	2
Public service (lower grades)	128	....	61	2.9	....	....	67	4.3	....	....	..	..
Agriculture	64	....	52	2.5	....	....	12	.8	....	....	..	..
Transportation	40	....	23	1.0	....	....	17	1.1	....	....	..	..
Navigation	40	....	30	1.4	....	....	10	.6	....	....	..	..
Unskilled	446	123	184	8.7	40	1.9	256	16.3	83	4.9	6	..
Grand Total	**3698**	**3698**	**2108**	**100.0**	**2014**	**100.0**	**1572**	**100.0**	**1662**	**100.0**	**18**	**22**

XIV. SUMMARY OF SIGNIFICANT FACTS

The significant facts found in the course of the analysis can now be summarized as follows:

(1) The ratio of intermarriage for men and women of all nationalities, as a group, is about 14, (13.59) out of every 100 marriages, (10,835 intermarriages out of 79,704 marriages.)

(2) There is a strong tendency for intermarriages to occur within identical generations.[43] The first generation tends to intermarry with the first, the second generation with the second.

(3) The proportion of intermarriage between persons of different generations decreases as the interval between the generations increases. Thus, intermarriages are more frequent between *men* of the *first* generation and *women* of the *first* generation, than between *men* of the first generation and *women* of the *second* generation. This is true also of intermarriage between *men* of the *second* generation and *women* of the *second* generation, as compared with intermarriages between *men* of the *second* generation and *women* of the *first* generation.

(4) In the second generation, both men and women, each considered as a group, irrespective of national descent, intermarry approximately three times as often as men and women of the first generation. In other words, the increase in proportion of intermarriage of the second generation over the first is about 300%.

(5) The ratio of intermarriage for women is slightly lower than that for men.

(6) There are three main forces at work in each group tending to produce amalgamation with other groups: preponderance of marriageable men over marriageable women, rise in economic status, and diminution in the intensity of the group consciousness or in the attitude of group solidari-

[43] For definition of the term "generation" see Chapter II, p. 16, Note 3.

ty. In the first generation, the first of these factors is most effective; in the second generation, the last plays the most important rôle. The factor of economic status remains about constant between the other two.

(7) With regard to the ratio of intermarriage, the various nationalities range themselves in an ascending scale. Of the most important groups represented, the Jews and the Negroes are lowest, the Italians are next, the Irish are higher than the Italians, and the Northern, North Western and some Central European peoples are highest.

(8) Distinctions of religion and of color respectively, account for the low proportion of intermarriage among Jews and Negroes. Lack of these barriers and the presence of a numerous variety of similar cultural groups in the population accelerate the fusion of the Northern and North Western European peoples. A shifting population and a somewhat lower social prestige prevent the Italian from rising higher in the scale as yet. Strong religious preferences tend to limit the range of intermarriage among the Irish who otherwise might be higher in the scale.

(9) The lower the ratio of intermarriage in the first generation, the greater the tendency for the ratio to be high in the second generation, and consequently the greater the tendency for the proportion of increase to be high. For the lowest group, the Jews, the increase is a little over 700%; for the middle groups, the Italians and the Irish, it is somewhat over 300% and somewhat over 200% respectively; for the Northern, North-Western and some Central European peoples it is from 100% to 300%.

(10) While in the second generation there is a striking increase in the proportion of intermarriage, there is a correspondingly striking decrease in the number of nationalities with which individuals of the second generation intermarry. The average number of nationalities for the first generation (for both men and women) is 12; for the second generation (for both men and women) it is 6.

(11) The apparent process of selection in the second

generation results in the choice of a group of nationalities predominantly Northern and Northwestern European. This choice may be determined primarily by the preponderance of Teutonic population elements or by a combination of this with the factor of higher social prestige and economic stability of these groups.

(12) More than two-thirds of the intermarriages among men and over 60% among women take place in the higher economic classes.

(13) The largest proportion of the intermarriages takes place among persons on the middle or mediocre culture plane rather than on the high or low cultural level. Thus, three-fourths of the men who intermarry are found in the occupation groups corresponding to the middle level, namely in commerce and trade, in manufacturing and mechanical pursuits and in personal and domestic service, while only about 10% are professional men and about 12% unskilled workers. The same is true of the women who intermarry, almost 87% of them being found in the middle occupation and culture groups.

XV. FURTHER SUGGESTED USES OF DERIVED TABLES AND ORIGINAL DATA

The statistical tables which form the basis of the discussion in Chapter III are of two kinds: derived tables[44] and tables containing the original data.[45] But since no effort has been made to present an exhaustive analysis, neither the derived tables nor the original data have been fully utilized, though this is far less the case with the former than with the latter. Thus, for example, from Tables (IVa—IVi) only five ethnic groups were selected for discussion,[46] whereas the remaining 24 ethnic groups could

[44] See Tables I-V inclusive, VII, VIII, IX-XIII inclusive. Chapter II, pp. 23-25.

[45] See Table VI, Series 1-91 and Series 1-88; Statistical Appendix, pp. 101-207.

[46] For the reasons directing the choice, see Chapter III, p. 46.

also be considered, one by one, were the requisite information upon each one at hand. Similarly, the detailed explanation of why in one ethnic group the proportion of increase in intermarriage for the second generation is greater or less than the proportion of increase in another ethnic group, was omitted, owing to the lack of certain basic population figures. Only the *general trend* was noted, based upon the consideration of the mass figures.

A similar explanation holds of the use of the original data. Aside from the obvious necessity of presenting in a scientific work the original figures from which the working tables are derived (since the original figures may possibly be recombined by other students in ways different from those of the present author, and thus yield new results) the series of tables referred to are of value because

1) They indicate for each ethnic group separately the number of intermarriages according to generations, the nationalities with which the persons intermarried, the nationalities with which they intermarried most often and the nationalities with which they failed to intermarry. Before any further detailed studies of particular ethnic groups can be undertaken, such figures as those presented in these tables are indispensable as a beginning.

2) They furnish the data for a comparison between linguistic or culture groups and may possibly be used to indicate the general trend of amalgamation within broad racial groups such as the Baltic, Mediterranean and Alpine racial subvarieties in the United States.

3) They lay the basis for comparative studies over larger or shorter periods of time.

Finally, the data for New York City presented thus far and the type of discussion followed, may serve as a guide for similar studies for other large cities, for smaller towns and for rural districts, for which intermarriage statistics have not yet been compiled. This monograph suggests what kinds of facts are to be gathered to obtain significant results, what are the statistical forms into which the facts can be thrown to yield such results, and what are the possible hypotheses that can be framed to explain the facts.

Results obtained for other centres of population can be profitably compared with those for New York City and thus the basis can be laid for generalizations and possibly also forecasts as to the process of amalgamation in the United States.

CHAPTER IV.

INTERPRETATIONS: THE BEARING OF THE RESULTS UPON PUBLIC POLICIES OF ASSIMILATION

I. NEED FOR SEPARATING SCIENTIFIC EXPLANATIONS OF FACTS FROM THEIR ETHICAL EVALUATION

The chief aim in the preceding pages has been to make clear the method and scope of this study, to indicate its limitations and to present objectively the significant facts and the probable explanations of these facts. The attempt was consciously made to exclude interpretations or ethical evaluations, for in the case of scientific explanation there can be only one aim, namely the discovery of the true causal relations between the phenomena studied, while in the case of the ethical evaluation of the facts the aim may differ with the ideal of progress set up as the final goal.

Inasmuch, however, as the original purpose of this study was to gain facts that could be used for guidance in the framing of public policies of assimilation, it seems desirable to indicate the larger bearings of the data even though strictly speaking, it does not fall within the province of this study to do so.

The facts enumerated here show one thing almost conclusively. Amalgamation of the European peoples in the United States is going on, and gathering momentum on the way. But while the facts themselves may be incontrovertible, their meaning may vary with the point of view adopted for their interpretation.

II. THE IDEAL OF ETHNIC PURITY

To the *advocate of ethnic purity*[1] the facts may point to a fatal "mongrelization" of the American people proceeding at a dangerously rapid pace. According to this view, an intermarriage ratio of 14 per 100 (and probably much higher in the smaller communities and rural sections), with a range of increase in the second generation of from 100% to 1000%, the rapid dilution particularly of the North European stocks, the disproportionate fusion in the middle economic groups, producing a drab cultural product, are facts to be viewed with grave concern by the American people.

When carried to a logical limit this point of view must result in a complete restriction of immigration on the one hand, and in the deliberate intensification of group consciousness among immigrant peoples on the other. The aim of the first policy would be to cut off the inflow of all additional ethnic groups that must needs be fused with those already here. The second policy would be expected to reduce materially the present rate of amalgamation, and tend to hold it down to a minimum.

III. THE IDEAL OF RAPID AND THOROUGH ETHNIC AMALGAMATION

But while there is no specific evidence as yet to disprove

[1] For expressions of this view see among others, E. A. Ross, *The Old World in the New;* "Racial Consequences of Immigration," *Century Magazine,* Dec., 1913, Vol. 87; "Significance of Immigration," *The American Economic Review Supplement,* Vol. II, No. 1, March, 1912, p. 37; Chas. B. Davenport, *Heredity in Relation to Eugenics,* Ch. V, Migrations and their Eugenic Significance, pp. 212-220; Edwin G. Conklin, *Heredity and Environment,* pp. 434-435; "The Effect of Race Intermingling" *Proceedings of the American Philosophical Association,* Nov. 4, 1917; Chas. E. Woodruff, *Expansion of Races,* p. 389, and p. 390; Paul Popenoe and R. H. Johnson, *Applied Eugenics,* Ch. XV, p. 304; A. Alleman, "Immigration and the Future American Race," *Popular Science Monthly,* Vol. 75, p. 592.

the harmful effects of intermarriage among the various divergent varieties of the European peoples in America, it appears reasonably certain, judging from general biologic principles and from results in analagous historical processes, that such amalgamation is not only not harmful but may even be highly desirable[2]. At any rate, the danger of "mongrelization" is remote, especially as the fusion is taking place under rather favorable economic and social conditions. Building upon such premises as these the *ideal of ethnic homogeneity* and *consequent thorough social assimilation,* achieved through a rapid and thorough mixture of the immigrant peoples, may be opposed to that of ethnic isolation. If now the facts are interpreted from this point of view, the *advocate of ethnic amalgamation* finds much encouragement but also much that remains to be achieved. For, his argument may shape itself thus: An intermarriage ratio of 14 per 100 in a city like New York is rather high, but in view of the ever-present tendency towards the formation of self sufficient immigrant

[2] For expressions of pertinent views, see, for example, Th. Waitz, *Anthropologie der Naturvölker,* Vol. I, pp. 422-24; F. H. Giddings, *Principles of Sociology,* p. 324, 325; "The American People," *The International Quarterly,* June, 1903, Vol. VII, p. 291; G. E. Smith, "The Influence of Racial Admixture in Egypt," *The Eugenics Review,* Vol. 7, 1915-1916, pp. 163-183; U. G. Weatherly, "Race and Marriage," *American Journal of Sociology,* Vol. XV, pp. 433-53, Jan., 1910; Papers on "The Effects of Racial Miscegenation" by Earl Finch, and on "Anthropological View of Race," by Felix von Luschan, in *Papers on Interracial Problems communicated to the First Universal Races Congress at London, July,* 1911, edited by Gustav Spiller; Ignaz Zollschan, *Das Rassen-Problem,* 5. Abschnitt, Die Folgen von Inzucht und Rassenmischung; Hans Fehlinger, "Kreuzungen beim Menschen," *Archiv für Rassen und Gesellschaftsbiologie,* 1911, pp. 447-457; Wm. Z. Ripley, "The European Population of the United States," Huxley Memorial Lecture for 1908. *Journal of the Royal Anthropological Institute,* Vol. XXXVIII, 1908. Race Progress and Immigration, *Annals of the American Academy of Political and Social Science,* Vol. XXXIV, July-Dec., 1909, p. 135; Franz Boas, *The Mind of Primitive Man,* p. 260; Jerome Dowd, "The Racial Element in Social Assimilation," *American Journal of Sociology,* Vol. 16, p. 633.

colonies, it is not by any means high enough. True, there is an increase of approximately 300% in intermarriage among the second generation, and a broad range of increase up to 1000%. But it would be preferable to have a fairly high *uniform* rate of fusion, rather than some nationalities with a *low* index of intermarriage at one end of the scale and some with a *high* index at the other end, as is the case at present. The children of the immigrants must amalgamate even faster than they are doing now, if a homogeneous American people is to be created within the shortest possible period of time. Moreover, he may continue, while fusion among the various nationalities is indeed going on, it is nevertheless very largely within identical generations. First generation mixes with first and second generation with second. There is a tendency to fix certain general habits of life reminiscent of the old world rather than of the new. Should immigration continue, this tendency would be further aggravated. A thorough-going fusion would involve a much more frequent crossing of the generation lines than is indicated by the figures, and would thus facilitate further the process of assimilation of the foreign-born and the native-born. This applies with equal force to the number of nationalities with which persons of each group intermarry. Instead of reduction of the number in the second generation, as appears to be the case now, there should be even a greater dispersion or at least the same scattering of intermarriage among various groups as there is in the first generation. Furthermore, he may argue, while it is reassuring to discover that it is in the higher economic groups that two-thirds of the intermarriages occur, the aim must be to raise this proportion to even a higher level in order to safeguard absolutely the process of amalgamation as far as its economic and social setting is concerned. And finally, as to the fact that it is the mediocre culture groups which show the largest proportion of intermarriage rather than the highest and the lowest groups, it may be asserted that from the point of view of the *thorough-*

going miscegenationist it makes comparatively little difference what the relative proportions are. The supreme aim is to produce a perfect blend of ethnic stocks. Cultural contributions, being primarily dependent on native capacity for culture-building, will result naturally from a virile and versatile mixed people. Even if in the rapid process of fusion the cultural achievements of the mixing peoples should be largely discarded, and there should result a temporary general lowering of the culture level of the new stock, the loss would surely be made up by leaps and bounds once the homogeneous nation has settled down to a unified national life.

Now, how is this process of amalgamation to be consciously accelerated? Here, too, the advocate of rapid and complete fusion may point out, the facts themselves suggest the methods that would logically have to be employed. Three forces, it was found, were at work, mainly responsible for the intermingling of men and women of various ethnic groups: preponderance of marriageable men over women, rise in economic status and a diminution of the intensity of group consciousness. Whatever strengthens these forces also hastens the process of fusion. The first factor finds its freest field of operation in the first generation, the last operates most effectively in the second generation. It is not inconceivable that through conscious social control each of these forces could be so manipulated as to be raised indefinitely in its potency. Through a preferential treatment of single male immigrants, a wider and wider disparity might be created between the number of marriageable men and the number of marriageable women among persons of the first generation. This would act as an indirect compulsion upon both men and women to intermarry, as indeed it already does, although to a much smaller extent under the present conditions. The factor of economic status is even more amenable to control. Every step taken in advancing the living and working conditions of the masses of immigrants, along with that of the native-born tends to augment their mobility, to create wider and wider contacts and thus to increase the probability of more frequent fusion among the various nationalities.

But while the possibility of controlling the first factor (disparity of sex ratios among the marriageable) may be somewhat illusory and its advisability open to serious doubt, and while the control of the second factor (rise in economic status) for the specific purpose of accelerating ethnic fusion may be somewhat irrelevant, the conscious accentuation of the third and apparently most powerful factor, (decrease of intensity of group consciousness) is not only more feasible, but will in the long run produce the desired effect with unerring certainty. One need only examine carefully, so the argument may run, the forces that tend to sap the spirit of group solidarity among the immigrant peoples to see how easily the task might be accomplished.[3] Encourage dispersion of the foreign-born populations within the individual communities and throughout the land, discourage on the part of the younger generation especially, affiliation with specifically immigrant communal activities, frown upon educational and cultural undertakings calculated to impart to the younger generation a knowledge and an appreciation of the cultural heritage of the immigrant group, condemn nationalistic leaders who persistently stir up in the immigrant the remembrances and the passions of a life left behind, treat with fine scorn the vain attempts of the intellectuals to formulate theories of "adjustment" to American life; above all, foster in school, in civic life and in international relations a positive ideal of national unity, national homogeneity, singleness of political as well as cultural allegiance—do all this, so argues the ethnic fusionist, do it steadily and systematically, and in two generations, at the most in three, the polyglot American people will be a mere memory and a fully blended, unified nation an accomplished fact.

[3] See Chapter III, p. 41.

IV. THE IDEAL OF GRADUAL AMALGAMATION

To this reading of the facts still another may be opposed, taking as its *basic premise* that *too sudden and too great* a *rupture* of *ethnic bonds* is *not only undesirable* but *may turn out* to *be dangerous*. Were there involved in intermarriage nothing but the stark fact of biologic fusion of individuals of not very dissimilar ethnic varieties, there might perhaps be no serious consequences, even if the process went ahead on a large scale and with increasing rapidity. Much more, however, is involved. Intermarriage, it may be urged, is equally a sociological fact. It is a blending of different cultures, through the medium of specific representatives of these cultures. In the newly created home life two civilizations in miniature are contending for supremacy. On the one hand, the more dissimilar are the attitudes, the outlooks, the habits of the mating persons, the more difficult will it be to create a harmonious composite.[4] On the other hand, the more colorless, the more de-vitalized the cultural equipment of either husband or wife or both, the surer will the new family life be characterized by lack of color, lack of insight into and appreciation of the culture values inherent in the ethnic backgrounds of the parties to the marriage. Violent transitions in mental and social life, then, are to be

[4] See for example Fishberg's conclusion that mixed marriages between Jews and non-Jews are three to four times more likely to be dissolved than pure marriages. Maurice Fishberg, *The Jews*, p. 217. Also Karl Walcker, *Grundriss der Statistik*, p. 138, quoted by Hoffman in *Race Traits and Tendencies of the American Negro*: "It has been found that the number of children to a marriage was 4.35 where both persons were of the same religion (Christian) but only 1.58 where the father was Christian and the mother was a Jewess. When both were Jews the number of births to a marriage was 4.21 but only 1.78 where the father was evangelized, and 1.66 where the father was a Catholic," p. 192. Walcker believes that the barriers which make marriage of Jews and Christians less fruitful are psychological rather than physiological. For a statement of the general underlying principle, see Edward Westermark, *The History of Human Marriage*, Ch. XIII, The Law of Similarity, pp. 278-289.

avoided as much as possible. The passage from one phase to another, must be relatively smooth to avoid the deteriorating effects of the shock that must come to the nervous system and to the complex social organism.[5]

One who interprets the facts in the light of these principles, feels considerable apprehension in reviewing them. According to his view, the striking increase in the proportion of intermarriage in the second generation, far from being a cause for rejoicing, should make one pause and ask if not more is lost than gained by the sudden snapping of group bonds which this indicates. For, it must be repeated, the intermarriage ratio marks only the *lower limit* of group disruption, so to speak, and as a rule the higher the intermarriage ratio, the more extensive the breaking away from the group life in all its phases. The adherent of gradual amalgamation would observe further, that in spite of the powerful centrifugal forces operating within the groups there are counteracting centripetal tendencies present. This is shown by the occurrence of intermarriages to a large extent within identical generations, and also by the fact that the proportion of mixed marriages between persons of different generations decreases as the interval between the generations increases. Rather than decrying this tendency as leading towards a fixation of types instead of making for thoroughgoing amalgamation, it should be looked upon as a wholesome brake upon too precipitate a process, thus providing in a small measure the more gradual transition from one generation to another, which is so greatly needed. Homogeneity achieved more slowly in this fashion will be more genuine and more permanent than the apparent unification resulting from too quick a fusion.

One who holds this point of view may go further and say: That there is an irresistible impulse making for eth-

[5] For an analysis of neurotic symptoms growing out of the intense mental conflict due to violent transitions from one type of thought-life to another, radically different type, see the instructive case cited in A. A. Brill's *Psychanalysis*, p. 102, Second Edition.

nic amalgamation can hardly be doubted in the face of the facts as a whole. Now since this amalgamation is probably inevitable and will proceed at a cumulative speed, there ought to be some effort to save as much as possible from the wreckage that results from the collapse of the cultural heritages of the fusing groups. This is all the more urgent since the mixture is going on primarily in the mediocre culture groups. Here there is neither the cultural equipment nor a keen enough self-consciousness to produce the desire to transmit to the rising generation culture values worth while conserving and incorporating into American life. While the biologic products of the union will in all probability be of virile stock, the cultural atmosphere into which the new generation is born will be nondescript. The result will be not so much a deterioration of cultural life, for, where there is little or none of it, it is hardly accurate to speak of deterioration. The result will rather be that at the critical moment in the life of the growing second generation there will be nothing to offer it but a drab outlook upon life. But what is far more to be regretted, the unique opportunity that America has of utilizing the rich cultural heritages of the immigrant groups and weaving them into the texture of its growing civilization,—an opportunity such as no other nation ever was offered under the same circumstances—will inevitably be lost. To be consoled by the thought that the new versatile nation resulting from the fusion of many peoples will soon replace, by the potency of its own genius, what may have been discarded or neglected or deliberately ignored in the culture of the immigrant groups, is very much like justifying the barbarities the invading Germanic tribes committed upon the civilization of ancient Rome, on the basis that they ruthlessly cleared the ground for the creation of a newer and more virile culture, irrespective of the high achievements already recorded in the Greco-Roman world. That a thousand years later the more civilized descendants of these empire wreckers should rediscover the ruined remnants of a glorious past and cherish them as long-lost treasures is ample proof of the original sin and madness of the fathers.

And finally, he may argue, this faith in the spontaneous creation of a new culture lacks a firm scientific basis, as it is grounded in an erroneous view of the nature of progress. Uncontrolled, unguided social movements tend to level down, whereas the essence of progress is conscious, deliberate selection and accentuation of those social forces that tend in the direction of improvement and perfection of group life.

Quite naturally the methods by which this point of view is to be translated into action will differ from those of the radical fusionist.

Amalgamation being inevitable, it is needless to increase, through preferential immigration of single males, for example, the disparity between the number of marriageable men and of marriageable women of the first generation. To do so would be to encourage the growth of difficult social problems arising out of an unsettled type of population, such as these unmarried male immigrants are bound to be. Experience in the past in the congested American cities, has shown the grave dangers both to the community and to the immigrant.

To the improvement of the economic status of the groups there can be no objection. But the facts show that only a comparatively small share can be assigned to this force in the production of amalgamation. There is not much promise, then, in this method, even though it could be applied on a larger scale and more consciously than is likely to be the case.

As to assiduously inducing a lack of group consciousness among immigrants, or undermining group solidarity in whatever form found, quite the opposite attitude is to be assumed. The fundamental objection to congested immigrant quarters is not that they tend to keep alive old-world habits and old-world interests. Far greater and more immediately menacing evils are the unsanitary and overcrowded tenements, the lack of recreational facilities for the youth and educational opportunities for the immigrant adult, the poorly lighted, ill-ventilated shops and factories, the inadequate protection to life—conditions over which the immigrant as such has practically no control, but must accept as he finds them upon his arrival. In a more favorable physical and economic setting much, if not all, of the apparent unsavoriness of immigrant life would fall away, as it actually does, as soon as circumstances are changed for the better. Moreover, rather than discourage affiliation with immigrant communal activities on the part of the younger generation, every effort should be made to foster among them an intelligent and appreciative interest in the cultural activities of their elders. The educational efforts of the immigrant community directed to this end are to be commended as contributions to the spiritual enrichment of the rising generation of Americans; if need be, constructively criticized, but hardly frowned upon as unworthy of a free democratic life. Nationalistic leaders in the group, instead of being condemned as unwelcome and misguided enthusiasts are rather to be brought into closer contact with the aspirations of the larger American community, thus enabling them to reinterpret for their own people, the life in the new environment. Efforts of leaders of thought among the immigrants to formulate "theories of adjustment," instead being relegated to the class of intellectual vaporings, should rather be examined as reasoned expressions of a deep-seated desire to fit into the new life and yet preserve the individuality of the group. The net result of this more sympathetic attitude, may possibly turn out to be a considerable heightening of group consciousness and perhaps a temporary retardation of actual fusion. But ultimately amalgamation will take place and with a younger generation, inheriting something of the cultural past of its group, the process will go ahead on a progressively higher cultural plane. America will thus gain far more in the long run than she loses.

V. THE IDEAL OF INTELLECTUAL AND EMOTIONAL HARMONY

One other point of view is possible. It is to ignore the fact of intermarriage. Or if not ignore it, at least to minimize its importance. Accordingly, it may be said, whether the group fuse or not biologically is really of no consequence. Intermarriage is not an absolute essential of assimilation. The co-existence of racial varieties with a strong spirit of national unity in France, Switzerland, Italy and even Germany would tend to prove that racial homogeneity is not an absolute essential of national unity. If then, the former is not to be considered the *summum bonum* of national development, then failure to fuse biologically need not be counted as something running counter to the democratic ideal. The concept of democracy, must, therefore, be further expanded to include ethnic stocks, which, though mentally and morally adjusted, nevertheless remain biologically more or less distinct. Whether in any specific case it would have been more advantageous for the group to have fused or to have remained intact is as impossible to ascertain as it is profitless to speculate upon. For, if the group disappears there is no way of telling what it might have contributed if it had not fused. And similarly, if the group has kept intact, there is no means of finding out what its contributions would have been if it had fused.

But even if racial homogeneity were a desirable national ideal it is extremely doubtful if it can ever be achieved completely. Thus far the fusion of the various white ethnic stocks does not seem to have produced a real blend.[6]

[6] "Study of Old Americans," by Dr. Ales Hrdlicka, curator of Physical Anthropology of the Smithsonian Institution, *Journal of Heredity*, VI, page 509, Nov., 1914. Also "The Old White Americans" in the *Proceedings of XIXth International Congress of Americanists*, Washington, 1917. "One of the main objects of his study was to determine whether the descendants of the early American settlers, living in a new environment, and more or less constantly intermarrying were being amalgamated into a distinct sub-type of the white race. Enough has already been found, as this preliminary report shows, to prove that such amalgamation has not taken place to any important degree. The

Moreover, the highest form of assimilation exists not where one individuality swallows up another, or one group merges indistinguishably with another, but where each side adapts to its own personality the unique contributions of the other.[7] That is, each side utilizes the other as a stimulus for a continuous creative life. The number of dis-

persistence in heredity of certain features, which run down even through six or eight generations is one of the remarkable results brought out by the study. If the process could continue for a few hundred years, Dr. Hrdlicka thinks, it might reach a point where one could speak of the members of old American families as of a distinct stock. But so far this point has not been reached; the Americans are almost as diverse and variable, it appears, as were their first ancestors in this country." From the *Journal of Heredity,* March, 1917, p. 104-105. "The Melting Pot a Myth."

[7] Assimilation conceived in this form seems to be the central thought of Prof. Dewey in his address on "Nationalizing Education," *Addresses and Proceedings of the National Education Association,* New York, 1916, Vol. IV, p. 185. He says: "I find that many who talk the loudest about the need of a supreme and unified Americanism of spirit really mean some special code or tradition to which they happen to be attached. They have some pet tradition which they would impose upon all. In thus measuring the scope of Americanism by some single element which enters into it they are themselves false to the spirit of America. Neither Englandism nor New-Englandism, neither Puritan nor Cavalier, any more than Teuton or Slav, can do anything but furnish one note in a vast symphony.

"The way to deal with hyphenism, in other words, is to welcome it in the sense of extracting from each people its special good, so that it shall surrender into a common fund of wisdom and experience what it especially has to contribute. All of these surrenders and contributions taken together create the national spirit of America. The dangerous thing is for each factor to isolate itself, to try to live off its past, and then to attempt to impose itself upon other elements, or, at least, to keep itself intact and thus refuse to accept what other cultures have to offer, so as thereby to be transmuted into authentic Americanism." Or, even in a more vigorous vein: "No matter how loudly any one proclaims his Americanism, if he assumes that any one racial strain, any one component culture, no matter how early settled it was in our territory, or how effective it has proven in its own land, is to furnish a pattern to which all other strains and cultures are to conform, he is a traitor to an American nationalism." p. 184-185.

tinctive individualities is then constantly multiplied instead of reduced and the only problem worthy of attention is the harmonization of the lives of these unique individualities.

But a deeper objection, by far, can be raised. It is, that to strive for racial homogeneity would divert the national imagination and the national will from the ideal of intellectual and emotional harmony among the masses of diverse elements, to the ideal of physical commingling and unity of blood relationship. Doubtless the latter is easier of attainment. But in the spiritual struggles for the realization of the former, profounder levels of unity are constantly reached and the national ideal thus approaches step by step the all-embracing human ideal. Herein is to be found the only adequate answer to the insistent and rightly insistent cry for national unity and the dread of America as a "polyglot boarding-house."

To encourage, then, the growth of cultural consciousness among the various immigrant groups with the aid of their ultimate disappearance is like calling upon them to make elaborate preparation for their own burial ceremonies. Why not leave the question of biologic fusion open for the decision of each individual and each group? The burden of conserving cultural individuality rests after all upon the group as such. If it has a virile cultural life, no artificial stimulants will be needed to keep it alive. If it lacks vitality and melts away in contact with other superior cultures, then it has surely merited its fate. According to this view, one duty only can rightfully be laid upon the immigrant groups. It is, that they must become an integral part of American life, in the sense of not holding aloof from its broad, common interests, but sharing by sentiment and by deed in the common aspirations and enterprises of the whole people. Thus as a phase of a comprehensive American national consciousness, cultural group consciousness becomes an asset in the expanding life of the nation, and its furtherance a distinct service towards the creation of a unique and rich civilization.

VI. IMPLICATIONS FOR GENERAL SOCIOLOGICAL THEORY

Finally, attention may be called in a few words to the deeper implications for sociological theory of the problem discussed in this monograph. Amalgamation of divergent ethnic stocks in the United States is proceeding within a democratic setting. There is no attempt to produce national unity and solidarity through compulsion, as was the case, for example, in some of the European countries, such as Austria-Hungary, Russia and Germany. This situation offers to the United States the unique opportunity of experimenting in the field of conscious social control of the transmission through education of the varied cultural heritages of the immigrant peoples. It opens up the possibility of consciously creating a synthetic culture. Moreover, it suggests the larger possibilities of world organization upon the basis of harmonious co-operation of racial and cultural groups within the State, rather than upon the basis of forced unification.

CHAPTER V.

STATISTICAL APPENDIX

INTRODUCTORY NOTE

This Appendix contains all statistical tables enumerated on pp. 23-25 in *Chapter II, Method and Scope,* with the exception of Tables I, II, III, IVa, VIII, IX, X, XI, XII. These tables were inserted into the body of the text for purposes of more convenient reference in following the argument at various successive points.

Tables IVb-IVi (pp. 93-100) supplement Table IVa (p. 43) by presenting the proportions of intermarriage arranged in order of magnitude in five classes (Class I-Class V) for men and women separately and for each generation separately. These tables, together with Table IVa form the basis of the general conclusion that the Jews and Negroes are at the lowest point of the scale of proportions of intermarriage, the Italians, Irish, Poles (Russian and Austrian), Greeks, Finns, at the middle point, while the Northern, Northwestern and some Central European peoples tend to gather near the highest point.

Table V is a summary table giving in alphabetical order the nationalities studied in this monograph, indicating the number of marriages and number of intermarriages recorded for each national group and for each "generation" within each group, and the proportion of intermarriage for each nationality and for each "generation" within the group. The alphabetical arrangement makes reference to a particular nationality easy, while the basic figures from which the proportions of intermarriage were calculated make it possible to evaluate correctly in each individual case the true significance of the ratio of intermarriage.

Table VI, Series 1-91 (for men) (pp. 101-154) and Series 1-88 (for women) (pp. 155-207) show the number of intermarriages for each nationality separately, the nationalities with which men and women respectively intermarried and the generations of the persons intermarrying. Each of the nine possible combinations of the three generation groups (1st, 2nd, 3rd generation) is noted and the cases of marriage are classified under them. In the case of the men the combinations are: marriages between 1st generation men and 1st generation women (of the same or of a different nationality); 1st generation men and 2nd generation women; 2nd generation men and 1st generation women; 1st generation men and 3rd generation women; 3rd generation men and 1st generation women; 2nd generation men and 2nd generation women; 2nd generation men and 3rd generation women; 3rd generation men and 2nd generation women; 3rd generation men and 3rd generation women. Similarly for the women where the order is reversed in each combination.

Thus, for example, in Table I, Series 1-91, (p. 103) the figures giving the number of intermarriages between Armenian men and Irish women (the seventh line below the caption) are to be read as follows: Number of intermarriages between Armenian men of the 1st generation and Irish women of the 2nd generation—2; total number of in-marriages between Armenian men of the 1st generation and Irish women of the 2nd generation—2; total number of intermarriages between Armenian men and Irish women—4.

Or, in the case of the tables in Series 1-88 (for women): In Table II, Series 1-88 (p. 157), the figures giving the number of intermarriages between Bohemian women and Italian men (the sixteenth line below the caption) are to be read as follows: Number of intermarriages between Bohemian women of the 1st generation and Italian men of the 1st generation—3; number of intermarriages between Bohemian women of the 1st generation and Italian men of the 2nd generation—1; number of intermarriages between Bohemian women of the 2nd generation and Italian men of the 1st generation—2; number of intermarriages between Bohemian women of the 2nd generation and Italian men of the 2nd generation—2; total number of intermarriages between Bohemian women and Italian men—8.

For a statement of the value of these two series of tables for further study see p. 69.

Table VII (p. 208) gives the percentage of increase in intermarriage of the 2nd generation over the 1st generation. The proportions of increase are grouped into 8 classes, with an additional class indicating proportions of decrease. In this table are presented, in a re-grouping, the figures in Table V (opp. p. 100) giving the percentage of increase and decrease in proportion of intermarriage of the 2nd generation over the first. Table VII, taken in conjunction with Tables IVa-IVi and Table V form the basis for the general conclusion that the lower the ratio of intermarriage in the first generation, the greater the ratio in the second, and therefore the greater the relative increase.

Tables (XIV-XVII) present figures on the basis of which the general conclusion is reached that, while in the first generation there is a general preponderance of marriageable men and women, there is a definite approach to an equality of sex ratios of marriageable persons in the second generation. (For the application of this result to the argument, see Chapter III, p. 36.)

ABBREVIATIONS

I. F B F P=foreign born of foreign parents=1st generation.

N B F P=native born of foreign parents=2nd generation.

N B N P=native born of native parents=3rd generation.

II. Austria (Boh.)=Austria (Bohemian); Austria (Germ.) =Austria (German); Austria (Ital.)=Austria (Italian); Austria (Jew.)=Austria (Jewish); Austria (Pol.)=Austria (Polish); B. W. I (Col.)=British West Indies (Colored); B. W. I. (Engl.)=British West Indies (English); Bulgaria (Jew.)=Bulgaria (Jewish); Canada (Col.)=Canada (Colored); Canada (Engl.)=Canada (English); Cuba (Col.)=Cuba (Colored); Cuba (Span.)=Cuba (Spanish); D. W. I. (Col.)=Dutch West Indies (Colored); England (Jew.)= England (Jewish); France (Jew.)=France (Jewish); Germany (Jew.)=Germany (Jewish); Germany (N.)= Germany (North); Germany (S.)=Germany (South); Holland (Jew.)=Holland (Jewish); Hungary (Germ.) =Hungary (German); Hungary (Hung.)=Hungary (Hungarian); Hungary (Jew.)=Hungary (Jewish); Hungary (Sl.)=Hungary (Slovak); Mexico (Span.)= Mexico (Spanish); Porto Rico (Span.)=Porto Rico (Spanish); Rumania (Jew.)=Rumania (Jewish); Russia (Jew.)=Russia (Jewish); Russia (Pol.)=Russia (Polish); Switzerland (Germ.)=Switzerland (German); Switzerland (Ital.)=Switzerland (Italian); Turkey (Jew.)=Turkey (Jewish); U. S. (Jew.)=United States (Jewish); U. S. (Col.)=United States (Colored); Venezula (Span.)=Venezuela (Spanish).

Table IV b

Classification of Nationalities according to Proportion of Intermarriage
Men and Women of the First Generation
(considered as one group)
(1908 - 1912)

(For the number of cases upon which the computation of the percentages is based, see Table V, p.100)

CLASS I (0 to 4.99 Intermarriages per 100 marriages)		CLASS II (5 to 9.99 Intermarriages per 100 marriages)		CLASS III (10 to 24.99 Intermarriages per 100 marriages)		CLASS IV (25 to 49.99 Intermarriages per 100 marriages)		CLASS V (50 to 100 Intermarriages per 100 marriages)	
Nationality	No. of Intermarriages per 100 marriages	Nationality	No. of Intermarriages per 100 marriages	Nationality	No. of Intermarriages per 100 marriages	Nationality	No. of Intermarriages per 100 marriages	Nationality	No. of Intermarriages per 100 marriages
Syria	4.63	Armenia	9.14	Hungary (Germ.)	23.51	France	40.39	Serbia	100*
England (Jew.)	4.57	Hungary (Hung.)	7.84	Greece	22.00	Denmark	40.37	Mexico (Span.)	91.30*
Cuba (Col.)	4.00*	Italy (South)	5.95	Russia (Polish)	19.70	Brit. West. Ind. (Engl.)	40.15	Switzerland (French)	88.70
Germany (Jew.)	3.74	Italy (Combined groups)	5.72	Germany (Not located)	19.50	Norway	37.74	Portugal	85.71*
Holland (Jew.)	3.70			Austria (Boh.)	17.71	Austria (Ital.)	36.84*	Canada (Engl.)	76.47
Italy (Not located)	3.69			Finland	16.27	Spain	29.79	Japan	72.41*
France (Jew.)	3.44*			Italy (North)	15.73	Germany (Combined groups)	28.66	Switzerland (Ital.)	68.42*
Hungary (Jew.)	2.09			Ireland	14.54	Sweden	26.61	Cuba (Span.)	67.53
Turkey (Jew.)	.80			Roumania	13.88*			Canada (French)	65.62
Dutch West Ind. (Col.)	.75			Hungary (Sl.)	13.65			Switzerland (Germ.)	59.92
Jews (Combined groups)	.64			Austria (Pol.)	12.51			China	60.00*
Austria (Jew.)	.57			Turkey	12.38			Austria (Germ.)	55.20
Brit. West Ind. (Col.)	.48			Canada (Col.)	11.11*			Germany (South)	55.16
Russia (Jew.)	.36							England	54.69
Rumania (Jew.)	.35							Holland	53.53
								Germany (North)	52.04
								Belgium	51.81
								Wales	50.50
								Scotland	50.46
								Porto Rico (Span.)	50.00

*Based on less than 50 marriage records

Table IV c

Classification of Nationalities according to Proportion of Intermarriage
Men and Women of the Second Generation
(considered as one group)
(1908 - 1912)

(For the number of cases upon which the computation of the percentages is based, see Table V. p.100)

CLASS I (0 to 4.99 Intermarriages per 100 Marriages)		CLASS II (5 to 9.99 Intermarriages per 100 Marriages)		CLASS III (10 to 24.99 Intermarriages per 100 Marriages)		CLASS IV (25 to 49.99 Intermarriages per 100 Marriages)		CLASS V (50 to 100 Intermarriages per 100 Marriages)	
NATIONALITY	No. of Intermarriages per 100 Marriages	NATIONALITY	No. of Intermarriages per 100 Marriages	NATIONALITY	No. of Intermarriages per 100 Marriages	NATIONALITY	No. of Intermarriages per 100 Marriages	NATIONALITY	No. of Intermarriages per 100 Marriages
Jews (Combined groups)	4.51	France (Jew.)	8.06	Italy (not located)	22.05	Austria (Boh.)	48.57	Greece	100.*
Holland (Jew.)	4.34	Germany (Jew.)	6.02	Dutch West Ind. (Col.)	20.00*	Hungary (Sl.)	44.28	Portugal	100.*
United States (Jew.)[(1)]	3.68	Austria (Jew.)	5.68	Italy (combined groups)	18.88	Germany (combined groups)	38.74	Turkey	100.*
Italy (South)	3.51					Germany (not located)	37.19	Cuba (Span.)	95.45
Russia (Jew.)	3.40					Ireland	35.99	Holland	92.78
Hungary (Jew.)	3.31					China	33.34*	Denmark	90.00
England (Jew.)	2.72					Switzerland (Ital.)	33.33*	Switzerland (Germ.)	89.79
Roumania (Jew.)	2.52					Austria (Pol.)	31.60	Canada (French)	89.70
United States (Col.)[(1)]	1.08					Italy (North)	30.57	Canada (Eng.)	89.38
								Scotland	88.88
								Austria (Germ.)	86.72
								France	85.78
								Hungary (Hung.)	85.71*
								Norway	85.24
								Spain	84.21
								England	82.56
								Belgium	80.00
								Wales	79.54
								Finland	75.00*
								Hungary (Germ.)	73.68
								Sweden	73.56
								Germany (South)	71.87
								Germany (North)	70.58
								Porto Rico (Span.)	66.66*
								Russia (Pol.)	65.21
								Armenia	50.*

Note: The following nationalities are here omitted because the percentage of intermarriage was zero: Austria (Ital.); Brit. West Ind. (Col.); Brit. West Ind. (Engl.); Canada (Col.); Cuba (Col.); Japan; Mexico (Span.); Roumania; Serbia; Switzerland (French); Syria; Turkey (Jew.).

*Based on less than 50 marriage records

(1) Third Generation

TABLE IVd

Classification of Nationalities according to Proportion of Intermarriage
Men of the 1st and 2nd Generations
(considered as one group)
(1908 - 1912)

(For the number of cases upon which the computation of the percentages is based, see Table V, p.100)

CLASS I (0 to 4.99 Intermarriages per 100 Marriages)		CLASS II (5 to 9.99 Intermarriages per 100 Marriages)		CLASS III (10 to 24.99 Intermarriages per 100 Marriages)		CLASS IV (25 to 49.99 Intermarriages per 100 Marriages)		CLASS V (50 to 100 Intermarriages per 100 Marriages)	
Nationality	No. of Inter-marri-ages per 100 marri-ages	Nationality	No. of Inter-marri-ages per 100 Marri-ages	Nationality	No. of Inter-marri-ages per 100 marri-ages	Nationality	No. of Inter-marri-ages per 100 marri-ages	Nationality	No. of Inter-marri-ages per 100 marri-ages
Hungary (Sl.)	4.86	Austria (Pol.)	9.25	Roumania	25.80*	France	46.88	Serbia	100.*
Hungary (Hung.)	4.28	Italy (South)	9.25	Hungary (Germ.)	18.82	Spain	36.96	Portugal	88.23*
England (Jew.)	3.77	Italy (combined groups)	9.03	Armenia	17.58	Norway	35.45	Mexico (Span.)	87.50*
Cuba (Col.)	3.44*	Canada (Col.)	8.34*	Ireland	17.48	Germany (combined groups)	35.33	Switzerland (French)	81.31*
United States (Col.)[1]	1.78	Finland	8.09	Italy (North)	14.83	Greece	34.75	Canada (Eng.)	79.82
Jews (combined groups)	1.12	Italy (not located)	7.92	Austria (Boh.)	12.12	Germany (not located)	30.9	Canada (French)	78.26
Turkey (Jew.)	1.05	Germany (Jew.)	7.37	France (Jew.)	11.11*	Russia (Pol.)	27.30	Cuba (Span.)	75.92
Hungary (Jew.)	.97	Holland (Jew.)	5.71			Sweden	26.79	Japan	72.41*
Austria (Jew.)	.84	Syria	5.26			Turkey	22.04	Holland	67.45
Brit. West Ind. (Col.)	.64	United States (Jew.)[1]	5.14					England	66.09
Russia (Jew.)	.50							Switzerland (Germ.)	65.98
Roumania (Jew.)	.41							Wales	62.82
								Scotland	61.92
								Switzerland (Ital.)	61.11*
								Belgium	61.05
								Porto Rico (Span.)	60.97*
								Germany (South)	59.91
								Germany (North)	57.14
								Austria (Germ.)	55.97
								China	55.56*
								Denmark	53.75
								Brit. West Ind. (Eng.)	48.31
								Austria (Ital.)	47.82*

Note. Dutch West Ind. (Col.) is omitted because the percentage of intermarriage was zero.

*Based on less than 50 marriage records

(1) Third Generation

TABLE IVe

Classification of Nationalities according to Proportion of Intermarriage
Men of the First Generation

(1908 - 1912)

(For the number of cases upon which the computation of the percentages is based, see Table V p. 100)

CLASS I (0 to 4.99 Intermarriages per 100 Marriages)		CLASS II (5 to 9.99 Intermarriages per 100 Marriages)		CLASS III (10 to 24.99 Intermarriages per 100 Marriages)		CLASS IV (25 to 49.99 Intermarriages per 100 Marriages)		CLASS V 50 to 100 Intermarriages per 100 Marriages	
Nationality	No. of Intermarriages per 100 Marriages	Nationality	No. of Intermarriages per 100 Marriages	Nationality	No. of Intermarriages per 100 Marriages	Nationality	No. of Intermarriages per 100 Marriages	Nationality	No. of Intermarriages per 100 Marriages
Germany (Jew.)	4.85	Ireland	9.61	Roumania	23.80	Brit. West Ind. (Engl.)	48.51	Serbia	100.*
Hungary (Sl.)	4.61	Italy (South)	9.13	Sweden	22.46	Denmark	48.15	Mexico (Span.)	91.30*
Hungary (Hung.)	4.28	Austria	8.87	Germany (not located)	21.32	Austria (Ital.)	47.82	Switzerland (French)	90.*
Cuba (Col.)	4.00*	Italy (combined groups)	7.45	Turkey	20.80	France	37.36	Portugal	85.71*
England (Jew.)	3.60	Finland	7.38	Hungary (Germ.)	18.10	Greece	34.55	Canada (Engl.)	75.00
Turkey (Jew.)	1.05	Italy (not located)	5.52	Armenia	14.67	Spain	34.39	Japan	72.42*
Hungary (Jew.)	.82	Holland (Jew.)	5.24*	Italy (North)	11.89	Norway	32.02	Cuba (Span.)	72.09*
Brit. West Ind. (Col.)	.65	Syria	5.26	Canada (Col.)	11.11*	Germany (combined groups)	31.22	Switzerland (Ital.)	64.70*
Austria (Jew.)	.55			Austria (Boh.)	10.69	Russia (Pol.)	27.00	Canada (French)	64.58*
Jews (combined groups)	.50							Holland	62.23
Roumania (Jew.)	.43							Switzerland (Germ.)	61.05
Russia (Jew.)	.26							England	60.71
								China	60.00*
								Germany (South)	59.60
								Porto Rico (Span.)	58.97*
								Belgium	58.41
								Germany (North)	57.08
								Wales	54.54
								Scotland	53.77
								Austria (Germ.)	51.98

Note: The following nationalities were omitted because the percentage of intermarriage was zero: France (Jew.); Dutch West Ind. (Col.)

*Based on less than 50 marriage records

TABLE IVf

Classification of Nationalities according to Proportion of Intermarriage
Men of the Second Generation
(1908 - 1912)

(For the number of cases upon which the computation of the percentages is based, see Table V, p. 100)

CLASS I (0 to 4.99 Intermarriages per 100 Marriages)		CLASS II (5 to 9.99 Intermarriages per 100 Marriages)		CLASS III (10 to 24.99 Intermarriages per 100 Marriages)		CLASS IV (25 to 49.99 Intermarriages per 100 Marriages)		CLASS V (50 to 100 Intermarriages per 100 Marriages)	
Nationality	No. of Intermarriages per 100 Marriages	Nationality	No. of Intermarriages per 100 Marriages	Nationality	No. of Intermarriages per 100 Marriages	Nationality	No. of Intermarriages per 100 Marriages	Nationality	No. of Intermarriages per 100 Marriages
England (Jew.)	3.96	Germany (Jew.)	8.85	Austria (Boh.)	17.69	Germany (combined groups)	40.90	Armenia	100.*
Russia (Jew.)	3.76	Holland (Jew.)	6.25	France (Jew.)	17.24	Germany (not located)	40.69	Greece	100.*
Hungary (Jew.)	2.35	Jews (combined groups)	5.67	Austria (Pol.)	16.80	China	33.34*	Italy (North)	100.
		Austria (Jew.)	5.15			Ireland	29.85	Porto Rico (Span.)	100.*
						Hungary (Sl.)	25.00	Portugal	100.*
								Turkey	100.*
								Holland	96.15
								Canada (French)	93.18
								Switzerland (Germ.)	91.07
								Cuba (Span.)	90.90*
								Canada (Eng.)	90.17
								Scotland	89.78
								Austria (Germ.)	89.58
								Denmark	88.63
								France	88.37
								Spain	87.50*
								Belgium	85.34
								Wales	82.60
								England	81.96
								Norway	79.16
								Finland	75.00*
								Russia (Pol.)	71.42*
								Sweden	70.00
								Germany (South)	69.56
								Hungary (Germ.)	62.50*
								Italy (South)	60.00*
								Germany (North)	58.82
								Italy (combined groups)	45.49
								Italy (not located)	40.69

Note: The following nationalities were omitted because the percentage of intermarriage was zero: - Austria (Ital.); Brit. West Ind. (Col.); Brit. West Ind. (Engl.); Canada (Col.); Cuba (Col.); Dutch West Ind. (Col.); Hungary (Hung.); Japan; Mexico (Span.); Roumania; Roumania (Jew.); Serbia; Switzerland (French); Switzerland (Ital.); Syria; Turkey (Jew.).

*Based on less than 50 marriage records

TABLE IV c

Classification of Nationalities according to Proportion of Intermarriage
Women of the 1st and 2nd Generations
(considered as one group)
(1908 - 1912)

(For the number of cases upon which the computation of the percentages is based, see Table V, p. 100)

CLASS I (0 to 4.99 Intermarriages per 100 Marriages)		CLASS II (5 to 9.99 Intermarriages per 100 Marriages)		CLASS III (10 to 24.99 Intermarriages per 100 Marriages)		CLASS IV (25 to 49.99 Intermarriages per 100 Marriages)		CLASS V (50 to 100 Intermarriages per 100 Marriages)	
Nationality	No. of Intermarriages per 100 Marriages	Nationality	No. of Intermarriages per 100 Marriages	Nationality	No. of Intermarriages per 100 Marriages	Nationality	No. of Intermarriages per 100 Marriages	Nationality	No. of Intermarriages per 100 Marriages
Italy (combined groups)	4.35			Finland	23.98	Denmark	39.09	Switzerland (French)	82.35*
Syria	4.00			Hungary (Sl.)	21.69	Sweden	34.83	Canada (Engl.)	79.88
United States (Jew.) (1)	3.68			Austria (Ital.)	18.75*	Porto Rico (Span.)	33.33*	Canada (French)	72.22
Greece	3.53			Austria (Pol.)	17.48	Germany (combined groups)	31.18	Cuba (Span.)	71.11
Dutch West Ind. (Col.)	3.27			Hungary (Hung.)	12.50	Austria (Boh.)	30.52	Switzerland (Ital.)	69.56*
Hungary (Jew.)	3.24			Russia (Pol.)	11.68	Hungary (Germ.)	29.27	Switzerland (Germ.)	66.66
England (Jew.)	3.14			Italy (North)	10.15	Spain	28.76	Austria (Germ.)	62.87
Italy (Not located)	3.09					Germany (Not located)	28.10	England	58.54
Germany (Jew)	2.83					Brit. West Ind. (Engl.)	28.00	Belgium	58.09
France (Jew)	2.17*					Ireland	25.31	Scotland	57.41
Italy (South)	2.14							Holland	56.00
Turkey	1.98							Wales	55.38
Jews (Combined groups)	1.21							France	51.96
Austria (Jew.)	1.12							Germany (South)	51.17
Russia (Jew.)	.74							Germany (North)	48.10
Turkey (Jew.)	.56							Norway	42.43
Roumania (Jew.)	.48								
United States (Col.) (1)	.44								
Brit. West Ind. (Col.)	.27								

Note: The following nationalities are omitted here because the percentage of intermarriage was zero: - Armenia; China; Canada (Col.); Cuba (Col.); Holland (Jew.); Japan; Mexico (Span.); Portugal; Roumania; Serbia.

* Based on less than 50 marriage records.

(1) Third Generation

TABLE IVb

Classification of Nationalities according to Proportion of Intermarriage
Women of the 1st Generation
(1908 - 1912)

(For the number of cases upon which the computation of the percentages is based, see Table V. p.100)

CLASS I (0 to 4.99 Intermarriages per 100 Marriages)		CLASS II (5 to 9.99 Intermarriages per 100 Marriages)		CLASS III (10 to 24.99 Intermarriages per 100 Marriages)		CLASS IV (25 to 49.99 Intermarriages per 100 Marriages)		CLASS V (50 to 100 Intermarriages per 100 Marriages)	
Nationality	No. of Intermarriages per 100 marriages	Nationality	No. of Intermarriages per 100 marriages	Nationality	No. of Intermarriages per 100 marriages	Nationality	No. of Intermarriages per 100 marriages	Nationality	No. of Intermarriages per 100 marriages
Syria	4.05	France (Jew.)	7.69*	Spain	24.44	Germany (South)	49.54	Switzerland (French)	97.50*
Italy (combined groups)	3.69	England (Jew.)	5.55	Austria (Boh.)	23.65	Scotland	46.59	Canada (Engl.)	73.26
Greece	3.53			Finland	23.54	England	46.36	Switzerland (Ital.)	71.42*
Hungary (Jew.)	3.10			Hungary (Sl.)	21.12	Germany (North)	45.61	Canada (French)	65.67*
Germany (Jew.)	2.62			Austria (Ital.)	20.00*	Wales	45.45*	Cuba (Span.)	61.76*
Italy (South)	2.15			Italy (North)	19.68	France	43.23	Switzerland (Germ.)	58.66
Turkey	1.98			Ireland	18.66	Holland	37.80	Austria (Germ.)	56.09
Dutch West Ind. (Col.)	1.69			Germany (not located)	17.17	Norway	37.23	Belgium	55.45
Italy (not located)	1.58			Austria (Pol.)	15.37	Porto Rico (Span.)	34.78*		
Jews (combined groups)	.78			Hungary (Hung.)	11.17	Sweden	30.33		
Turkey (Jew.)	.56			Russia (Pol.)	10.71	Denmark	29.95		
Austria (Jew.)	.50					Brit. West Ind. (Engl.)	28.57		
Russia (Jew.)	.47					Hungary (Germ.)	28.23		
Roumania (Jew.)	.29					Germany (combined groups)	25.36		
Brit. West Ind. (Col.)	.27								

Note: The following nationalities are omitted here because the percentage of intermarriage was zero; Armenia; Canada (Col.); China; Cuba (Col.); Holland (Jew.); Japan; Mexico (Span.); Portugal; Roumania; Serbia.

*Based on less than 50 marriage records.

TABLE IVi

Classification of Nationalities according to Proportion of Intermarriage
Women of the Second Generation
(1908 - 1912).

(For the number of cases upon which the computation of the percentages was based, see Table V. p. 100)

CLASS I (0 to 4.99 intermarriages per 100 marriages).		CLASS II (5 to 9.99 intermarriages per 100 marriages).		CLASS III (10 to 24.99 intermarriages per 100 marriages).		CLASS IV (25 to 49.99 intermarriages per 100 marriages).		CLASS V (50 to 100 intermarriages per 100 marriages).	
Nationality	No. of Intermarriages per 100 marriages	Nationality	No. of Intermarriages per 100 marriages	Nationality	No. of Intermarriages per 100 marriages	Nationality	No. of Intermarriages per 100 marriages	Nationality	No. of Intermarriages per 100 marriages
Hungary (Jew.)	3.89	Italy (combined groups)	9.16	Italy (not located)	12.37	Austria (Pol.)	42.67	Cuba (Span.)	100.*
Roumania (Jew.)	3.75	Italy (North)	8.39			Ireland	38.31	Denmark	91.66
Jews (combined groups)	3.58	Austria (Jew.)	6.00			Germany (combined groups)	36.74	Holland	90.69
Russia (Jew.)	3.14					Germany (not located)	35.95	Norway	89.19
Germany (Jew.)	2.96							Switzerland (Germ.)	89.01
Italy (South)	2.06							Canada (Engl.)	88.74
England (Jew.)	1.67							Austria (Germ.)	88.23
								Scotland	88.02
								Hungary (Hung.)	86.71*
								France	85.65
								Canada (French)	85.34
								England	85.11
								Hungary (Germ.)	81.81*
								Spain	81.81*
								Belgium	76.92
								Germany (North)	76.47
								Wales	76.19
								Sweden	76.14
								Finland	75.00*
								Germany (South)	75.17
								Austria (Boh.)	64.81
								Russia (Pol.)	62.50
								Hungary (Sl.)	56.25
								Dutch West Ind. (Col.)	50.00*
								Switzerland (Ital.)	50.00*

Note: The following nationalities [illegible] omitted her[illegible] because the percentage of intermar[illegible] was zero. Armenia: [illegible] Ital[illegible]; British West Indies (colored); British West Indies

... gener. (FBFP+NBFP)	1st gener. (FBFP)	... gener. (NBFP)	... of 2nd gener. over 1st gener.	... gener. (FBFP+NBFP)	1st gener. (FBFT)	... gener. (NBFP)	... of 2nd gener. over 1st gener.	... gener. (FBFP+NBFP)	... gener. (FBFP)	... gener. (NBFP)	... gener. (FBFP+NBFP)	... gener. (FBFP)	... gener. (NBFP)	... gener. (FBFP+NBFP)	... gener. (FBFP)	... gener. (NBFP)	... gener. (FBFP+NBFP)
17.56	16.67	100.	599.8	0	0	0	0	166	164	2	91	90	1	75	74	1	16
12.12	10.69	17.69	165.4	30.52	23.65	66.81	282.4	1451	1101	350	635	505	130	816	596	220	365
55.97	51.96	89.58	172.3	62.87	58.09	88.23	151.8	988	855	133	452	404	48	536	451	85	590
47.82	0	0	0	18.75	20.00	0	0	39	38	1	23	23	0	16	15	1	14
.84	.55	5.15	936.3	1.12	.50	6.00	1200.	14032	12890	1142	6767	6341	426	7265	6549	716	159
9.25	8.87	16.80	189.4	17.48	15.87	42.67	268.8	5197	4914	283	2475	2356	119	2722	2558	164	705
61.06	58.41	83.34	142.6	58.09	55.43	76.92	138.7	218	193	25	113	101	12	105	92	13	130
.64	.65	0	0	.27	.27	0	0	1666	1638	28	925	916	9	741	722	19	8
40.31	48.31	0	0	28.12	28.57	0	0	153	152	1	89	89	0	64	63	1	61
0	0	0	0	0	0	0	0	10	10	0	10	10	0	0	0	0	0
8.34	11.11	0	0	0	0	0	0	12	9	3	12	9	3	0	0	0	1
79.82	75.00	90.17	120.2	79.88	73.26	88.74	121.1	705	442	263	352	240	112	353	202	151	565
78.26	64.58	93.18	144.2	72.22	66.67	83.34	125.0	164	96	68	92	46	44	72	43	24	124
55.56	60.00	33.34	-179.9	0	0	0	0	18	15	3	18	15	3	0	0	0	10
3.44	4.00	0	0	0	0	0	0	29	25	4	29	25	4	0	0	0	1
75.92	72.09	90.90	126.0	71.11	61.76	100.00	161.9	99	77	22	54	43	11	45	34	11	73
53.75	48.18	88.63	183.9	39.09	29.95	91.66	306.0	563	483	80	320	276	44	243	207	36	267
0	0	0	0	3.27	1.69	50.00	2958.5	138	133	5	77	74	3	61	59	2	2
56.09	60.71	81.96	135.0	58.54	46.36	83.11	179.2	3614	2576	1038	1988	1489	499	1626	1087	539	2266
3.77	3.60	3.96	110	3.14	5.55	1.67	-332.3	403	183	220	212	111	101	191	72	119	14
8.09	7.38	75.00	1016.2	23.98	23.54	75.00	318.6	850	842	8	383	379	4	467	463	4	143
46.88	37.36	88.37	236.5	51.96	43.25	85.63	193.4	1455	1161	294	691	562	129	764	599	165	721
11.11	0	17.24	0	2.17	7.69	0	0	91	29	62	45	16	29	46	13	33	6
35.33	31.22	40.90	131.0	31.18	25.58	36.74	144.7	14979	8031	6948	7780	4503	3277	7199	3528	3671	4994
57.14	57.08	58.82	103.0	48.10	45.61	76.47	167.6	933	882	51	511	494	17	422	388	34	495
59.91	59.60	69.56	116.7	51.17	49.54	73.17	147.6	1322	1258	64	726	703	23	596	555	41	740
30.9	21.32	40.68	190.8	28.10	17.17	35.95	209.3	12724	5891	6833	6543	3306	3237	6181	2585	3596	3759
7.37	4.05	8.85	183.2	2.88	2.62	2.96	112.9	3486	1310	2176	1792	662	1130	1694	648	1046	180
34.73	34.53	100.00	289.6	3.53	3.53	0	0	560	559	1	334	333	1	226	226	0	124
57.45	62.23	96.15	154.5	56.00	37.80	90.69	239.6	294	225	69	169	143	26	125	82	43	184
5.71	5.26	6.25	118.8	0	0	0	0	100	54	46	70	38	32	30	16	14	4
18.82	18.10	62.5	345.3	29.27	28.25	81.81	289.7	1061	1042	19	494	486	8	567	556	11	259
4.28	4.28	0	0	12.50	11.17	85.71	767.3	733	726	7	350	350	0	383	376	7	65
.97	.82	2.33	284.1	3.24	3.10	3.89	125.4	4862	4289	573	2153	1939	214	2709	2350	359	109
4.86	4.61	25.00	542.1	21.69	21.12	56.25	266.3	3597	3545	52	1624	1604	20	1973	1941	32	507
7.48	9.61	29.85	310.6	25.31	18.66	38.31	205.3	18547	11826	6721	8812	5385	3427	9735	6441	3294	4005
9.03	7.45	45.49	610.6	4.35	3.69	9.16	248.2	23881	21975	1906	12281	11771	510	11600	10204	1396	1615
4.83	11.82	100.0	841.0	10.15	19.68	8.39	-234.5	2330	2173	157	1139	1101	38	1193	1072	119	390
9.25	9.13	60.00	657.1	2.14	2.15	2.06	-104.3	8411	8013	398	4364	4354	10	4047	3659	388	491
7.92	5.52	40.69	777.3	3.09	1.58	12.37	782.9	13140	11789	1351	6778	6316	462	6362	5473	889	734
2.41	72.41	0	0	0	0	0	0	29	29	0	29	29	0	0	0	0	21
1.12	.50	5.67	1134.0	1.21	.78	3.58	458.9	65198	56231	7558	32491	28520	3827	32707	27709	4211	763
7.50	91.30	0	0	0	0	0	0	24	25	1	26	25	1	0	0	0	21
35.45	32.02	79.16	247.2	42.43	37.23	89.19	239.5	700	639	61	330	306	24	370	333	37	274
30.97	58.97	100.0	169.5	33.33	34.78	0	0	65	62	3	41	39	2	24	23	1	33
8.23	85.71	100.0	116.7	0	0	0	0	17	14	3	17	14	3	0	0	0	15
23.80	23.80	0	0	0	0	0	0	37	36	1	21	21	0	16	15	1	5
.41	.43	0	0	.48	.29	2.75	1293.1	2646	2527	119	1196	1157	39	1450	1370	80	12
.50	.26	3.76	1446.1	.74	.47	3.14	668.0	37768	34568	3200	19411	18055	1356	18357	16513	1844	235
27.30	27.00	71.42	264.4	11.68	10.71	62.50	583.5	1898	1875	23	1040	1033	7	856	840	16	384
100.00	100.00	0	0	0	0	0	0	11	11	0	11	11	0	0	0	0	11
54.92	55.77	89.78	166.9	57.41	46.59	88.02	188.9	1557	1179	378	822	636	186	735	543	192	931
36.96	34.39	87.50	248.6	28.76	24.44	81.81	334.7	311	292	19	165	157	8	146	135	11	103
26.79	22.46	70.00	311.6	34.63	30.33	76.14	251.0	2100	1901	199	989	899	90	1111	1002	109	652
91.81	90.00	0	0	82.55	87.50	0	0	67	62	5	33	30	3	34	32	2	55
65.98	61.05	91.07	149.1	66.66	58.66	89.01	151.7	686	539	147	341	285	56	345	254	91	455

TABLE VI

Series 1—91

MEN

(For a discussion of the method of reading these tables and of their further utilization, see Introductory Note, page 87.)

TABLE VI, SERIES 1—91

(Heavy type in caption indicates generation of **MAN**)

NATIONALITY		GENERATION									
MAN	WOMAN	**1st Gen.** (FBFP) with 1st Gen. (FBFP)	**1st Gen.** (FBFP) with 2nd Gen. (NBFP)	**2nd Gen.** (NBFP) with 1st Gen. (FBFP)	**1st Gen.** (FBFP) with 3rd Gen. (NBNP)	**3rd Gen.** (NBNP) with 1st Gen. (FBFP)	**2nd Gen.** (NBFP) with 2nd Gen. (NBFP)	**2nd Gen.** (NBFP) with 3rd Gen. (NBNP)	**3rd Gen.** (NBNP) with 2nd Gen. (NBFP)	**3rd Gen.** (NBNP) with 3rd Gen. (NBNP)	TOTALS
		1—ARMENIA									
Armenia	Armenia	74	1								75
Armenia	Austria (Pol.)	2									2
Armenia	Canada (Engl.)		1								1
Armenia	England	1									1
Armenia	Germany		3				1				4
Armenia	Hungary (Sl.)	1									1
Armenia	Ireland	2	2								4
Armenia	Russia (Pol.)	2									2
Armenia	Sweden	1									1
Totals		**83**	**7**				**1**				**91**
		2—AUSTRIA (BOH.)									
Austria (Boh.)	Austria (Boh.)	421	30	34			73				558
Austria (Boh.)	Austria (Jew)						2				2
Austria (Boh.)	England						1				1
Austria (Boh.)	France	2									2
Austria (Boh.)	Germany	12	7	1			7				27
Austria (Boh.)	Germany (North)	3									3
Austria (Boh.)	Germany (South)	2		1							3
Austria (Boh.)	Hungary (Sl.)	21					1				22
Austria (Boh.)	Ireland	3		3			4				10
Austria (Boh.)	Italy						2				2
Austria (Boh.)	Russia (Jew)		1								1
Austria (Boh.)	Scotland			1							1
Austria (Boh.)	Switzerland (Germ.)	2	1								3
Totals		**466**	**39**	**40**			**90**				**635**

NATIONALITY		GENERATION									
Man	Woman	1st Gen. (FBFP) with 1st Gen. (FBFP)	1st Gen. (FBFP) with 2nd Gen. (NBFP)	2nd Gen. (NBFP) with 1st Gen. (FBFP)	1st Gen. (FBFP) with 3rd Gen. (NBNP)	3rd Gen. (NBNP) with 1st Gen. (FBFP)	2nd Gen. (NBFP) with 2nd Gen. (NBFP)	2nd Gen. (NBFP) with 3rd Gen. (NBNP)	3rd Gen. (NBNP) with 2nd Gen. (NBFP)	3rd Gen. (NBNP) with 3rd Gen. (NBNP)	Totals
	3—AUSTRIA (GERM.)										
Austria (Germ.)	Austria (Germ.)	189	5				5				199
Austria (Germ.)	Austria (Boh.)	6									6
Austria (Germ.)	Austria (Ital.)	2									2
Austria (Germ.)	Austria (Jew)			1							1
Austria (Germ.)	Belgium	1									1
Austria (Germ.)	Austria (Pol.)	6					1				7
Austria (Germ.)	Canada (Engl.)		2				2				4
Austria (Germ.)	Canada (French)	1									1
Austria (Germ.)	Denmark	1	1				1				3
Austria (Germ.)	England	4	4	1			2				11
Austria (Germ.)	France	2	1								3
Austria (Germ.)	Germany	34	24	4			16				78
Austria (Germ.)	Germany (North)	5	1				1				7
Austria (Germ.)	Germany (South)	35	1				1				37
Austria (Germ.)	Holland	1									1
Austria (Germ.)	Hungary (Germ.)	14									14
Austria (Germ.)	Hungary (Hung.)			1							1
Austria (Germ.)	Hungary (Jew)	15									15
Austria (Germ.)	Hungary (Sl.)	12									12
Austria (Germ.)	Ireland	16	3				10				29
Austria (Germ.)	Italy	1									1
Austria (Germ.)	Italy (North)	1									1
Austria (Germ.)	Luxemburg	1									1
Austria (Germ.)	Norway	2									2
Austria (Germ.)	Scotland	2									2
Austria (Germ.)	Sweden	2		1							3
Austria (Germ.)	Switzerland (Germ.)	8									8
Austria (Germ.)	Russia (Jew)	1		1							2
Totals		362	42	9			39				452

NATIONALITY		GENERATION									
MAN	WOMAN	1st Gen. (FBFP) with 1st Gen. (FBFP)	1st Gen. (FBFP) with 2nd Gen. (NBFP)	2nd Gen. (NBFP) with 1st Gen. (FBFP)	1st Gen. (FBFP) with 3rd Gen. (NBNP)	3rd Gen. (NBNP) with 1st Gen. (FBFP)	2nd Gen. (NBFP) with 2nd Gen. (NBFP)	2nd Gen. (NBFP) with 3rd Gen. (NBNP)	3rd Gen. (NBNP) with 2nd Gen. (NBFP)	3rd Gen. (NBNP) with 3rd Gen. (NBNP)	TOTALS
			4—AUSTRIA (ITAL.)								
Austria (Ital.)	Austria (Ital.)	11	1								12
Austria (Ital.)	Austria (Germ.)	2									2
Austria (Ital.)	Germany		1								1
Austria (Ital.)	Germany (Jew)	2									2
Austria (Ital.)	Hungary (Jew)	1									1
Austria (Ital.)	Ireland	1									1
Austria (Ital.)	Italy	2									2
Austria (Ital.)	Italy (North)	1									1
Austria (Ital.)	Switzerland (Germ.)	1									1
Totals		21	2								23
			5—AUSTRIA (POL.)								
Austria (Pol.)	Austria (Pol.)	2121	26	31			68				2246
Austria (Pol.)	Austria (Boh.)	15	2				1				18
Austria (Pol.)	Austria (Germ.)	2									2
Austria (Pol.)	England	2	1								3
Austria (Pol.)	France						1				1
Austria (Pol.)	Germany	13	9				6				28
Austria (Pol.)	Germany (North)	1									1
Austria (Pol.)	Germany (South)	8									8
Austria (Pol.)	Hungary (Germ.)	1									1
Austria (Pol.)	Hungary (Hung.)	1									1
Austria (Pol.)	Hungary (Sl.)	99	1	2							102
Austria (Pol.)	Ireland	10	4	2			4				20
Austria (Pol.)	Italy						1				1
Austria (Pol.)	Norway			1							1
Austria (Pol.)	Russia (Pol.)	33	1	1							35
Austria (Pol.)	Scotland	2	2				1				5
Austria (Pol.)	Sweden	1									1
Austria (Pol.)	Switzerland (Germ.)		1								1
Totals		2309	47	37			82				2475

NATIONALITY		GENERATION									
MAN	WOMAN	1st Gen. (FBFP) with 1st Gen. (FBFP)	1st Gen. (FBFP) with 2nd Gen. (NBFP)	2nd Gen. (NBFP) with 1st Gen. (FBFP)	1st Gen. (FBFP) with 3rd Gen. (NBNP)	3rd Gen. (NBNP) with 1st Gen. (FBFP)	2nd Gen. (NBFP) with 2nd Gen. (NBFP)	2nd Gen. (NBFP) with 3rd Gen. (NBNP)	3rd Gen. (NBNP) with 2nd Gen. (NBFP)	3rd Gen. (NBNP) with 3rd Gen. (NBNP)	TOTALS
6—BELGIUM											
Belgium	Belgium	41	1				2				44
Belgium	Austria (Pol.)	1									1
Belgium	Canada (Engl.)	1									1
Belgium	Denmark	1									1
Belgium	England	2					1				3
Belgium	France	19									19
Belgium	Germany	11	6				5				22
Belgium	Holland	3									3
Belgium	Hungary (Sl.)	1		1							2
Belgium	Ireland	6	2	1			1				10
Belgium	Italy	1					1				2
Belgium	Luxemburg	1									1
Belgium	Switzerland (Germ.)	1									1
Belgium	Switzerland (French)	1									1
Belgium	Porto Rico (Span.)	1									1
Belgium	Russia (Jew)		1								1
Totals		91	10	2			10				113
7—BRITISH WEST INDIES (COL.)											
B. W. I. (Col.)	British West Ind. (Col.)	672	15	1							688
B. W. I. (Col.)	Cuba (Col.)	2									2
B. W. I. (Col.)	Germany (South)	1									1
B. W. I. (Col.)	Hungary (Sl.)	2									2
B. W. I. (Col.)	Ireland	1									1
B. W. I. (Col.)	Norway	[illegible]									1
B. W. I. (Col.)	Porto Rico (Col.)	2									2
B. W. I. (Col.)	Switzerland (Germ.)	1									1
B. W. I. (Col.	United States (Col.)				219			8			227
Totals		682	15	1	219			8			925

NATIONALITY		GENERATION									
MAN	WOMAN	1st Gen. (FBFP) with 1st Gen. (FBFP)	1st Gen. (FBFP) with 2nd Gen. (NBFP)	2nd Gen. (NBFP) with 1st Gen. (FBFP)	1st Gen. (FBFP) with 3rd Gen. (NBNP)	3rd Gen. (NBNP) with 1st Gen. (FBFP)	2nd Gen. (NBFP) with 2nd Gen. (NBFP)	2nd Gen. (NBFP) with 3rd Gen. (NBNP)	3rd Gen. (NBNP) with 2nd Gen. (NBFP)	3rd Gen. (NBNP) with 3rd Gen. (NBNP)	TOTALS
8—BRITISH WEST INDIES (ENGL.)											
B. W. I. (Engl.)	British West Indies (Engl.)	46									46
B. W. I. (Engl.)	Austria (Germ.)	1									1
B. W. I. (Engl.)	Belgium		1								1
B. W. I. (Engl.)	British West Indies (Col.)	2									2
B. W. I. (Engl.)	Canada (Engl.)		2								2
B. W. I. (Engl.)	England	5	2								7
B. W. I. (Engl.)	Germany		4								4
B. W. I. (Engl.)	Germany (South)	1									1
B. W. I. (Engl.)	Hungary (Jew)	1									1
B. W. I. (Engl.)	Ireland	12	6								18
B. W. I. (Engl.)	Italy	1									1
B. W. I. (Engl.)	Scotland	1	1								2
B. W. I. (Engl.)	Sweden	2									2
B. W. I. (Engl.)	United States (Jew)				1						1
Totals		72	16		1						89
9—CANADA (COL.)											
Canada (Col.)	British West Indies (Col.)			1							1
Canada (Col.)	Cuba (Col.)	1									1
Canada (Col.)	Scotland	1									1
Canada (Col.)	United States (Col.)				7			2			9
Totals		2		1	7			2			12

NATIONALITY		GENERATION									
MAN	WOMAN	1st Gen. (FBFP) with 1st Gen. (FBFP)	1st Gen. (FBFP) with 2nd Gen. (NBFP)	2nd Gen. (NBFP) with 1st Gen. (FBFP)	1st Gen. (FBFP) with 3rd Gen. (NBNP)	3rd Gen. (NBNP) with 1st Gen. (FBFP)	2nd Gen. (NBFP) with 2nd Gen. (NBFP)	2nd Gen. (NBFP) with 3rd Gen. (NBNP)	3rd Gen. (NBNP) with 2nd Gen. (NBFP)	3rd Gen. (NBNP) with 3rd Gen. (NBNP)	TOTALS
				10—CANADA (ENGL.)							
Canada (Engl.)	Canada (Engl.	48	12	6			5				71
Canada (Engl.)	Austria (Pol.)	1	2	1							4
Canada (Engl.)	B. W. I. (Engl.)	2									2
Canada (Engl.)	Belgium		1								1
Canada (Engl.)	Canada (French)	6		1							7
Canada (Engl.)	Cuba						1				1
Canada (Engl.)	Denmark						1				1
Canada (Engl.)	England	22	6	6			12				46
Canada (Engl.)	France	3									3
Canada (Engl.)	Germany	4	22	1			23				50
Canada (Engl.)	Germany (North)	1									1
Canada (Engl.)	Germany (South)			1							1
Canada (Engl.)	Holland			1							1
Canada (Engl.)	Hungary (Germ.)	2		1							3
Canada (Engl.)	Hungary (Sl.)	2									2
Canada (Engl.)	Ireland	54	26	13			18				111
Canada (Engl.)	Italy			1			3				4
Canada (Engl.)	Hungary (Jew)	1									1
Canada (Engl.)	Norway	1									1
Canada (Engl.)	Portugal						1				1
Canada (Engl.)	Russia (Jew)	1		1							2
Canada (Engl.)	Russia (Pol.)	1									1
Canada (Engl.)	Scotland	10	6	2			4				22
Canada (Engl.)	Sweden	1		2			3				6
Canada (Engl.)	Switzerland (French)	1									1
Canada (Engl.)	Switzerland (Germ.)	2		1			1				4
Canada (Engl.)	United States (Col.)				2			1			3
Canada (Engl.)	Wales						1				1
Totals		163	75	38	2		73	1			352

NATIONALITY		GENERATION									
MAN	WOMAN	1st Gen. (FBFP) with 1st Gen. (FBFP)	1st Gen. (FBFP) with 2nd Gen. (NBFP)	2nd Gen. (NBFP) with 1st Gen. (FBFP)	1st Gen. (FBFP) with 3rd Gen. (NBNP)	3rd Gen. (NBNP) with 1st Gen. (FBFP)	2nd Gen. (NBFP) with 2nd Gen. (NBFP)	2nd Gen. (NBFP) with 3rd Gen. (NBNP)	3rd Gen. (NBNP) with 2nd Gen. (NBFP)	3rd Gen. (NBNP) with 3rd Gen. (NBNP)	TOTALS
11—CANADA (FR.)											
Canada (French)	Canada (French	14	3	2			1				20
Canada (French)	Austria (Boh.)	1									1
Canada (French)	Austria (Pol.)			1							1
Canada (French)	England	2	1	1							4
Canada (French)	England (Jew)		1								1
Canada (French)	France	2					1				3
Canada (French)	Germany	2	2	3			2				9
Canada (French)	Germany (North)	2		1							3
Canada (French)	Germany (South)	1									1
Canada (French	Ireland	7	6	4			24				41
Canada (French)	Italy						1				1
Canada (French)	Italy (South)	2									2
Canada (French)	Scotland		1				2				3
Canada (French)	Sweden						1				1
Canada (French)	Syria	1									1
Totals		34	14	12			32				92
12—CHINA											
China	China	5	1				2				8
China	Canada (Engl.)	1									1
China	France	1									1
China	Germany (North)	2									2
China	Germany (Jew)	1									1
China	Ireland	1									1
China	Norway	1									1
China	Russia (Jew)		1								1
China	Scotland						1				1
China	Spain	1									1
Totals		13	2				3				18

NATIONALITY		GENERATION									
Man	Woman	1st Gen. (FBFP) with 1st Gen. (FBFP)	1st Gen. (FBFP) with 2nd Gen. (NBFP)	2nd Gen. (NBFP) with 1st Gen. (FBFP)	1st Gen. (FBFP) with 3rd Gen. (NBNP)	3rd Gen. (NBNP) with 1st Gen. (FBFP)	2nd Gen. (NBFP) with 2nd Gen. (NBFP)	2nd Gen. (NBFP) with 3rd Gen. (NBNP)	3rd Gen. (NBNP) with 2nd Gen. (NBFP)	3rd Gen. (NBNP) with 3rd Gen. (NBNP)	Totals
13—CUBA (COL.)											
Cuba (Col.)	Cuba (Col.)	2									2
Cuba (Col.)	D. W. I. (Col.)	1									1
Cuba (Col.)	Italy (North)	1									1
Cuba (Col.)	Porto Rico (Col.)	2									2
Cuba (Col.)	United States (Col.)				19			4			23
Totals		6			19			4			29
14—CUBA (SPAN.)											
Cuba (Span.)	Cuba (Span.)	12		1							13
Cuba (Span.)	Belgium	1									1
Cuba (Span.)	Canada (Engl.)	2									2
Cuba (Span.)	England	2									2
Cuba (Span.)	Finland	2									2
Cuba (Span.)	France	1	1	1							3
Cuba (Span.)	Germany	1	4				3				8
Cuba (Span.)	Germany (South)	1									1
Cuba (Span.)	Holland	1		1							2
Cuba (Span.)	Ireland		3	1			2				6
Cuba (Span.)	Italy	2									2
Cuba (Span.)	Italy (South)	1									1
Cuba (Span.)	Porto Rico (Span.)	2									2
Cuba (Span.)	Scotland			1			1				2
Cuba (Span.)	Spain	6									6
Cuba (Span.)	Venezuela (Span.)	1									1
Totals		35	8	5			6				54

NATIONALITY		GENERATION									
MAN	WOMAN	1st Gen. (FBFP) with 1st Gen. (FBFP)	1st Gen. (FBFP) with 2nd Gen. (NBFP)	2nd Gen. (NBFP) with 1st Gen. (FBFP)	1st Gen. (FBFP) with 3rd Gen. (NBNP)	3rd Gen. (NBNP) with 1st Gen. (FBFP)	2nd Gen. (NBFP) with 2nd Gen. (NBFP)	2nd Gen. (NBFP) with 3rd Gen. (NBNP)	3rd Gen. (NBNP) with 2nd Gen. (NBFP)	3rd Gen. (NBNP) with 3rd Gen. (NBNP)	TOTALS
15—DENMARK											
Denmark	Denmark	143		2			3				148
Denmark	Austria (Boh.)	3									3
Denmark	Austria (Germ.)	2					2				4
Denmark	Austria (Pol.)	7		1							8
Denmark	Belgium	1									1
Denmark	Canada (Engl.)	2					1				3
Denmark	England	9	4	3							16
Denmark	Finland	5									5
Denmark	France	1					1				2
Denmark	Germany	7	8	3			9				27
Denmark	Germany (North)	4									4
Denmark	Germany (South)	4									4
Denmark	Hungary (Sl.)	2									2
Denmark	Ireland	22	2	4			7				35
Denmark	Hungary (Jew)	1									1
Denmark	Norway	16	1	2			1				20
Denmark	Russia (Jew)	1									1
Denmark	Russia (Pol.)	1									1
Denmark	Scotland	2		1			1				4
Denmark	Sweden	20									20
Denmark	Switzerland (Germ.)	4		1							5
Denmark	United States (Col.)				2			2			4
Denmark	Wales	1	1								2
Totals		258	16	17	2		25	2			320
16—DANISH WEST INDIES (COL.)											
D. W. I. (Col.)	Danish West Indies (Col.)	54					1				55
D. W. I. (Col.)	British West Indies (Col.)	2					2				4
D. W. I. (Col.)	United States (Col.)				18						18
Totals		56			18		3				77

NATIONALITY		GENERATION									
MAN	WOMAN	1st Gen. (FBFP) with 1st Gen. (FBFP)	1st Gen. (FBFP) with 2nd Gen. (NBFP)	2nd Gen. (NBFP) with 1st Gen. (FBFP)	1st Gen. (FBFP) with 3rd Gen. (NBNP)	3rd Gen. (NBNP) with 1st Gen. (FBFP)	2nd Gen. (NBFP) with 2nd Gen. (NBFP)	2nd Gen. (NBFP) with 3rd Gen. (NBNP)	3rd Gen. (NBNP) with 2nd Gen. (NBFP)	3rd Gen. (NBNP) with 3rd Gen. (NBNP)	TOTALS
					17—ENGLAND						
England	England	549	35	34			56				674
England	Austria (Boh.)	1	2	4			1				8
England	Austria (Germ.)	2	5	1			3				11
England	Austria (Jew)	2					1				3
England	Austria (Pol.)	6		2			2				10
England	Belgium	3		1							4
England	British West Indies (Engl.)	7									7
England	Canada (Engl.)	39	6	4			14				63
England	Canada (French)	2		2							4
England	Cuba (Span.)		1				2				3
England	Denmark	8	2	1			3				14
England	Danish West Indies (Col.)		1								1
England	England (Jew)	1									1
England	Finland	7					1				8
England	France	35	5	6			7				53
England	Germany	68	92	13			101				274
England	Germany (Jew)		3				1				4
England	Germany (North)	9		3			8				20
England	Germany (South)	13	2	4							19
England	Greece	1									1
England	Holland			1			2				3
England	Hungary (Germ.)	2									2
England	Hungary (Hung.)	3									3
England	Hungary (Jew)	3	3				1				7
England	Hungary (Sl.)	5		2			2				9
England	Ireland	284	100	58			110				552
England	Italy	7	7	1			1				16
England	Italy (North)	1	1								2
England	Italy South)			1							1
England	Norway	9	2	3			2				16
England	Rumania (Jew)	1					1				2
England	Russia (Jew)	4	1								5

NATIONALITY		GENERATION									
MAN	WOMAN	1st Gen. (FBFP) with 1st Gen. (FBFP)	1st Gen. (FBFP) with 2nd Gen. (NBFP)	2nd Gen. (NBFP) with 1st Gen. (FBFP)	1st Gen. (FBFP) with 3rd Gen. (NBNP)	3rd Gen. (NBNP) with 1st Gen. (FBFP)	2nd Gen. (NBFP) with 2nd Gen. (NBFP)	2nd Gen. (NBFP) with 3rd Gen. (NBNP)	3rd Gen. (NBNP) with 2nd Gen. (NBFP)	3rd Gen. (NBNP) with 3rd Gen. (NBNP)	TOTALS
17—ENGLAND—*Continued*											
England	Russia (Pol.)	3									3
England	Scotland	66	16	2			15				99
England	Spain	3									3
England	Sweden	47	3	5			7				62
England	Switzerland (Germ.)	7	1	1			6				15
England	Wales	3	1	1			2				7
Totals		**1201**	**289**	**150**			**349**				**1989**
18—FINLAND											
Finland	Finland	350	1	1							352
Finland	Austria (Germ.)	1									1
Finland	Denmark	2									2
Finland	England	1									1
Finland	Germany (North)	2					2				4
Finland	Germany (South)			1							1
Finland	Holland	1									1
Finland	Hungary (Jew)	1									1
Finland	Hungary (Sl.)	1									1
Finland	Ireland	4	1								5
Finland	Norway	1									1
Finland	Scotland		1								1
Finland	Sweden	10	1								11
Finland	Switzerland (Germ.)	1									1
Totals		**375**	**4**	**2**			**2**				**383**
19—FRANCE											
France	France	331	21	9			6				367
France	Austria (Boh.)	1	1								2
France	Austria (Germ.)	3		2							5
France	Austria (Pol.)	1	2				1				4
France	Belgium	17		1			2				20

NATIONALITY		GENERATION									
Man	Woman	1st Gen. (FBFP) with 1st Gen. (FBFP)	1st Gen. (FBFP) with 2nd Gen. (NBFP)	2nd Gen. (NBFP) with 1st Gen. (FBFP)	1st Gen. (FBFP) with 3rd Gen. (NBNP)	3rd Gen. (NBNP) with 1st Gen. (FBFP)	2nd Gen. (NBFP) with 2nd Gen. (NBFP)	2nd Gen. (NBFP) with 3rd Gen. (NBNP)	3rd Gen. (NBNP) with 2nd Gen. (NBFP)	3rd Gen. (NBNP) with 3rd Gen. (NBNP)	Totals
19—FRANCE—*Continued*											
France	British West Indies (Engl.)	1									1
France	Canada (Engl.)						4				4
France	Canada (French)	5									5
France	Chile						1				1
France	Cuba (Span.)			1							1
France	Denmark	1									1
France	England	10	4	4			6				24
France	Finland	3		1							4
France	France (Jew)	1									1
France	Germany	19	13	6			29				67
France	Germany (North)	1									1
France	Germany (South)	12		4							16
France	Holland	1									1
France	Hungary (Jew)	1	1	1							3
France	Hungary (Sl.)	1									1
France	Ireland	23	15	14			26				78
France	Italy	13		2			1				16
France	Luxemburg	1									1
France	Russia (Jew)	5		2			1				8
France	Scotland	6	2	2			2				12
France	Spain	3									3
France	Sweden	6	1								7
France	Switzerland (French)	20					1				21
France	Switzerland (Germ.)	13	1								14
France	Venezuela (Span.)	1									1
France	United States (Jew)				1						1
Totals		500	61	49	1		80				691

NATIONALITY		GENERATION									
Man	Woman	1st Gen. (FBFP) with 1st Gen. (FBFP)	1st Gen. (FBFP) with 2nd Gen. (NBFP)	2nd Gen. (NBFP) with 1st Gen. (FBFP)	1st Gen. (FBFP) with 3rd Gen. (NBNP)	3rd Gen. (NBNP) with 1st Gen. (FBFP)	2nd Gen. (NBFP) with 2nd Gen. (NBFP)	2nd Gen. (NBFP) with 3rd Gen. (NBNP)	3rd Gen. (NBNP) with 2nd Gen. (NBFP)	3rd Gen. (NBNP) with 3rd Gen. (NBNP)	Totals
				20—GERMANY							
Germany	Germany	1902	699	278			1642				4521
Germany	Argentine			1							1
Germany	Austria (Boh.)	26	6	7			30				69
Germany	Austria (Germ.)	98	3	19			32				152
Germany	Austria (Jew)	6	1	3			6				16
Germany	Austria (Pol.)	29	6	13			23				71
Germany	Belgium	4	1	2			1				8
Germany	British West Indies (Engl.)	1		1			1				3
Germany	Canada (Engl.)	9	3	9			32				53
Germany	Canada (French)	2	2	2			4				10
Germany	Cuba (Span.)	2		1			1				4
Germany	Denmark	9	2	3			11				25
Germany	England	35	20	47			119				221
Germany	Finland	5		3			1				9
Germany	France	37	7	12			34				90
Germany	Germany (Jew)		1				1				2
Germany	Holland	1	1				5				7
Germany	Hungary (Germ.)	55	2	5			4				66
Germany	Hungary (Hung.)	4					1				5
Germany	Hungary (Jew)	5		2							7
Germany	Hungary (Sl.)	75	2	10			2				89
Germany	Ireland	77	42	147			481				747
Germany	Italy (North)	1		4							5
Germany	Italy	10	6	9			28				53
Germany	Italy (South)	1					1				2
Germany	Norway	7	2	4			9				22
Germany	Porto Rico (Span.)	1									1
Germany	Portugal			1							1
Germany	Russia (Jew)	2	4	6			8				20
Germany	Russia (Pol.)	6		3			2				11
Germany	Scotland	10	3	22			35				70
Germany	Spain	1		1			2				4

Nationality: Man	Nationality: Woman	1st Gen. (FBFP) with 1st Gen. (FBFP)	1st Gen. (FBFP) with 2nd Gen. (NBFP)	2nd Gen. (NBFP) with 1st Gen. (FBFP)	1st Gen. (FBFP) with 3rd Gen. (NBNP)	3rd Gen. (NBNP) with 1st Gen. (FBFP)	2nd Gen. (NBFP) with 2nd Gen. (NBFP)	2nd Gen. (NBFP) with 3rd Gen. (NBNP)	3rd Gen. (NBNP) with 2nd Gen. (NBFP)	3rd Gen. (NBNP) with 3rd Gen. (NBNP)	Totals
20—GERMANY—*Continued*											
Germany	Sweden	31	5	23			32				91
Germany	Switzerland (Germ.)	26	8	14			25				73
Germany	Venezuela (Span.)	2									2
Germany	Wales			5			3				8
Germany	United States (Jew)							4			4
Totals		2480	826	657			2576	4			6543
21—GERMANY (NORTH)											
Germany (N.)	Germany (N.)	209	3	2			5				219
Germany (N.)	Austria (Boh.)	24	3								27
Germany (N.)	Austria (Pol.)	13	1	1							15
Germany (N.)	Australia (Engl.)	1									1
Germany (N.)	Canada (Engl.)	7	1				1				9
Germany (N.)	Canada (French)	1	1								2
Germany (N.)	Denmark	3		1							4
Germany (N.)	England	12	8				1				21
Germany (N.)	Finland	2	1								3
Germany (N.)	France	1									1
Germany (N.)	Germany (S.)	91	1	4							96
Germany (N.)	Holland	2									2
Germany (N.)	Hungary (Germ.)	13									13
Germany (N.)	Hungary (Hung.)	2									2
Germany (N.)	Hungary (Jew)	2									2
Germany (N.)	Hungary (Sl.)	16									16
Germany (N.)	Ireland	24	13	1							38
Germany (N.)	Italy	2	1								3
Germany (N.)	Italy (North)	3									3
Germany (N.)	Norway	2	1	1							4
Germany (N.)	Russia (Pol.)	4	1								5
Germany (N.)	Scotland	2	1								3
Germany (N.)	Sweden	9									9

NATIONALITY		GENERATION									
MAN	WOMAN	1st Gen. (FBFP) with 1st Gen. (FBFP)	1st Gen. (FBFP) with 2nd Gen. (NBFP)	2nd Gen. (NBFP) with 1st Gen. (FBFP)	1st Gen. (FBFP) with 3rd Gen. (NBNP)	3rd Gen. (NBNP) with 1st Gen. (FBFP)	2nd Gen. (NBFP) with 2nd Gen. (NBFP)	2nd Gen. (NBFP) with 3rd Gen. (NBNP)	3rd Gen. (NBNP) with 2nd Gen. (NBFP)	3rd Gen. (NBNP) with 3rd Gen. (NBNP)	TOTALS
21—GERMANY (NORTH)—*Continued*											
Germany (N.)	Switzerland (Germ.)	8	4								12
Germany (N.)	Venezuela (Span.)		1								1
Totals		453	41	10			7				511
22—GERMANY (SOUTH)											
Germany (S.)	Germany (S.)	278	6	2			5				291
Germany (S.)	Austria (Boh.)	14	3				2				19
Germany (S.)	Austria (Germ.)	64	3	2			1				70
Germany (S.)	Austria (Jew)	3									3
Germany (S.)	Austria (Pol.)	34		1							35
Germany (S.)	British West Indies (Engl.)	2									2
Germany (S.)	Canada (Engl.)	2									2
Germany (S.)	Canada (French)	2									2
Germany (S.)	Denmark	2									2
Germany (S.)	England	17	3				3				23
Germany (S.)	Finland	3									3
Germany (S.)	France	1	12								13
Germany (S.)	Germany (North)	77	2	1			2				82
Germany (S.)	Holland	2									2
Germany (S.)	Hungary (Germ.)	37									37
Germany (S.)	Hungary (Hung.)	1									1
Germany (S.)	Hungary (Sl.)	28									28
Germany (S.)	Ireland	29	26	1							56
Germany (S.)	Norway	2	1								3
Germany (S.)	Russia (Pol.)	7									7
Germany (S.)	Scotland	4									4
Germany (S.)	Spain	1									1
Germany (S.)	Sweden	10		1							11
Germany (S.)	Switzerland (Germ.)	25	1	1			1				28
Germany (S.)	Turkey	1									1
Totals		646	57	9			14				726

NATIONALITY		GENERATION									
Man	Woman	1st Gen. (FBFP) with 1st Gen. (FBFP)	1st Gen. (FBFP) with 2nd Gen. (NBFP)	2nd Gen. (NBFP) with 1st Gen. (FBFP)	1st Gen. (FBFP) with 3rd Gen. (NBNP)	3rd Gen. (NBNP) with 1st Gen. (FBFP)	2nd Gen. (NBFP) with 2nd Gen. (NBFP)	2nd Gen. (NBFP) with 3rd Gen. (NBNP)	3rd Gen. (NBNP) with 2nd Gen. (NBFP)	3rd Gen. (NBNP) with 3rd Gen. (NBNP)	Totals
					23—GREECE						
Greece	Greece	218									218
Greece	Austria (Boh.)	1									1
Greece	Austria (Germ.)	1	1								2
Greece	Austria (Jew)	1									1
Greece	Austria (Pol.)	6									6
Greece	Canada (Engl.)		1								1
Greece	Canada (French)		1								1
Greece	Denmark	1									1
Greece	England	5	1								6
Greece	France	5									5
Greece	Germany	4	4				1				9
Greece	Germany (North)	4									4
Greece	Germany (South)	2	4								6
Greece	Holland	1									1
Greece	Hungary (Germ.)	1									1
Greece	Hungary (Hung.)	1									1
Greece	Hungary (Jew)	2									2
Greece	Hungary (Sl.)	10									10
Greece	Ireland	23	5								28
Greece	Italy	8	4								12
Greece	Italy (North)	1									1
Greece	Italy (South)	3									3
Greece	Norway	1									1
Greece	Russia (Jew)		1								1
Greece	Russia (Pol.)	3									3
Greece	Scotland	2									2
Greece	Sweden	5									5
Greece	Turkey (Jew)	1									1
Greece	Wales		1								1
Totals		310	23				1				334

Nationality		Generation									
Man	Woman	1st Gen. (FBFP) with 1st Gen. (FBFP)	1st Gen. (FBFP) with 2nd Gen. (NBFP)	2nd Gen. (NBFP) with 1st Gen. (FBFP)	1st Gen. (FBFP) with 3rd Gen. (NBNP)	3rd Gen. (NBNP) with 1st Gen. (FBFP)	2nd Gen. (NBFP) with 2nd Gen. (NBFP)	2nd Gen. (NBFP) with 3rd Gen. (NBNP)	3rd Gen. (NBNP) with 2nd Gen. (NBFP)	3rd Gen. (NBNP) with 3rd Gen. (NBNP)	Totals
24—HOLLAND											
Holland	Holland	50	4	1							55
Holland	Austria (Boh.)	2									2
Holland	Austria (Pol.)						1				1
Holland	Belgium	3									3
Holland	Canada (Engl.)		1				1				2
Holland	Canada (French)		1								1
Holland	Cuba (Span.)	1									1
Holland	Denmark	1									1
Holland	England	1	7	2			3				13
Holland	France	12					1				13
Holland	Germany	19	8				5				32
Holland	Germany (North)	1									1
Holland	Germany (South)	1		1			4				6
Holland	Greece	1									1
Holland	Hungary (Jew)	3									3
Holland	Hungary (Sl.)	2									2
Holland	Ireland	10	3	1			1				15
Holland	Italy		1								1
Holland	Luxemburg		1								1
Holland	Norway						1				1
Holland	Russia (Pol.)	1									1
Holland	Scotland	1		2							3
Holland	Sweden	6		1							7
Holland	Switzerland (Germ.)	1	1				1				3
Totals		116	27	8			18				169
25—HUNGARY (GERM.)											
Hungary (Germ.)	Hungary (Germ.)	397	1	2			1				401
Hungary (Germ.)	Austria (Boh.)	2									2
Hungary (Germ.)	Austria (Germ.)	16	1								17
Hungary (Germ.)	Austria (Pol.)	2									2

NATIONALITY		GENERATION									
Man	Woman	1st Gen. (FBFP) with 1st Gen. (FBFP)	1st Gen. (FBFP) with 2nd Gen. (NBFP)	2nd Gen. (NBFP) with 1st Gen. (FBFP)	1st Gen. (FBFP) with 3rd Gen. (NBNP)	3rd Gen. (NBNP) with 1st Gen. (FBFP)	2nd Gen. (NBFP) with 2nd Gen. (NBFP)	2nd Gen. (NBFP) with 3rd Gen. (NBNP)	3rd Gen. (NBNP) with 2nd Gen. (NBFP)	3rd Gen. (NBNP) with 3rd Gen. (NBNP)	Totals
25—HUNGARY (GERM.)—*Continued*											
Hungary (Germ.)	Belgium	1									1
Hungary (Germ.)	Finland	2									2
Hungary (Germ.)	France	1									1
Hungary (Germ.)	Germany	10	5								15
Hungary (Germ.)	Germany (North)	5									5
Hungary (Germ.)	Germany (South)	9									9
Hungary (Germ.)	Hungary (Hung.)	17									17
Hungary (Germ.)	Hungary (Sl.)	11									11
Hungary (Germ.)	Ireland	2					3				5
Hungary (Germ.)	Scotland			2							2
Hungary (Germ.)	Sweden	2									2
Hungary (Germ.)	Switzerland (Germ.)	1									1
Hungary (Germ.)	Switzerland (Ital.)	1									1
Totals		**479**	**7**	**4**			**4**				**494**
26—HUNGARY (HUNG.)											
Hungary (Hung.)	Hungary (Hung.)	334	1								335
Hungary (Hung.)	Austria (Germ.)	1									1
Hungary (Hung.)	Canada (Engl.)		1								1
Hungary (Hung.)	England	2									2
Hungary (Hung.)	Germany (South)	1									1
Hungary (Hung.)	Hungary (Germ.)	6									6
Hungary (Hung.)	Hungary (Sl.)	2									2
Hungary (Germ.)	Ireland	2									2
Totals		**348**	**2**								**350**
27—HUNGARY (SL.)											
Hungary (Sl.)	Hungary (Sl.)	1522	8	9			6				1545
Hungary (Sl.)	Austria (Boh.)	13	2								15
Hungary (Sl.)	Austria (Germ.)	3									3

NATIONALITY		GENERATION									
MAN	WOMAN	1st Gen. (FBFP) with 1st Gen. (FBFP)	1st Gen. (FBFP) with 2nd Gen. (NBFP)	2nd Gen. (NBFP) with 1st Gen. (FBFP)	1st Gen. (FBFP) with 3rd Gen. (NBNP)	3rd Gen. (NBNP) with 1st Gen. (FBFP)	2nd Gen. (NBFP) with 2nd Gen. (NBFP)	2nd Gen. (NBFP) with 3rd Gen. (NBNP)	3rd Gen. (NBNP) with 2nd Gen. (NBFP)	3rd Gen. (NBNP) with 3rd Gen. (NBNP)	TOTALS
		27—HUNGARY (SL.)—*Continued*									
Hungary (Sl.)	Austria (Jew)	1									1
Hungary (Sl.)	Austria (Pol.)	23	2	1							26
Hungary (Sl.)	France	2	1								3
Hungary (Sl.)	Germany	9	2				1				12
Hungary (Sl.)	Germany (North)	1									1
Hungary (Sl.)	Hungary (Germ.)	5									5
Hungary (Sl.)	Hungary (Hung.)	2									2
Hungary (Sl.)	Ireland		2	2							4
Hungary (Sl.)	Italy (South)						1				1
Hungary (Sl.)	Russia (Pol.)	5									5
Hungary (Sl.)	Switzerland (Germ.)	1									1
Totals		**1587**	**17**	**12**			**8**				**1624**
		28—IRELAND									
Ireland	Ireland	4455	412	784			1620				7271
Ireland	Austria (Boh.)	3	49	3			9				64
Ireland	Austria (Germ.)	1	3	4							8
Ireland	Austria (Jew)	2		2			5				9
Ireland	Austria (Pol.)	5		12			9				26
Ireland	Belgium	1		1			3				5
Ireland	Canada (Engl.)	16	8	11			28				63
Ireland	Canada (French)	1		4			6				11
Ireland	Cuba (Span.)		1	2			3				6
Ireland	Denmark	2	1	2			4				9
Ireland	England	84	30	64			114				292
Ireland	Finland	3		7							10
Ireland	France	12	6	6			26				50
Ireland	Germany	25	78	38			437				578
Ireland	Germany (Jew)		1	2			6				9
Ireland	Germany (North)	13		7							20

NATIONALITY		GENERATION									
MAN	WOMAN	1st Gen. (FBFP) with 1st Gen. (FBFP)	1st Gen. (FBFP) with 2nd Gen. (NBFP)	2nd Gen. (NBFP) with 1st Gen. (FBFP)	1st Gen. (FBFP) with 3rd Gen. (NBNP)	3rd Gen. (NBNP) with 1st Gen. (FBFP)	2nd Gen. (NBFP) with 2nd Gen. (NBFP)	2nd Gen. (NBFP) with 3rd Gen. (NBNP)	3rd Gen. (NBNP) with 2nd Gen. (NBFP)	3rd Gen. (NBNP) with 3rd Gen. (NBNP)	TOTALS
				28—IRELAND—*Continued*							
Ireland	Germany (South)	14		8							22
Ireland	Holland	2		2			4				8
Ireland	Hungary (Germ.)	2	1	1							4
Ireland	Hungary (Hung.)	1					5				6
Ireland	Hungary (Jew)	1	1								2
Ireland	Hungary (Sl.)	8		2			2				12
Ireland	Italy	5	15	6			24				50
Ireland	Italy (North)	1		1							2
Ireland	Italy (South)	1		4							5
Ireland	Norway	9		5			8				22
Ireland	Portugal						1				1
Ireland	Russia (Jew)						8				8
Ireland	Russia (Pol.)			4			3				7
Ireland	Scotland	55	19	33			33				140
Ireland	Spain	1	2				1				4
Ireland	Sweden	20	5	13			9				47
Ireland	Switzerland (French)						1				1
Ireland	Switzerland (Germ.)	3	2	3			17				25
Ireland	Venezuela (Span.)		1								1
Ireland	Wales	3	1	4			4				12
Ireland	United States (Jew)							2			2
Totals		**4749**	**636**	**1035**			**2390**	**2**			**8812**
				29—ITALY							
Italy	Italy	5317	650	107			167				6241
Italy	Austria (Boh.)	3	2	1			2				8
Italy	Austria (Germ.)	8	5	1			7				21
Italy	Austria (Jew)	4		2			2				8
Italy	Austria (Pol.)	10	5				2				17
Italy	Belgium	1		1							2

NATIONALITY		GENERATION									
MAN	WOMAN	1st Gen. (FBFP) with 1st Gen. (FBFP)	1st Gen. (FBFP) with 2nd Gen. (NBFP)	2nd Gen. (NBFP) with 1st Gen. (FBFP)	1st Gen. (FBFP) with 3rd Gen. (NBNP)	3rd Gen. (NBNP) with 1st Gen. (FBFP)	2nd Gen. (NBFP) with 2nd Gen. (NBFP)	2nd Gen. (NBFP) with 3rd Gen. (NBNP)	3rd Gen. (NBNP) with 2nd Gen. (NBFP)	3rd Gen. (NBNP) with 3rd Gen. (NBNP)	TOTALS
				29—ITALY—*Continued*							
Italy	Canada (Engl.)	3					2				5
Italy	Canada (French)		1				1				2
Italy	Cuba (Span.)	1									1
Italy	Denmark	1	1	1							3
Italy	England	15	8	5			8				36
Italy	England (Jew)	1					1				2
Italy	Finland			1							1
Italy	France	11	6	2			6				25
Italy	Germany	31	43	7			45				126
Italy	Germany (Jew)	5	1				2				8
Italy	Germany (South)	11	7	1			3				22
Italy	Greece	1									1
Italy	Holland	2	2				4				8
Italy	Hungary (Germ.)	3									3
Italy	Hungary (Hung.)	2									2
Italy	Hungary (Jew)	9		4							13
Italy	Hungary (Sl.)	18	1	5			1				25
Italy	Ireland	35	20	12			24				91
Italy	Luxemburg	1									1
Italy	Norway	3	1	1							5
Italy	Rumania (Jew)		1				1				2
Italy	Russia (Jew)	18	4	7			8				37
Italy	Russia (Pol.)	8	1	1			1				11
Italy	Scotland	1	7	1			5				14
Italy	Spain	1	2								3
Italy	Sweden	10		2			3				15
Italy	Switzerland (Germ.)	2		1							3
Italy	Switzerland (Ital.)	11									11
Italy	United States (Jew)				1			4			5
Totals		**5547**	**768**	**163**	**1**		**295**	**4**			**6778**

NATIONALITY		GENERATION									
MAN	WOMAN	1st Gen. (FBFP) with 1st Gen. (FBFP)	1st Gen. (FBFP) with 2nd Gen. (NBFP)	2nd Gen. (NBFP) with 1st Gen. (FBFP)	1st Gen. (FBFP) with 3rd Gen. (NBNP)	3rd Gen. (NBNP) with 1st Gen. (FBFP)	2nd Gen. (NBFP) with 2nd Gen. (NBFP)	2nd Gen. (NBFP) with 3rd Gen. (NBNP)	3rd Gen. (NBNP) with 2nd Gen. (NBFP)	3rd Gen. (NBNP) with 3rd Gen. (NBNP)	TOTALS
30—ITALY (NORTH)											
Italy (N.)	Italy (N.)	861	109								970
Italy (N.)	Austria (Germ.)	1									1
Italy (N.)	Austria (Jew)	2									2
Italy (N.)	Austria (Ital.)	1									1
Italy (N.)	Austria (Pol.)	3	1								4
Italy (N.)	Belgium	1									1
Italy (N.)	Canada (Engl.)	1									1
Italy (N.)	Cuba (Span.)	1									1
Italy (N.)	England	5	4								9
Italy (N.)	Finland	1									1
Italy (N.)	France	14									14
Italy (N.)	Germany	1	8								9
Italy (N.)	Germany (North)	1									1
Italy (N.)	Germany (South)	2					1				3
Italy (N.)	Hungary (Sl.)	2									2
Italy (N.)	Ireland	5	3				36				44
Italy (N.)	Italy (South)	58	5								63
Italy (N.)	Russia (Jew)	3		1							4
Italy (N.)	Russia (Pol.)	1									1
Italy (N.)	Spain	2									2
Italy (N.)	Sweden	2									2
Italy (N.)	Switzerland (Ital.)	2									2
Italy (N.)	United States (Jew)				1						1
Totals		**970**	**130**	**1**	**1**		**37**				**1139**

31—ITALY (SOUTH)

Man	Woman	1st Gen. (FBFP) with 1st Gen. (FBFP)	1st Gen. (FBFP) with 2nd Gen. (NBFP)	2nd Gen. (NBFP) with 1st Gen. (FBFP)	1st Gen. (FBFP) with 3rd Gen. (NBNP)	3rd Gen. (NBNP) with 1st Gen. (FBFP)	2nd Gen. (NBFP) with 2nd Gen. (NBFP)	2nd Gen. (NBFP) with 3rd Gen. (NBNP)	3rd Gen. (NBNP) with 2nd Gen. (NBFP)	3rd Gen. (NBNP) with 3rd Gen. (NBNP)	Totals
Italy (S.)	Italy (S.)	3580	576				4				3960
Italy (S.)	Austria (Germ.)	2									2
Italy (S.)	Austria (Jew)	6	2				1				9
Italy (S.)	Austria (Pol.)	15	6								21
Italy (S.)	Belgium		1								1
Italy (S.)	Canada (Engl.)	2	1								3
Italy (S.)	Canada (French)		1								1
Italy (S.)	England	7	6								13
Italy (S.)	France	7	6								13
Italy (S.)	England (Jew)	1									1
Italy (S.)	Germany	11	30				3				44
Italy (S.)	Germany (North)	4									4
Italy (S.)	Germany (South)	2									2
Italy (S.)	Germany (Jew)	2	1								3
Italy (S.)	Hungary (Hung.)	2									2
Italy (S.)	Hungary (Jew)	8									8
Italy (S.)	Hungary (Sl.)	10	1								11
Italy (S.)	Ireland	19	20				2				41
Italy (S.)	Italy (North)	185	2								187
Italy (S.)	Norway	3	1								4
Italy (S.)	Russia (Jew)	10	6								16
Italy (S.)	Russia (Pol.)	4									4
Italy (S.)	Scotland		1								1
Italy (S.)	Spain	5									5
Italy (S.)	Sweden	1	1								2
Italy (S.)	Switzerland (French)	1									1
Italy (S.)	Switzerland (Germ.)		1								1
Italy (S.)	Switzerland (Ital.)	2									2
Italy (S.)	Syria	1									1
Italy (S.)	United States (Col.)				1						1
Totals		3890	463		1		10				4364

NATIONALITY		GENERATION									
MAN	WOMAN	1st Gen. (FBFP) with 1st Gen. (FBFP)	1st Gen. (FBFP) with 2nd Gen. (NBFP)	2nd Gen. (NBFP) with 1st Gen. (FBFP)	1st Gen. (FBFP) with 3rd Gen. (NBNP)	3rd Gen. (NBNP) with 1st Gen. (FBFP)	2nd Gen. (NBFP) with 2nd Gen. (NBFP)	2nd Gen. (NBFP) with 3rd Gen. (NBNP)	3rd Gen. (NBNP) with 2nd Gen. (NBFP)	3rd Gen. (NBNP) with 3rd Gen. (NBNP)	TOTALS
32 JAPAN											
Japan	Japan	8									8
Japan	Canada (Engl.)		1								1
Japan	England	1									1
Japan	Finland	2									2
Japan	France	1									1
Japan	Germany	1									1
Japan	Germany (South)	2	1								3
Japan	Ireland	2									2
Japan	Mexico (Span.)	1									1
Japan	Norway	1									1
Japan	Scotland	2	1								3
Japan	Spain	1									1
Japan	Sweden	2									2
Japan	Switzerland (Germ.)	2									2
Totals		26	3								29
33 MEXICO (SPAN.)											
Mexico (Span.)	Austria (Pol.)	1									1
Mexico (Span.)	Cuba (Span.)	2									2
Mexico (Span.)	France	2									2
Mexico (Span.)	Scotland	2									2
Mexico (Span.)	Mexico (Span.)	2	1								3
Mexico (Span.)	Germany	1	1								2
Mexico (Span.)	Germany (North)	1									1
Mexico (Span.)	Germany (South)	1									1
Mexico (Span.)	Ireland	2	2				1				5
Mexico (Span.)	Spain	3									3
Mexico (Span.)	Sweden	1									1
Mexico (Span.)	Switzerland (Germ.)	1									1
Totals		19	4				1				24

NATIONALITY		GENERATION									
MAN	WOMAN	1st Gen. (FBFP) with 1st Gen. (FBFP)	1st Gen. (FBFP) with 2nd Gen. (NBFP)	2nd Gen. (NBFP) with 1st Gen. (FBFP)	1st Gen. (FBFP) with 3rd Gen. (NBNP)	3rd Gen. (NBNP) with 1st Gen. (FBFP)	2nd Gen. (NBFP) with 2nd Gen. (NBFP)	2nd Gen. (NBFP) with 3rd Gen. (NBNP)	3rd Gen. (NBNP) with 2nd Gen. (NBFP)	3rd Gen. (NBNP) with 3rd Gen. (NBNP)	TOTALS
34—NORWAY											
Norway	Norway	206	2	3			2				213
Norway	Austria (Boh.)			1							1
Norway	Austria (Germ.)	2									2
Norway	Austria (Pol.)	3		1							4
Norway	Belgium	2									2
Norway	British West Indies (Engl.)	2									2
Norway	Canada (Engl.)	1	1				2				4
Norway	Denmark	7		1							8
Norway	England	7	1				1				9
Norway	Finland	10									10
Norway	France		1				1				2
Norway	Germany	4	5				7				16
Norway	Germany (North)	3									3
Norway	Hungary (Jew)	1									1
Norway	Hungary (Sl.)	1	1								2
Norway	Ireland	12	4	1			1				18
Norway	Italy		1								1
Norway	Italy (South)	1									1
Norway	Scotland	2									2
Norway	Sweden	24	2	2			1				29
Totals		288	18	9			15				330
35—PORTO RICO (SPAN.)											
Porto Rico (Span.)	Porto Rico (Span.)	15	1								16
Porto Rico (Span.)	Austria (Boh.)		1								1
Porto Rico (Span.)	Austria (Germ.)	1									1
Porto Rico (Span.)	Austria (Pol.)	1									1
Porto Rico (Span.)	Belgium	1									1
Porto Rico (Span.)	Cuba (Col.)	1									1
Porto Rico (Span.)	Cuba (Span.)	3	1								4
Porto Rico (Span.)	Denmark		1								1

NATIONALITY		GENERATION									
MAN	WOMAN	1st Gen. (FBFP) with 1st Gen. (FBFP)	1st Gen. (FBFP) with 2nd Gen. (NBFP)	2nd Gen. (NBFP) with 1st Gen. (FBFP)	1st Gen. (FBFP) with 3rd Gen. (NBNP)	3rd Gen. (NBNP) with 1st Gen. (FBFP)	2nd Gen. (NBFP) with 2nd Gen. (NBFP)	2nd Gen. (NBFP) with 3rd Gen. (NBNP)	3rd Gen. (NBNP) with 2nd Gen. (NBFP)	3rd Gen. (NBNP) with 3rd Gen. (NBNP)	TOTALS
35—PORTO RICO (SPAN.)—*Continued*											
Porto Rico (Span.)	England		1				2				3
Porto Rico (Span.)	Germany	2									2
Porto Rico (Span.)	Ireland	3	2								5
Porto Rico (Span.)	Italy (South)	2									2
Porto Rico (Span.)	Spain	1									1
Porto Rico (Span.)	Sweden	1									1
Porto Rico (Span.)	Switzerland (Germ.)	1									1
Totals		32	7				2				41
36—PORTUGAL											
Portugal	Portugal	2									2
Portugal	Denmark						1				1
Portugal	England	1									1
Portugal	France	2									2
Portugal	Germany						1				1
Portugal	Hungary (Jew)	1									1
Portugal	Ireland	3	2								5
Portugal	Italy	2									2
Portugal	Norway	1									1
Portugal	Sweden			1							1
Totals		12	2	1			2				17
37—RUMANIA											
Rumania	Rumania	15	1								16
Rumania	Austria (Germ.)	1									1
Rumania	Germany	1									1
Rumania	Hungary (Sl.)	2									2
Rumania	Ireland		1								1
Totals		19	2								21

NATIONALITY		GENERATION									
MAN	WOMAN	1st Gen. (FBFP) with 1st Gen. (FBFP)	1st Gen. (FBFP) with 2nd Gen. (NBFP)	2nd Gen. (NBFP) with 1st Gen. (FBFP)	1st Gen. (FBFP) with 3rd Gen. (NBNP)	3rd Gen. (NBNP) with 1st Gen. (FBFP)	2nd Gen. (NBFP) with 2nd Gen. (NBFP)	2nd Gen. (NBFP) with 3rd Gen. (NBNP)	3rd Gen. (NBNP) with 2nd Gen. (NBFP)	3rd Gen. (NBNP) with 3rd Gen. (NBNP)	TOTALS
38—RUSSIA (POL.)											
Russia (Pol)	Russia (Pol)	750	4				2				756
Russia (Pol)	Austria (Boh)	1									1
Russia (Pol)	Austria (Germ)	2	1								3
Russia (Pol)	Austria (Jew)						1				1
Russia (Pol)	Austria (Pol)	192	1				1				194
Russia (Pol)	Denmark			1							1
Russia (Pol)	Finland	12		1							13
Russia (Pol)	Germany (North	12	5								17
Russia (Pol)	Hungary (Sl)	32	1								33
Russia (Pol)	Ireland	8	4				1				13
Russia (Pol)	Norway	1									1
Russia (Pol)	Russia (Jew)	1									1
Russia (Pol)	Scotland	1									1
Russia (Pol)	Sweden	3	1								4
Russia (Pol)	Switzerland (Germ)	1									1
Totals		**1016**	**17**	**2**			**5**				**1040**
39—SERVIA											
Servia	Austria (Boh)	2									2
Servia	Austria (Pol)	1									1
Servia	Hungary (Jew)	1									1
Servia	Hungary (Sl)	7									7
Servia	Ireland		1								1
Totals		11	1								**12**
40—SCOTLAND											
Scotland	Scotland	280	14	10			9				313
Scotland	Austria (Boh)	3									3
Scotland	Austria (Germ)		2								2
Scotland	Austria (Jew)			1							1

NATIONALITY		GENERATION									
MAN	WOMAN	1st Gen. (FBFP) with 1st Gen. (FBFP)	1st Gen. (FBFP) with 2nd Gen. (NBFP)	2nd Gen. (NBFP) with 1st Gen. (FBFP)	1st Gen. (FBFP) with 3rd Gen. (NBNP)	3rd Gen. (NBNP) with 1st Gen. (FBFP)	2nd Gen. (NBFP) with 2nd Gen. (NBFP)	2nd Gen. (NBFP) with 3rd Gen. (NBNP)	3rd Gen. (NBNP) with 2nd Gen. (NBFP)	3rd Gen. (NBNP) with 3rd Gen. (NBNP)	TOTALS
					40—SCOTLAND—*Continued*						
Scotland	Austria (Pol.)		1				1				2
Scotland	Belgium	1									1
Scotland	Canada (Engl.)	12	2	2			5				21
Scotland	Canada (French)			1			1				2
Scotland	Denmark	1	1								2
Scotland	England	59	11	7			17				94
Scotland	Finland	1									1
Scotland	France	4	3	1			1				9
Scotland	Germany	8	27	2			49				86
Scotland	Germany (North)						2				2
Scotland	Germany (South)	3	1	2							6
Scotland	Germany (Jew)		1								1
Scotland	Holland	1	1								2
Scotland	Hungary (Jew)	1	2								3
Scotland	Hungary (Sl.)	1									1
Scotland	Ireland	115	37	14			50				216
Scotland	Italy		1				1				2
Scotland	Italy (North)	1									1
Scotland	Italy (South)	1									1
Scotland	Norway	3					1				4
Scotland	Russia (Pol.)						1				1
Scotland	Spain	1									1
Scotland	Sweden	24	2	1			1				28
Scotland	Switzerland (Germ.)	1	4	3			3				11
Scotland	Wales	3	2								5
Totals		**524**	**112**	**44**			**142**				**822**

NATIONALITY		GENERATION									
MAN	WOMAN	1st Gen. (FBFP) with 1st Gen. (FBFP)	1st Gen. (FBFP) with 2nd Gen. (NBFP)	2nd Gen. (NBFP) with 1st Gen. (FBFP)	1st Gen. (FBFP) with 3rd Gen. (NBNP)	3rd Gen. (NBNP) with 1st Gen. (FBFP)	2nd Gen. (NBFP) with 2nd Gen. (NBFP)	2nd Gen. (NBFP) with 3rd Gen. (NBNP)	3rd Gen. (NBNP) with 2nd Gen. (NBFP)	3rd Gen. (NBNP) with 3rd Gen. (NBNP)	TOTALS
		41—SPAIN									
Spain	Spain	102	1				1				104
Spain	Algeria	2									2
Spain	Austria (Germ)						1				1
Spain	Austria (Pol)						1				1
Spain	Belgium	2									2
Spain	Canada (Engl)	2									2
Spain	Cuba (Span)	5									5
Spain	Denmark	1									1
Spain	France	7	1								8
Spain	England	2									2
Spain	Germany	4	3				1				8
Spain	Germany (South)	1	1				1				3
Spain	Hungary (Sl)	1									1
Spain	Ireland	2	3				2				7
Spain	Italy	3	1				1				5
Spain	Italy (South)	1	1								2
Spain	Luxemburg	1									1
Spain	Mexico (Span)	1									1
Spain	Portugal	1									1
Spain	Porto Rico (Span)	3									3
Spain	Russia (Jew)		1								1
Spain	Sweden	2									2
Spain	Syria	1									1
Spain	United States (Col)							1			1
Totals		144	12				8				165

NATIONALITY		GENERATION									
Man	Woman	1st Gen. (FBFP) with 1st Gen. (FBFP)	1st Gen. (FBFP) with 2nd Gen. (NBFP)	2nd Gen. (NBFP) with 1st Gen. (FBFP)	1st Gen. (FBFP) with 3rd Gen. (NBNP)	3rd Gen. (NBNP) with 1st Gen. (FBFP)	2nd Gen. (NBFP) with 2nd Gen. (NBFP)	2nd Gen. (NBFP) with 3rd Gen. (NBNP)	3rd Gen. (NBNP) with 2nd Gen. (NBFP)	3rd Gen. (NBNP) with 3rd Gen. (NBNP)	Totals
					42—SWEDEN						
Sweden	Sweden	681	16	17			10				724
Sweden	Austria (Boh.)	2									2
Sweden	Austria (Germ.)	2	1				1				4
Sweden	Austria (Pol.)	3									3
Sweden	Canada (Engl.)	2					1				3
Sweden	Denmark	7	2				1				10
Sweden	England	7	3	2			2				14
Sweden	Finland	35		1							36
Sweden	France	9		1			4				14
Sweden	Germany	11	10				26				47
Sweden	Germany (North)	7					1				8
Sweden	Germany (South)	3									3
Sweden	Holland	1					1				2
Sweden	Hungary (Germ.)						1				1
Sweden	Hungary (Hung.)	4									4
Sweden	Hungary (Sl.)	3	1								4
Sweden	Ireland	30	8	6			13				57
Sweden	Italy	1									1
Sweden	Luxemburg	1									1
Sweden	Norway	36	1	1							38
Sweden	Russia (Jew)			1							1
Sweden	Servia		1								1
Sweden	Scotland	4	1								5
Sweden	Switzerland (Germ.)	5	1								6
Totals		**854**	**45**	**29**			**61**				**989**
					43—SWITZERLAND (GERM.)						
Switzerland (Germ.)	Switzerland (Germ.)	103	8	3			2				116
Switzerland (Germ.)	Austria (Boh.)	1									1
Switzerland (Germ.)	Austria (Germ.)	13									13
Switzerland (Germ.)	Austria (Pol.)	1	1	1							3

NATIONALITY		GENERATION									
MAN	WOMAN	1st Gen. (FBFP) with 1st Gen. (FBFP)	1st Gen. (FBFP) with 2nd Gen. (NBFP)	2nd Gen. (NBFP) with 1st Gen. (FBFP)	1st Gen. (FBFP) with 3rd Gen. (NBNP)	3rd Gen. (NBNP) with 1st Gen. (FBFP)	2nd Gen. (NBFP) with 2nd Gen. (NBFP)	2nd Gen. (NBFP) with 3rd Gen. (NBNP)	3rd Gen. (NBNP) with 2nd Gen. (NBFP)	3rd Gen. (NBNP) with 3rd Gen. (NBNP)	TOTALS
43—SWITZERLAND (GERM.)—*Continued*											
Switzerland (Germ.)	Belgium	3									3
Switzerland (Germ.)	Canada (Engl.)	1					1				2
Switzerland (Germ.)	Canada (French)						1				1
Switzerland (Germ.)	Cuba (Span.)						1				1
Switzerland (Germ.)	England	12	3	1			2				18
Switzerland (Germ.)	Finland	4									4
Switzerland (Germ.)	France	12					1				13
Switzerland (Germ.)	Germany	41	26	2			20				89
Switzerland (Germ.)	Germany (North)	3		1			1				5
Switzerland (Germ.)	Germany (South)	16		3			1				20
Switzerland (Germ.)	Hungary (Germ.)	6									6
Switzerland (Germ.)	Hungary (Sl.)	5	1								6
Switzerland (Germ.)	Ireland	11	4	3			9				27
Switzerland (Germ.)	Italy	3					1				4
Switzerland (Germ.)	Norway	2					1				3
Switzerland (Germ.)	Russia (Pol.)	1									1
Switzerland (Germ.)	Scotland						1				1
Switzerland (Germ.)	Sweden	1	1								2
Switzerland (Germ.)	Switzerland (French)	1									1
Switzerland (Germ.)	Switzerland (Ital.)		1								1
Totals		**240**	**45**	**14**			**42**				**341**
44—SWITZERLAND (FRENCH)											
Switz. (French)	Switzerland (French)	6									6
Switz. (French)	England	1									1
Switz. (French)	France	10									10
Switz. (French)	Ireland	6	3								9
Switz. (French)	Italy (South)	1									1
Switz. (French)	Norway	1									1
Switz. (French)	Sweden	2									2
Switz. (French)	Switzerland (Germ.)	3									3
Totals		**30**	**3**								**33**

NATIONALITY		GENERATION									
MAN	WOMAN	1st Gen. (FBFP) with 1st Gen. (FBFP)	1st Gen. (FBFP) with 2nd Gen. (NBFP)	2nd Gen. (NBFP) with 1st Gen. (FBFP)	1st Gen. (FBFP) with 3rd Gen. (NBNP)	3rd Gen. (NBNP) with 1st Gen. (FBFP)	2nd Gen. (NBFP) with 2nd Gen. (NBFP)	2nd Gen. (NBFP) with 3rd Gen. (NBNP)	3rd Gen. (NBNP) with 2nd Gen. (NBFP)	3rd Gen. (NBNP) with 3rd Gen. (NBNP)	TOTALS
		45—SWITZERLAND (ITAL.)									
Switzerland (Ital.)	Switzerland (Ital.)	6	1								7
Switzerland (Ital.)	Hungary (Sl.)	1									1
Switzerland (Ital.)	Ireland		1	1							2
Switzerland (Ital.)	Italy	6	1								7
Switzerland (Ital.)	Italy (North)	1									1
Totals		**14**	**3**	**1**							**18**
		46—SYRIA									
Syria	Canada (Engl.)	1									1
Syria	Syria	71	1								72
Syria	Russia (Jew)		1								1
Syria	Sweden	1									1
Syria	Switzerland (French)	1									1
Totals		**74**	**2**								**76**
		47—TURKEY									
Turkey	Turkey	99									99
Turkey	Austria (Pol.)	2									2
Turkey	Belgium	1									1
Turkey	Bulgaria	1									1
Turkey	British West Indies (Engl.)	1									1
Turkey	Egypt	1									1
Turkey	France	1									1
Turkey	Germany (North)	1					1				2
Turkey	Greece	5									5
Turkey	Hungary (Sl.)	2									2
Turkey	Ireland	5	1	1							7
Turkey	Italy (South)	2									2
Turkey	Norway	1									1
Turkey	Spain	1									1
Turkey	Switzerland (Germ.)	1									1
Totals		**124**	**1**	**1**			**1**				**127**

NATIONALITY		GENERATION									
Man	Woman	1st Gen. (FBFP) with 1st Gen. (FBFP)	1st Gen. (FBFP) with 2nd Gen. (NBFP)	2nd Gen. (NBFP) with 1st Gen. (FBFP)	1st Gen. (FBFP) with 3rd Gen. (NBNP)	3rd Gen. (NBNP) with 1st Gen. (FBFP)	2nd Gen. (NBFP) with 2nd Gen. (NBFP)	2nd Gen. (NBFP) with 3rd Gen. (NBNP)	3rd Gen. (NBNP) with 2nd Gen. (NBFP)	3rd Gen. (NBNP) with 3rd Gen. (NBNP)	Totals
48—UNITED STATES											
United States	United States									9542	9542
United States	Austria (Boh.)					20			29		49
United States	Austria (Germ.)					31			18		49
United States	Austria (Jew)					11			13		24
United States	Austria (Pol.)					37			31		68
United States	Belgium					6			2		8
United States	British West Indies (Engl.)					8					8
United States	Canada (Engl.)					152			126		278
United States	Canada (French)					11			18		29
United States	Cuba (Span.)					10			7		17
United States	Denmark					25			24		49
United States	England					264			417		681
United States	England (Jew)								1		1
United States	Finland					17			6		23
United States	France					43			81		124
United States	Germany					193			1489		1682
United States	Germany (Jew)					3			15		18
United States	Germany (North)					44			13		57
United States	Germany (South)					78			6		84
United States	Greece								1		1
United States	Holland					6			20		26
United States	Hungary (Germ.)					10			1		11
United States	Hungary (Jew)					7			6		13
United States	Hungary (Hung.)					2					2
United States	Hungary (Sl.)					29			6		35
United States	Ireland					694			1662		2356
United States	Italy (North)					8			1		9
United States	Italy (South)					14			4		18
United States	Italy					34			83		117
United States	Mexico (Span.)								2		2
United States	Norway					26			17		43
United States	Porto Rico (Span.)					1					1

NATIONALITY		GENERATION									
MAN	WOMAN	1st Gen. (FBFP) with 1st Gen. (FBFP)	1st Gen. (FBFP) with 2nd Gen. (NBFP)	2nd Gen. (NBFP) with 1st Gen. (FBFP)	1st Gen. (FBFP) with 3rd Gen. (NBNP)	3rd Gen. (NBNP) with 1st Gen. (FBFP)	2nd Gen. (NBFP) with 2nd Gen. (NBFP)	2nd Gen. (NBFP) with 3rd Gen. (NBNP)	3rd Gen. (NBNP) with 2nd Gen. (NBFP)	3rd Gen. (NBNP) with 3rd Gen. (NBNP)	TOTALS
48—UNITED STATES—*Continued*											
United States	Portugal								1		1
United States	Rumania (Jew)					3					3
United States	Russia (Jew)					14			12		26
United States	Russia (Pol.)					6			9		15
United States	Scotland					124			157		281
United States	Spain					5			9		14
United States	Sweden					70			53		123
United States	Switzerland (French)					4			4		8
United States	Switzerland (Germ.)					20			49		69
United States	Syria					1					1
United States	United States (Col.)									1	1
United States	United States (Jew)									14	14
United States	Venezuela (Span.)								1		1
United States	Wales					9			16		25
Totals						2040			4410	9557	16007
49—UNITED STATES (COL.)											
United States (Col.)	United States (Col.)									2206	2206
United States (Col.)	British West Indies (Col.)					41			2		43
United States (Col.)	Canada (Engl.)					13			3		16
United States (Col.)	Cuba (Col.)					3			2		5
United States (Col.)	Denmark					1					1
United States (Col.)	Danish West Indies (Col.)					3					3
United States (Col.)	England					1					1
United States (Col.)	Germany								3		3
United States (Col.)	Haiti (Col.)								2		2
United States (Col.)	Hungary (Jew)					1					1
United States (Col.)	Hungary (Sl.)					1					1
United States (Col.)	Ireland					1			4		5
United States (Col.)	Italy								1		1

NATIONALITY		GENERATION									
MAN	WOMAN	1st Gen. (FBFP) with 1st Gen. (FBFP)	1st Gen. (FBFP) with 2nd Gen. (NBFP)	2nd Gen. (NBFP) with 1st Gen. (FBFP)	1st Gen. (FBFP) with 3rd Gen. (NBNP)	3rd Gen. (NBNP) with 1st Gen. (FBFP)	2nd Gen. (NBFP) with 2nd Gen. (NBFP)	2nd Gen. (NBFP) with 3rd Gen. (NBNP)	3rd Gen. (NBNP) with 2nd Gen. (NBFP)	3rd Gen. (NBNP) with 3rd Gen. (NBNP)	TOTALS
49—UNITED STATES (COL.)—*Continued*											
United States (Col.)	Porto Rico (Col.)					1					1
United States (Col.)	Sweden					1					1
United States (Col.)	United States									11	11
Totals						67			17	2217	2301
50—WALES											
Wales	Wales	23	2	1			3				29
Wales	Austria (Germ.)	1									1
Wales	Austria (Jew)	1									1
Wales	Canada (Engl.)	1									1
Wales	England	9		3			2				14
Wales	Germany	1	2				5				8
Wales	Germany (North)			1							1
Wales	Hungary (Jew)	1									1
Wales	Ireland	4	5	1			7				17
Wales	Scotland	4									4
Wales	Sweden	1									1
Totals		46	9	6			17				78
51—AUSTRIA (JEW)											
Austria (Jew)	Austria (Jew)	4465	60	31			56				4612
Austria (Jew)	Austria (Boh.)	1									1
Austria (Jew)	Austria (Germ.)	1									1
Austria (Jew)	Canada (Engl.)	1	2				1				4
Austria (Jew)	Canada (Jew)	1									1
Austria (Jew)	Denmark	2									2
Austria (Jew)	England	1	2				2				5
Austria (Jew)	England (Jew)	8	8	2			11				29
Austria (Jew)	France (Jew)	2		1							3
Austria (Jew)	France	1	1								2

NATIONALITY		GENERATION									
MAN	WOMAN	1st Gen. (FBFP) with 1st Gen. (FBFP)	1st Gen. (FBFP) with 2nd Gen. (NBFP)	2nd Gen. (NBFP) with 1st Gen. (FBFP)	1st Gen. (FBFP) with 3rd Gen. (NBNP)	3rd Gen. (NBNP) with 1st Gen. (FBFP)	2nd Gen. (NBFP) with 2nd Gen. (NBFP)	2nd Gen. (NBFP) with 3rd Gen. (NBNP)	3rd Gen. (NBNP) with 2nd Gen. (NBFP)	3rd Gen. (NBNP) with 3rd Gen. (NBNP)	TOTALS
51—AUSTRIA (JEW)—*Continued*											
Austria (Jew)	Germany	3	3	1			2				9
Austria (Jew)	Germany (Jew)	80	71	7			69				227
Austria (Jew)	Germany (South)	2		1							3
Austria (Jew)	Holland (Jew)	1					1				2
Austria (Jew)	Hungary (Jew)	328	32	16			22				398
Austria (Jew)	Hungary (Sl.)			1							1
Austria (Jew)	Ireland	3	1	3			2				9
Austria (Jew)	Rumania (Jew)	154	10	5			5				174
Austria (Jew)	Russia (Jew)	876	133	44			77				1130
Austria (Jew)	Spain (Jew)						1				1
Austria (Jew)	Turkey (Jew)	1									1
Austria (Jew)	United States				11			9			20
Austria (Jew)	United States (Jew)				76			56			132
Totals		5931	323	112	87		249	65			6767
52—BULGARIA (JEW)											
Bulgaria (Jew)	Bulgaria (Jew)	3									3
Bulgaria (Jew)	Austria (Jew)	3									3
Bulgaria (Jew)	England (Jew)		1								1
Bulgaria (Jew)	Hungary (Jew)	1									1
Bulgaria (Jew)	Russia (Jew)	1									1
Bulgaria (Jew)	Turkey (Jew)	1									1
Totals		9	1								10
53—ENGLAND (JEW)											
England (Jew)	England (Jew)	10	2				4				16
England (Jew)	Austria (Jew)	12	5	3			10				30
England (Jew)	France (Jew)						3				3
England (Jew)	Germany						3				3
England (Jew)	Germany (South)	2									2

NATIONALITY		GENERATION									
MAN	WOMAN	1st Gen. (FBFP) with 1st Gen. (FBFP)	1st Gen. (FBFP) with 2nd Gen. (NBFP)	2nd Gen. (NBFP) with 1st Gen. (FBFP)	1st Gen. (FBFP) with 3rd Gen. (NBNP)	3rd Gen. (NBNP) with 1st Gen. (FBFP)	2nd Gen. (NBFP) with 2nd Gen. (NBFP)	2nd Gen. (NBFP) with 3rd Gen. (NBNP)	3rd Gen. (NBNP) with 2nd Gen. (NBFP)	3rd Gen. (NBNP) with 3rd Gen. (NBNP)	TOTALS
53—ENGLAND (JEW)—*Continued*											
England (Jew)	Germany (Jew)	5	14	6			24				49
England (Jew)	Holland (Jew)	2	1				1				4
England (Jew)	Hungary (Jew)	4		2			5				11
England (Jew)	Ireland						1				1
England (Jew)	Italy		1								1
England (Jew)	Russia (Jew)	28	13	7			16				64
England (Jew)	Switzerland (Jew)		1								1
England (Jew)	United States (Jew)				10			16			26
England (Jew)	United States				1						1
Totals		63	37	18	11		67	16			212
54—FRANCE (JEW)											
France (Jew)	France (Jew)			1							1
France (Jew)	Austria (Jew)	3	1				6				10
France (Jew)	England						1				1
France (Jew)	France			1							1
France (Jew)	Germany (Jew)	2	4	1			9				16
France (Jew)	Russia (Jew)		2	2							4
France (Jew)	Scotland						2				2
France (Jew)	United States							1			1
France (Jew)	United States (Jew)				4			5			9
Totals		5	7	5	4		18	6			45
55—GERMANY (JEW)											
Germany (Jew)	Germany (Jew)	213	61	117			329				720
Germany (Jew)	Austria (Germ.)						2				2
Germany (Jew)	Austria (Jew)	82	26	28			91				227
Germany (Jew)	Canada (Engl.)		2	3			1				6
Germany (Jew)	Canada (Jew)			1			1				2
Germany (Jew)	Denmark	1									1

NATIONALITY		GENERATION									
MAN	WOMAN	1st Gen. (FBFP) with 1st Gen. (FBFP)	1st Gen. (FBFP) with 2nd Gen. (NBFP)	2nd Gen. (NBFP) with 1st Gen. (FBFP)	1st Gen. (FBFP) with 3rd Gen. (NBNP)	3rd Gen. (NBNP) with 1st Gen. (FBFP)	2nd Gen. (NBFP) with 2nd Gen. (NBFP)	2nd Gen. (NBFP) with 3rd Gen. (NBNP)	3rd Gen. (NBNP) with 2nd Gen. (NBFP)	3rd Gen. (NBNP) with 3rd Gen. (NBNP)	TOTALS
55—GERMANY (JEW)—*Continued*											
Germany (Jew)	England	5	1	3			8				17
Germany (Jew)	England (Jew)	1	2	4			37				44
Germany (Jew)	France (Jew)		5	3			13				21
Germany (Jew)	Germany	1	4				8				13
Germany (Jew)	Germany (South)	2					1				3
Germany (Jew)	Holland	2		1			10				13
Germany (Jew)	Hungary (Hung.)			1							1
Germany (Jew)	Ireland	2	3	1			14				20
Germany (Jew)	Italy						2				2
Germany (Jew)	Hungary (Jew)	65	15	31			37				148
Germany (Jew)	Norway			2							2
Germany (Jew)	Rumania (Jew)	8		5			5				18
Germany (Jew)	Russia (Jew)	74	26	69			103				272
Germany (Jew)	Scotland		1								1
Germany (Jew)	Scotland (Jew)						1				1
Germany (Jew)	Spain						1				1
Germany (Jew)	Sweden		1				1				2
Germany (Jew)	Sweden (Jew)						1				1
Germany (Jew)	Switzerland (Germ.)						1				1
Germany (Jew)	Switzerland (Jew)	1					1				2
Germany (Jew)	Turkey (Jew)			1							1
Germany (Jew)	United States				7			41			48
Germany (Jew)	United States (Jew)				51			151			202
Totals		457	147	270	58		668	192			1792
56—HOLLAND (JEW)											
Holland (Jew)	Holland (Jew)	6	2	1			1				10
Holland (Jew)	Austria (Jew)	11	1	1			1				14
Holland (Jew)	England (Jew)			1			1				2
Holland (Jew)	Germany		1								1
Holland (Jew)	Germany (Jew)	3	2	1			6				12
Holland (Jew)	Hungary (Jew)	2	1								3

NATIONALITY		GENERATION									
MAN	WOMAN	1st Gen. (FBFP) with 1st Gen. (FBFP)	1st Gen. (FBFP) with 2nd Gen. (NBFP)	2nd Gen. (NBFP) with 1st Gen. (FBFP)	1st Gen. (FBFP) with 3rd Gen. (NBNP)	3rd Gen. (NBNP) with 1st Gen. (FBFP)	2nd Gen. (NBFP) with 2nd Gen. (NBFP)	2nd Gen. (NBFP) with 3rd Gen. (NBNP)	3rd Gen. (NBNP) with 2nd Gen. (NBFP)	3rd Gen. (NBNP) with 3rd Gen. (NBNP)	TOTALS
		56—HOLLAND (JEW)—*Continued*									
Holland (Jew)	Ireland		1								1
Holland (Jew)	Russia (Jew)	4	1	3			3				11
Holland (Jew)	Scotland			1							1
Holland (Jew)	United States							1			1
Holland (Jew)	United States (Jew)				3			11			14
Totals		26	9	8	3		12	12			70
		57—HUNGARY (JEW)									
Hungary (Jew)	Hungary (Jew)	1429	73	27			26				1555
Hungary (Jew)	Austria (Jew)	125	22	9			22				178
Hungary (Jew)	Austria (Boh.)		1								1
Hungary (Jew)	Canada (Jew)	1									1
Hungary (Jew)	England	1	1				2				4
Hungary (Jew)	England (Jew)	1					2				3
Hungary (Jew)	France (Jew)		2	1			1				4
Hungary (Jew)	Germany		2								2
Hungary (Jew)	Germany (Jew)	44	35	5			33				117
Hungary (Jew)	Germany (South)	2									2
Hungary (Jew)	Holland (Jew)	2	4	1			1				8
Hungary (Jew)	Hungary (Germ.)	2	1								3
Hungary (Jew)	Ireland	1	1				1				3
Hungary (Jew)	Italy		1								1
Hungary (Jew)	Rumania (Jew)	19		1			3				23
Hungary (Jew)	Russia (Jew)	82	30	25			30				167
Hungary (Jew)	Scotland		1	1							2
Hungary (Jew)	Switzerland (Germ.)	1									1
Hungary (Jew)	Switzerland (Jew)		1								1
Hungary (Jew)	United States				5			1			6
Hungary (Jew)	United States (Jew)				49			22			71
Totals		1710	175	70	54		121	23			2153

NATIONALITY		GENERATION									
Man	Woman	1st Gen. (FBFP) with 1st Gen. (FBFP)	1st Gen. (FBFP) with 2nd Gen. (NBFP)	2nd Gen. (NBFP) with 1st Gen. (FBFP)	1st Gen. (FBFP) with 3rd Gen. (NBNP)	3rd Gen. (NBNP) with 1st Gen. (FBFP)	2nd Gen. (NBFP) with 2nd Gen. (NBFP)	2nd Gen. (NBFP) with 3rd Gen. (NBNP)	3rd Gen. (NBNP) with 2nd Gen. (NBFP)	3rd Gen. (NBNP) with 3rd Gen. (NBNP)	Totals
					58—RUMANIA (JEW)						
Rumania (Jew)	Rumania (Jew)	769	6	2			3				780
Rumania (Jew)	Austria (Jew)	195	15	1			4				215
Rumania (Jew)	Bulgaria (Jew)	1									1
Rumania (Jew)	England	2									2
Rumania (Jew)	England (Jew)		1				1				2
Rumania (Jew)	Finland (Jew)	1									1
Rumania (Jew)	France	2									2
Rumania (Jew)	Germany (Jew)	7	12				1				20
Rumania (Jew)	Holland (Jew)	2									2
Rumania (Jew)	Hungary (Jew)	36	13				2				51
Rumania (Jew)	Russia (Jew)	245	29	8			15				297
Rumania (Jew)	Palestine (Jew)	2									2
Rumania (Jew)	Turkey (Jew)	1									1
Rumania (Jew)	United States				1						1
Rumania (Jew)	United States (Jew)				17			2			19
Totals		1263	76	11	18		26	2			1396
					59—RUSSIA (JEW)						
Russia (Jew)	Russia (Jew)	14510	777	328			455				16070
Russia (Jew)	Austria (Germ.)		1								1
Russia (Jew)	Austria (Jew)	1434	181	45			141				1801
Russia (Jew)	Austria (Pol.)	2									2
Russia (Jew)	Australia (Jew)						2				2
Russia (Jew)	Bulgaria (Jew)	1									1
Russia (Jew)	Canada (French)	2									2
Russia (Jew)	England	1	1				6				8
Russia (Jew)	England (Jew)	30	13	4			20				67
Russia (Jew)	Finland	1									1
Russia (Jew)	France	1	1								2
Russia (Jew)	France (Jew)		4	1			3				8
Russia (Jew)	Germany	1	3				8				12

NATIONALITY		GENERATION									
MAN	WOMAN	1st Gen. (FBFP) with 1st Gen. (FBFP)	1st Gen. (FBFP) with 2nd Gen. (NBFP)	2nd Gen. (NBFP) with 1st Gen. (FBFP)	1st Gen. (FBFP) with 3rd Gen. (NBNP)	3rd Gen. (NBNP) with 1st Gen. (FBFP)	2nd Gen. (NBFP) with 2nd Gen. (NBFP)	2nd Gen. (NBFP) with 3rd Gen. (NBNP)	3rd Gen. (NBNP) with 2nd Gen. (NBFP)	3rd Gen. (NBNP) with 3rd Gen. (NBNP)	TOTALS
		59—RUSSIA (JEW)—*Continued*									
Russia (Jew)	Germany (Jew)	101	141	25			101				368
Russia (Jew)	Germany (South)	1									1
Russia (Jew)	Holland	2	3	2			6				13
Russia (Jew)	Hungary (Jew)	283	57	27			43				410
Russia (Jew)	Ireland	7	3	6			10				26
Russia (Jew)	Italy	1					1				2
Russia (Jew)	Italy (North)	1									1
Russia (Jew)	Norway	1					1				2
Russia (Jew)	Palestine (Jew)	1									1
Russia (Jew)	Porto Rico (Span.)	1									1
Russia (Jew)	Portugal	1									1
Russia (Jew)	Rumania (Jew)	379	25	9			20				433
Russia (Jew)	Russia (Pol.)	1									1
Russia (Jew)	Scotland		1	2			1				4
Russia (Jew)	Spain	1									1
Russia (Jew)	Sweden	1		1			2				4
Russia (Jew)	Sweden (Jew)	1					1				2
Russia (Jew)	Switzerland (Jew)	1	2	1							4
Russia (Jew)	Turkey (Jew)	6									6
Russia (Jew)	United States				8			15			23
Russia (Jew)	United States (Jew)				61			69			130
Totals		**16773**	**1213**	**451**	**69**		**821**	**84**			**19411**

NATIONALITY		GENERATION									
MAN	WOMAN	1st Gen. (FBFP) with 1st Gen. (FBFP)	1st Gen. (FBFP) with 2nd Gen. (NBFP)	2nd Gen. (NBFP) with 1st Gen. (FBFP)	1st Gen. (FBFP) with 3rd Gen. (NBNP)	3rd Gen. (NBNP) with 1st Gen. (FBFP)	2nd Gen. (NBFP) with 2nd Gen. (NBFP)	2nd Gen. (NBFP) with 3rd Gen. (NBNP)	3rd Gen. (NBNP) with 2nd Gen. (NBFP)	3rd Gen. (NBNP) with 3rd Gen. (NBNP)	TOTALS
60—TURKEY (JEW)											
Turkey (Jew)	Turkey (Jew)	166									166
Turkey (Jew)	Austria (Jew)	3									3
Turkey (Jew)	Belgium	1									1
Turkey (Jew)	Bulgaria (Jew)	1									1
Turkey (Jew)	France (Jew)	1									1
Turkey (Jew)	Germany (Jew)		2								2
Turkey (Jew)	Hungary (Jew)	1									1
Turkey (Jew)	Rumania (Jew)	4									4
Turkey (Jew)	Russia (Jew)	12	1								13
Turkey (Jew)	United States				1						1
Totals		189	3		1						193
61—UNITED STATES (JEW)											
United States (Jew)	United States (Jew)									155	155
United States (Jew)	Austria (Jew)					48			38		86
United States (Jew)	Austria (Pol.)					1					1
United States (Jew)	Canada (Jew)					1					1
United States (Jew)	England (Jew)					7			12		19
United States (Jew)	France								1		1
United States (Jew)	France (Jew)					2			2		4
United States (Jew)	Germany					1			6		7
United States (Jew)	Germany (Jew)					15			97		112
United States (Jew)	Holland (Jew)					1			3		4
United States (Jew)	Hungary (Jew)					24			19		43
United States (Jew)	Ireland					2			1		3
United States (Jew)	Italy								1		1
United States (Jew)	Rumania (Jew)					7					7
United States (Jew)	Russia (Jew)					109			69		178
United States (Jew)	United States									19	19
Totals						218			250	174	642

NATIONALITY		GENERATION									
Man	Woman	1st Gen. (FBFP) with 1st Gen. (FBFP)	1st Gen. (FBFP) with 2nd Gen. (NBFP)	2nd Gen. (NBFP) with 1st Gen. (FBFP)	1st Gen. (FBFP) with 3rd Gen. (NBNP)	3rd Gen. (NBNP) with 1st Gen. (FBFP)	2nd Gen. (NBFP) with 2nd Gen. (NBFP)	2nd Gen. (NBFP) with 3rd Gen. (NBNP)	3rd Gen. (NBNP) with 2nd Gen. (NBFP)	3rd Gen. (NBNP) with 3rd Gen. (NBNP)	Totals
62 Marriages of men of various nationalities (1st and 2nd generations) to women, native born of native parents (United States)											
Austria (Engl.)	United States				3						3
Austria (Germ.)	United States				26			18			44
Armenia	United States				6						6
Argentina	United States				1						1
Austria (Boh.)	United States				6			9			15
Austria (Pol.)	United States				18			11			29
Brazil	United States				4						4
B. W. I. (Col.)	United States				2						2
B. W. I. (Engl.)	United States				26			1			27
Belgium	United States				2			1			3
Bolivia	United States				1						1
Bulgaria	United States				1						1
Canada (Engl.)	United States				152			113			265
Canada (French)	United States				23			15			38
Chile	United States				1						1
China	United States				5			3			8
Columbia	United States				1						1
Cuba (Span.)	United States				13			3			16
Denmark	United States				22			28			50
England	United States				419			378			797
Equador	United States				1						1
Egypt	United States				3						3
Finland	United States				1			4			5
France	United States				43			69			112
Germany (South)	United States				106			8			114
Germany (North)	United States				69			13			82
Germany	United States				256			1579			1835
Greece	United States				21						21
Holland	United States				19			13			32
Hungary (Sl.)	United States				6			4			10
Hungary (Germ.)	United States				2			1			3
Hungary (Hung.)	United States				3						3

NATIONALITY		GENERATION									
MAN	WOMAN	1st Gen. (FBFP) with 1st Gen. (FBFP)	1st Gen. (FBFP) with 2nd Gen. (NBFP)	2nd Gen. (NBFP) with 1st Gen. (FBFP)	1st Gen. (FBFP) with 3rd Gen. (NBNP)	3rd Gen. (NBNP) with 1st Gen. (FBFP)	2nd Gen. (NBFP) with 2nd Gen. (NBFP)	2nd Gen. (NBFP) with 3rd Gen. (NBNP)	3rd Gen. (NBNP) with 2nd Gen. (NBFP)	3rd Gen. (NBNP) with 3rd Gen. (NBNP)	TOTALS
Marriages of men of various nationalities (1st and 2nd generations) to women, native born of native parents (United States.) —*Continued.*											
India	United States				2						2
Ireland	United States				364			1486			1850
Italy (North)	United States				49			10			59
Italy	United States				105			118			223
Italy (South)	United States				56			2			58
Japan	United States				5						5
Mexico (Span.)	United States				6						6
Norway	United States				21			18			39
Portugal	United States				2			1			3
Russia (Pol.)	United States				9			3			12
Scotland	United States				118			149			267
Spain	United States				16			7			23
Sweden	United States				59			36			95
Switzerland (Germ.)	United States				32			35			67
Switzerland (French)	United States				3						3
Porto Rico (Span.)	United States				6						6
Porto Rico (Col.)	United States				1						1
Turkey	United States				5						5
Venezuela (Span.)	United States				2						2
Wales	United States				9			23			32
Australia (Jew)	United States				1						1
Canada (Jew)	United States				1						1
Portugal (Jew)	United States							1			
Totals					2134			4160			6294
Grand Total		57383		3348	2723	2345	8514	4628	4697	12038	101767

TABLE VI

Groups Represented by less than 10 Cases.

NATIONALITY		GENERATION									
Man	Woman	1st Gen. (FBFP) with 1st Gen. (FBFP)	1st Gen. (FBFP) with 2nd Gen. (NBFP)	2nd Gen. (NBFP) with 1st Gen. (FBFP)	1st Gen. (FBFP) with 3rd Gen. (NBNP)	3rd Gen. (NBNP) with 1st Gen. (FBFP)	2nd Gen. (NBFP) with 2nd Gen. (NBFP)	2nd Gen. (NBFP) with 3rd Gen. (NBNP)	3rd Gen. (NBNP) with 2nd Gen. (NBFP)	3rd Gen. (NBNP) with 3rd Gen. (NBNP)	Totals
63—AUSTRALIA (ENGL.)											
Australia (Engl.)	England	2									2
Australia (Engl.)	Ireland	1	1								2
Australia (Engl.)	Spain		1								1
Australia (Engl.)	Switzerland (Ital.)	1									1
Totals		4	2								6
64—BULGARIA											
Bulgaria	Bulgaria	1									1
Bulgaria	Hungary (Germ.)	1									1
Bulgaria	Hungary (Sl.)	1									1
Totals		3									3
65—BRAZIL											
Brazil	Cuba	1									1
Brazil	France	1									1
Brazil	Ireland	1									1
Brazil	Sweden	1									1
Totals		4									4
66—CHILE											
Chile	Ireland	3									3
Chile	France	1									1
Totals		4									4

NATIONALITY		GENERATION									
MAN	WOMAN	1st Gen. (FBFP) with 1st Gen. (FBFP)	1st Gen. (FBFP) with 2nd Gen. (NBFP)	2nd Gen. (NBFP) with 1st Gen. (FBFP)	1st Gen. (FBFP) with 3rd Gen. (NBNP)	3rd Gen. (NBNP) with 1st Gen. (FBFP)	2nd Gen. (NBFP) with 2nd Gen. (NBFP)	2nd Gen. (NBFP) with 3rd Gen. (NBNP)	3rd Gen. (NBNP) with 2nd Gen. (NBFP)	3rd Gen. (NBNP) with 3rd Gen. (NBNP)	TOTALS
67—COLOMBIA (SPAN.)											
Colombia (Span.)	Colombia (Span.)	1									1
Colombia (Span.)	France	1									1
Totals		2									2
68—COREA											
Corea	Corea	1									1
Corea	France	1									1
Totals		2									2
69—DALMATIA											
Dalmatia	Dalmatia	3									3
Totals		3									3
70—EGYPT											
Egypt	Egypt	1									1
Egypt	Ireland	1									1
Totals		2									2
71—EQUADOR											
Equador	Equador	1									1
Totals		1									1

Nationality: Man	Nationality: Woman	1st Gen. (FBFP) with 1st Gen. (FBFP)	1st Gen. (FBFP) with 2nd Gen. (NBFP)	2nd Gen. (NBFP) with 1st Gen. (FBFP)	1st Gen. (FBFP) with 3rd Gen. (NBNP)	3rd Gen. (NBNP) with 1st Gen. (FBFP)	2nd Gen. (NBFP) with 2nd Gen. (NBFP)	2nd Gen. (NBFP) with 3rd Gen. (NBNP)	3rd Gen. (NBNP) with 2nd Gen. (NBFP)	3rd Gen. (NBNP) with 3rd Gen. (NBNP)	Totals
72—GUATEMALA (SPAN.)											
Guatemala (Span.)	Guatemala (Span.)	1									1
Guatemala (Span.)	Germany	1									1
Totals		2									2
73—HAITI (COL.)											
Haiti (Col.)	British West Indies (Col.)	1									1
Haiti (Col.)	United States (Col.)				1						1
Totals		1			1						2
74—HONDURAS											
Honduras	United States (Jew)				1						1
Totals					1						1
75—INDIA											
India	Danish West Indies (Col.)	1									1
India	Hungary (Sl.)		1								1
India	United States (Col.)				1						1
Totals		1	1		1						3
76—LUXEMBURG											
Luxemburg	Luxemburg	1									1
Luxemburg	Austria (Germ.)	1									1
Luxemburg	France	3									3
Luxemburg	Germany	1									1
Luxemburg	Ireland	2									2
Luxemburg	Switzerland (French)	1									1
Totals		9									9

NATIONALITY		GENERATION									
Man	Woman	**1st Gen.** (FBFP) with 1st Gen. (FBFP)	**1st Gen.** (FBFP) with 2nd Gen. (NBFP)	**2nd Gen.** (NBFP) with 1st Gen. (FBFP)	**1st Gen.** (FBFP) with 3rd Gen. (NBNP)	**3rd Gen.** (NBNP) with 1st Gen. (FBFP)	**2nd Gen.** (NBFP) with 2nd Gen. (NBFP)	**2nd Gen.** (NBFP) with 3rd Gen. (NBNP)	**3rd Gen.** (NBNP) with 2nd Gen. (NBFP)	**3rd Gen.** (NBNP) with 3rd Gen. (NBNP)	Totals
		77—MONTENEGRO									
Montenegro	Montenegro	1									1
Montenegro	Hungary (Sl.)	1									1
Totals		2									2
		78—PHILIPPINE ISLANDS									
Philippine Isl.	Philippine Isl.	1									1
Philippine Isl.	England	1									1
Totals		2									2
		79—PERU									
Peru	France		1								1
Peru	Norway	1									1
Totals		1	1								2
		80—PERSIA									
Persia	Austria (Ital.)	1									1
Persia	Ireland	1									1
Persia	Turkey	1									1
Totals		3									3
		81—PORTO RICO (COL.)									
Porto Rico (Col.)	British West Indies (Col.)	2									2
Totals		2									2

NATIONALITY		GENERATION									
MAN	WOMAN	1st Gen. (FBFP) with 1st Gen. (FBFP)	1st Gen. (FBFP) with 2nd Gen. (NBFP)	2nd Gen. (NBFP) with 1st Gen. (FBFP)	1st Gen. (FBFP) with 3rd Gen. (NBNP)	3rd Gen. (NBNP) with 1st Gen. (FBFP)	2nd Gen. (NBFP) with 2nd Gen. (NBFP)	2nd Gen. (NBFP) with 3rd Gen. (NBNP)	3rd Gen. (NBNP) with 2nd Gen. (NBFP)	3rd Gen. (NBNP) with 3rd Gen. (NBNP)	TOTALS
82—VENEZUELA (SPAN.)											
Venezuela (Span.)	Austria (Germ.)	1									1
Venezuela (Span.)	Cuba (Span.)	1									1
Venezuela (Span.)	France	1									1
Totals		3									3
83—CANADA (JEW)											
Canada (Jew)	England (Jew)		1								1
Canada (Jew)	Germany (Jew)	1									1
Canada (Jew)	Ireland		1								1
Canada (Jew)	Russia (Jew)	1		1			1				3
Totals		2	2	1			1				6
84—DENMARK (JEW)											
Denmark (Jew)	Germany (Jew)						1				1
Totals							1				1
85—LUXEMBURG (JEW)											
Luxemburg (Jew)	Russia (Jew)		1								1
Totals			1								1
86—MOROCCO (JEW)											
Morocco (Jew)	Russia (Jew)			1							1
Totals				1							1

NATIONALITY		GENERATION									
MAN	WOMAN	1st Gen. (FBFP) with 1st Gen. (FBFP)	1st Gen. (FBFP) with 2nd Gen. (NBFP)	2nd Gen. (NBFP) with 1st Gen. (FBFP)	1st Gen. (FBFP) with 3rd Gen. (NBNP)	3rd Gen. (NBNP) with 1st Gen. (FBFP)	2nd Gen. (NBFP) with 2nd Gen. (NBFP)	2nd Gen. (NBFP) with 3rd Gen. (NBNP)	3rd Gen. (NBNP) with 2nd Gen. (NBFP)	3rd Gen. (NBNP) with 3rd Gen. (NBNP)	TOTALS
87—PALESTINE (JEW)											
Palestine (Jew)	Germany (Jew)		1								1
Palestine (Jew)	Rumania (Jew)	3									3
Palestine (Jew)	Russia (Jew)	2									2
Palestine (Jew)	Turkey (Jew)	1									1
Totals		6	1								7
88—SCOTLAND (JEW)											
Scotland (Jew)	Rumania (Jew)	1									1
Totals		1									1
89—SERVIA (JEW)											
Servia (Jew)	Servia (Jew)	1									1
Totals		1									1
90—SPAIN (JEW)											
Spain (Jew)	Russia (Jew)	1					1				2
Spain (Jew)	Austria (Jew)		1								1
Totals		1	1				1				3
91—SWEDEN (JEW)											
Sweden (Jew)	Austria (Jew)	2					1				3
Sweden (Jew)	England (Jew)						1				1
Sweden (Jew)	Russia (Jew)	1	3								4
Totals		3	3				2				8
Totals for groups represented by less than 10 cases		65	12	2	3		5				87
Totals for all groups		57448	6103	3350	2726	2345	8519	4628	4697	12038	101854

TABLE VI

Series 1—88

WOMEN

(For a discussion of the method of reading these tables and of their further utilization, see Introductory Note, page 87.)

TABLE VI, SERIES 1—88

(Heavy type in caption indicates generation of WOMAN)

NATIONALITY		GENERATION									
WOMAN	MAN	**1st Gen.** (FBFP) with 1st Gen. (FBFP)	**1st Gen.** (FBFP) with 2nd Gen. (NBFP)	**2nd Gen.** (NBFP) with 1st Gen. (FBFP)	**1st Gen.** (FBFP) with 3rd Gen. (NBNP)	**3rd Gen.** (NBNP) with 1st Gen. (FBFP)	**2nd Gen.** (NBFP) with 2nd Gen. (NBFP)	**2nd Gen.** (NBFP) with 3rd Gen. (NBNP)	**3rd Gen.** (NBNP) with 2nd Gen. (NBFP)	**3rd Gen.** (NBNP) with 3rd Gen. (NBNP)	TOTALS
1—ARMENIA											
Armenia	Armenia	74		1							75
Totals		**74**		**1**							**75**
2—AUSTRIA (BOH.)											
Austria (Boh.)	Austria (Boh.)	421	34	30			73				558
Austria (Boh.)	Austria (Germ.)	6									6
Austria (Boh.)	Austria (Pol.)	15		2			1				18
Austria (Boh.)	Canada (French)	1									1
Austria (Boh.)	Denmark	3									3
Austria (Boh.)	England	1	4	2			1				8
Austria (Boh.)	France	1		1							2
Austria (Boh.)	Germany	26	7	6			30				69
Austria (Boh.)	Germany (North)	24		3							27
Austria (Boh.)	Germany (South)	14		3			2				19
Austria (Boh.)	Greece	1									1
Austria (Boh.)	Holland	2									2
Austria (Boh.)	Hungary (Germ.)	2									2
Austria (Boh.)	Hungary (Sl.)	13		2							15
Austria (Boh.)	Ireland	3	3	49			9				64
Austria (Boh.)	Italy	3	1	2			2				8
Austria (Boh.)	Norway		1								1
Austria (Boh.)	Porto Rico (Span.)			1							1
Austria (Boh.)	Russia (Pol.)	1									1
Austria (Boh.)	Servia	2									2
Austria (Boh.)	Scotland	3									3
Austria (Boh.)	Sweden	2									2
Austria (Boh.)	Switzerland (Germ.)	1									1
Austria (Boh.)	Austria (Jew)	1									1
Austria (Boh.)	Hungary (Jew)			1							1
Totals		**546**	**50**	**102**			**118**				**816**

NATIONALITY		GENERATION									
WOMAN	MAN	1st Gen. (FBFP) with 1st Gen. (FBFP)	1st Gen. (FBFP) with 2nd Gen. (NBFP)	2nd Gen. (NBFP) with 1st Gen. (FBFP)	1st Gen. (FBFP) with 3rd Gen. (NBNP)	3rd Gen. (NBNP) with 1st Gen. (FBFP)	2nd Gen. (NBFP) with 2nd Gen. (NBFP)	2nd Gen. (NBFP) with 3rd Gen. (NBNP)	3rd Gen. (NBNP) with 2nd Gen. (NBFP)	3rd Gen. (NBNP) with 3rd Gen. (NBNP)	TOTALS
3—AUSTRIA (GERM.)											
Austria (Germ.)	Austria (Germ.)	189		5			5				199
Austria (Germ.)	Austria (Ital.)	2									2
Austria (Germ.)	Austria (Pol.)	2									2
Austria (Germ.)	British West Indies (Engl.)	1									1
Austria (Germ.)	Denmark	2					2				4
Austria (Germ.)	England	2	1	5			3				11
Austria (Germ.)	Finland	1									1
Austria (Germ.)	France	3	2								5
Austria (Germ.)	Germany	98	19	3			32				152
Austria (Germ.)	Germany (South)	64	2	3			1				70
Austria (Germ.)	Greece	1		1							2
Austria (Germ.)	Hungary (Germ.)	16		1							17
Austria (Germ.)	Hungary (Hung.)	1									1
Austria (Germ.)	Hungary (Sl.)	3									3
Austria (Germ.)	Ireland	1	4	3							8
Austria (Germ.)	Italy	8	1	5			7				21
Austria (Germ.)	Italy (North)	1									1
Austria (Germ.)	Italy (South)	2									2
Austria (Germ.)	Norway	2									2
Austria (Germ.)	Porto Rico (Span.)	1									1
Austria (Germ.)	Rumania	1									1
Austria (Germ.)	Russia (Pol.)	2		1							3
Austria (Germ.)	Scotland			2							2
Austria (Germ.)	Spain						1				1
Austria (Germ.)	Sweden	2		1			1				4
Austria (Germ.)	Switzerland (Germ.)	13									13
Austria (Germ.)	Wales	1									1
Austria (Germ.)	Austria (Jew)	1									1
Austria (Germ.)	Germany (Jew)						2				2
Austria (Germ.)	Russia (Jew)			1							1
Austria (Germ.)	Venezuela (Span.)	1									1
Austria (Germ.)	Luxemburg	1									1
Totals		422	29	31			54				536

NATIONALITY		GENERATION									
Woman	Man	1st Gen. (FBFP) with 1st Gen. (FBFP)	1st Gen. (FBFP) with 2nd Gen. (NBFP)	2nd Gen. (NBFP) with 1st Gen. (FBFP)	1st Gen. (FBFP) with 3rd Gen. (NBNP)	3rd Gen. (NBNP) with 1st Gen. (FBFP)	2nd Gen. (NBFP) with 2nd Gen. (NBFP)	2nd Gen. (NBFP) with 3rd Gen. (NBNP)	3rd Gen. (NBNP) with 2nd Gen. (NBFP)	3rd Gen. (NBNP) with 3rd Gen. (NBNP)	Totals
4—AUSTRIA (ITAL.)											
Austria (Ital.)	Austria (Ital.)	11		1							12
Austria (Ital.)	Austria (Germ.)	2									2
Austria (Ital.)	Italy (North)	1									1
Austria (Ital.)	Persia	1									1
Totals		15		1							16
5—AUSTRIA (POL.)											
Austria (Pol.)	Austria (Pol.)	2121	31	26			68				2246
Austria (Pol.)	Austria (Germ.)	6					1				7
Austria (Pol.)	Armenia	2									2
Austria (Pol.)	Belgium	1									1
Austria (Pol.)	Canada (Engl.)	1	1	2							4
Austria (Pol.)	Canada (French)		1								1
Austria (Pol.)	Denmark	7	1								8
Austria (Pol.)	England	6	2				2				10
Austria (Pol.)	France	1		2			1				4
Austria (Pol.)	Germany	29	13	6			23				71
Austria (Pol.)	Germany (North)	13	1	1							15
Austria (Pol.)	Germany (South)	34	1								35
Austria (Pol.)	Greece	6									6
Austria (Pol.)	Holland						1				1
Austria (Pol.)	Hungary (Germ.)	2									2
Austria (Pol.)	Hungary (Sl.)	23	1	2							26
Austria (Pol.)	Ireland	5	12				9				26
Austria (Pol.)	Italy	10		5			2				17
Austria (Pol.)	Italy (North)	3		1							4
Austria (Pol.)	Italy (South)	15		6							21
Austria (Pol.)	Mexico (Span.)	1									1
Austria (Pol.)	Norway	3	1								4
Austria (Pol.)	Porto Rico (Span.)	1									1
Austria (Pol.)	Russia (Pol.)	192		1			1				194
Austria (Pol.)	Servia	1									1
Austria (Pol.)	Scotland			1			1				2

NATIONALITY		GENERATION									
Woman	Man	1st Gen. (FBFP) with 1st Gen. (FBFP)	1st Gen. (FBFP) with 2nd Gen. (NBFP)	2nd Gen. (NBFP) with 1st Gen. (FBFP)	1st Gen. (FBFP) with 3rd Gen. (NBNP)	3rd Gen. (NBNP) with 1st Gen. (FBFP)	2nd Gen. (NBFP) with 2nd Gen. (NBFP)	2nd Gen. (NBFP) with 3rd Gen. (NBNP)	3rd Gen. (NBNP) with 2nd Gen. (NBFP)	3rd Gen. (NBNP) with 3rd Gen. (NBNP)	Totals
		5 AUSTRIA (POL.)—*Continued*									
Austria (Pol.)	Spain						1				1
Austria (Pol.)	Sweden	3									3
Austria (Pol.)	Switzerland (Germ.)	1	1	1							3
Austria (Pol.)	Turkey	2									2
Austria (Pol.)	United States (Jew)				1						1
Austria (Pol.)	Russia (Jew)	2									2
Totals		**2491**	**66**	**54**	**1**		**110**				**2722**
		6 BELGIUM									
Belgium	Belgium	41		1			2				44
Belgium	Austria (Germ.)	1									1
Belgium	British West Indies (Engl.)			1							1
Belgium	Canada (Engl.)			1							1
Belgium	Cuba (Span.)	1									1
Belgium	Denmark	1									1
Belgium	England	3	1								4
Belgium	France	17	1				2				20
Belgium	Germany	4	2	1			1				8
Belgium	Holland	3									3
Belgium	Hungary (Germ.)	1									1
Belgium	Ireland	1	1				3				5
Belgium	Italy	1	1								2
Belgium	Italy (North)	1									1
Belgium	Italy (South)			1							1
Belgium	Norway	2									2
Belgium	Porto Rico (Span.)	1									1
Belgium	Scotland	1									1
Belgium	Spain	2									2
Belgium	Switzerland (Germ.)	3									3
Belgium	Turkey	1									1
Belgium	Turkey (Jew)	1									1
Totals		**86**	**6**	**5**			**8**				**105**

NATIONALITY		GENERATION									
Woman	Man	1st Gen. (FBFP) with 1st Gen. (FBFP)	1st Gen. (FBFP) with 2nd Gen. (NBFP)	2nd Gen. (NBFP) with 1st Gen. (FBFP)	1st Gen. (FBFP) with 3rd Gen. (NBNP)	3rd Gen. (NBNP) with 1st Gen. (FBFP)	2nd Gen. (NBFP) with 2nd Gen. (NBFP)	2nd Gen. (NBFP) with 3rd Gen. (NBNP)	3rd Gen. (NBNP) with 2nd Gen. (NBFP)	3rd Gen. (NBNP) with 3rd Gen. (NBNP)	Totals
7—BRITISH WEST INDIES (COL.)											
B. W. I. (Col.)	British West Indies (Col.)	672	1	15							688
B. W. I. (Col.)	Danish West Indies (Col.)	2					2				4
B. W. I. (Col.)	British West Indies (Engl.)	2									2
B. W. I. (Col.)	Porto Rico (Col.)	2									2
B. W. I. (Col.)	United States (Col.)				41			2			43
B. W. I. (Col.)	Haiti (Col.)	1									1
B. W. I. (Col.)	Canada (Col.)		1								1
Totals		**679**	**2**	**15**	**41**		**2**	**2**			**741**
8—BRITISH WEST INDIES (ENGL.)											
B. W. I. (Engl.)	British West Indies (Engl.)	46									46
B. W. I. (Engl.)	Canada (Engl.)	2									2
B. W. I. (Engl.)	England	7									7
B. W. I. (Engl.)	France	1									1
B. W. I. (Engl.)	Germany	1	1				1				3
B. W. I. (Engl)	Germany (South)	2									2
B W I (Engl)	Norway	2									2
B W I (Engl)	Turkey	1									1
Totals		**62**	**1**				**1**				**64**
9—CANADA (ENGL.)											
Canada (Engl)	Canada (Engl)	48	6	12			5				71
Canada (Engl)	Armenia			1							1
Canada (Engl)	Austria (Germ)			2			2				4
Canada (Engl)	British West Indies (Engl)			2							2
Canada (Engl)	Belgium	1									1
Canada (Engl)	Cuba (Span)	2									2
Canada (Engl)	China	1									1
Canada (Engl)	Denmark	2					1				3
Canada (Engl)	England	39	4	6			14				63

NATIONALITY		GENERATION									
Woman	Man	1st Gen. (FBFP) with 1st Gen. (FBFP)	1st Gen. (FBFP) with 2nd Gen. (NBFP)	2nd Gen. (NBFP) with 1st Gen. (FBFP)	1st Gen. (FBFP) with 3rd Gen. (NBNP)	3rd Gen. (NBNP) with 1st Gen. (FBFP)	2nd Gen. (NBFP) with 2nd Gen. (NBFP)	2nd Gen. (NBFP) with 3rd Gen. (NBNP)	3rd Gen. (NBNP) with 2nd Gen. (NBFP)	3rd Gen. (NBNP) with 3rd Gen. (NBNP)	Totals
9—CANADA (ENGL.)—*Continued*											
Canada (Engl.)	France						4				4
Canada (Engl.)	Germany	9	9	3			32				53
Canada (Engl.)	Germany (North)	7		1			1				9
Canada (Engl.)	Germany (South)	2									2
Canada (Engl.)	Greece			1							1
Canada (Engl.)	Holland			1			1				2
Canada (Engl.)	Hungary (Hung.)			1							1
Canada (Engl.)	Ireland	16	11	8			28				63
Canada (Engl.)	Italy	3					2				5
Canada (Engl.)	Italy (North)	1									1
Canada (Engl.)	Italy (South)	2		1							3
Canada (Engl.)	Japan			1							1
Canada (Engl.)	Norway	1		1			2				4
Canada (Engl.)	Scotland	12	2	2			5				21
Canada (Engl.)	Spain	2									2
Canada (Engl.)	Sweden	2					1				3
Canada (Engl.)	Switzerland (Germ.)	1					1				2
Canada (Engl.)	Syria	1									1
Canada (Engl.)	Wales	1									1
Canada (Engl.)	United States (Col.)				13			3			16
Canada (Engl.)	Austria (Jew)	1		2			1				4
Canada (Engl.)	Germany (Jew)		3	2			1				6
Totals		154	35	47	13		101	3			353
10—CANADA (FRENCH)											
Canada (French)	Canada (French)	14	2	3			1				20
Canada (French)	Austria (Germ.)	1									1
Canada (French)	Canada (Engl.)	6	1								7
Canada (French)	England	2	2								4
Canada (French)	France	5									5
Canada (French)	Germany	2	2	2			4				10

NATIONALITY		GENERATION									
WOMAN	MAN	1st Gen. (FBFP) with 1st Gen. (FBFP)	1st Gen. (FBFP) with 2nd Gen. (NBFP)	2nd Gen. (NBFP) with 1st Gen. (FBFP)	1st Gen. (FBFP) with 3rd Gen. (NBNP)	3rd Gen. (NBNP) with 1st Gen. (FBFP)	2nd Gen. (NBFP) with 2nd Gen. (NBFP)	2nd Gen. (NBFP) with 3rd Gen. (NBNP)	3rd Gen. (NBNP) with 2nd Gen. (NBFP)	3rd Gen. (NBNP) with 3rd Gen. (NBNP)	TOTALS
		10—CANADA (FRENCH)—*Continued*									
Canada (French)	Germany (North)	1		1							2
Canada (French)	Germany (South)	2									2
Canada (French)	Greece			1							1
Canada (French)	Holland			1							1
Canada (French)	Ireland	1	4				6				11
Canada (French)	Italy			1			1				2
Canada (French)	Italy (South)			1							1
Canada (French)	Scotland		1				1				2
Canada (French)	Switzerland (Germ)						1				1
Canada (French)	Russia (Jew)	2									2
Totals		36	12	10			14				72
		11—CUBA (COL.)									
Cuba (Col)	Cuba (Col)	2									2
Cuba (Col)	British West Indies (Col)	2									2
Cuba (Col)	Porto Rico (Span)	1									1
Cuba (Col)	United States (Col)				3			2			5
Cuba (Col)	Canada (Col)	1									1
Totals		6			3			2			11
		12—CUBA (SPAN.)									
Cuba (Span)	Cuba (Span)	12	1								13
Cuba (Span)	Canada (Engl)						1				1
Cuba (Span)	England			1			2				3
Cuba (Span)	Germany	2	1				1				4
Cuba (Span)	Holland	1									1
Cuba (Span)	Ireland		2	1			3				6
Cuba (Span)	Italy	1									1
Cuba (Span)	Italy (North)	1									1
Cuba (Span)	Mexico (Span.)	2									2

NATIONALITY		GENERATION									
Woman	Man	1st Gen. (FBFP) with 1st Gen. (FBFP)	1st Gen. (FBFP) with 2nd Gen. (NBFP)	2nd Gen. (NBFP) with 1st Gen. (FBFP)	1st Gen. (FBFP) with 3rd Gen. (NBNP)	3rd Gen. (NBNP) with 1st Gen. (FBFP)	2nd Gen. (NBFP) with 2nd Gen. (NBFP)	2nd Gen. (NBFP) with 3rd Gen. (NBNP)	3rd Gen. (NBNP) with 2nd Gen. (NBFP)	3rd Gen. (NBNP) with 3rd Gen. (NBNP)	Totals
12—CUBA (SPAN.)—*Continued*											
Cuba (Span)	Porto Rico (Span)	3		1							4
Cuba (Span)	Spain	5									5
Cuba (Span)	Switzerland (Germ)						1				1
Cuba (Span)	France		1								1
Cuba (Span)	Brasil	1									1
Cuba (Span)	Venezuela (Span)	1									1
Totals		**29**	**5**	**3**			**8**				**45**
13—DENMARK											
Denmark	Denmark	143	2				3				148
Denmark	Austria (Germ)	1		1			1				3
Denmark	Belgium	1									1
Denmark	Canada (Engl)						1				1
Denmark	England	8	1	2			3				14
Denmark	Finland	2									2
Denmark	France	1									1
Denmark	Germany	9	3	2			11				25
Denmark	Germany (North)	3	1								4
Denmark	Germany (South)	2									2
Denmark	Greece	1									1
Denmark	Holland	1									1
Denmark	Ireland	2	2	1			4				9
Denmark	Italy	1	1	1							3
Denmark	Norway	7	1								8
Denmark	Porto Rico (Span)			1							1
Denmark	Portugal						1				1
Denmark	Russia (Pol)		1								1
Denmark	Scotland	1		1							2
Denmark	Spain	1									1
Denmark	Sweden	7		2			1				10
Denmark	United States (Col)				1						1

NATIONALITY		GENERATION									
Woman	Man	1st Gen. (FBFP) with 1st Gen. (FBFP)	1st Gen. (FBFP) with 2nd Gen. (NBFP)	2nd Gen. (NBFP) with 1st Gen. (FBFP)	1st Gen. (FBFP) with 3rd Gen. (NBNP)	3rd Gen. (NBNP) with 1st Gen. (FBFP)	2nd Gen. (NBFP) with 2nd Gen. (NBFP)	2nd Gen. (NBFP) with 3rd Gen. (NBNP)	3rd Gen. (NBNP) with 2nd Gen. (NBFP)	3rd Gen. (NBNP) with 3rd Gen. (NBNP)	Totals
					13—DENMARK—*Continued*						
Denmark	Austria (Jew)	2									2
Denmark	Germany (Jew)	1									1
Totals		194	12	11	1		25				243
					14—DUTCH WEST INDIES (COL.)						
D W I (Col)	Dutch West Indies (Col)	54					1				55
D W I (Col)	United States (Col)				3						3
D W I (Col)	Cuba (Col)	1									1
D W I (Col)	England			1							1
D W I (Col)	India	1									1
Totals		56		1	3		1				61
					15—ENGLAND						
England	England	549	34	35			56				674
England	Armenia	1									1
England	Austria (Boh)						1				1
England	Austria (Germ)	4	1	4			2				11
England	Austria (Pol)	2		1							3
England	British West Indies (Engl)	5		2							7
England	Belgium	2					1				3
England	Canada (Engl)	22	6	6			12				46
England	Canada (French)	2	1	1							4
England	Cuba (Span)	2									2
England	Denmark	9	3	4							16
England	Finland	1									1
England	France	9	4	4			6				23
England	Germany	35	47	20			119				221
England	Germany (North)	12		8			1				21
England	Germany (South)	17		3			3				23
England	Greece	5		1							6

NATIONALITY		GENERATION									
WOMAN	MAN	1st Gen. (FBFP) with 1st Gen. (FBFP)	1st Gen. (FBFP) with 2nd Gen. (NBFP)	2nd Gen. (NBFP) with 1st Gen. (FBFP)	1st Gen. (FBFP) with 3rd Gen. (NBNP)	3rd Gen. (NBNP) with 1st Gen. (FBFP)	2nd Gen. (NBFP) with 2nd Gen. (NBFP)	2nd Gen. (NBFP) with 3rd Gen. (NBNP)	3rd Gen. (NBNP) with 2nd Gen. (NBFP)	3rd Gen. (NBNP) with 3rd Gen. (NBNP)	TOTALS
15—ENGLAND—*Continued*											
England	Holland	1	2	7			3				13
England	Hungary (Hung)	2									2
England	Ireland	84	64	30			114				292
England	Italy	15	5	8			8				36
England	Italy (North)	5		4							9
England	Italy (South)	7		6							13
England	Japan	1									1
England	Norway	7		1			1				9
England	Porto Rico (Span)			1			2				3
England	Portugal	1									1
England	Scotland	59	7	11			17				94
England	Spain	2									2
England	Sweden	7	2	3			2				14
England	Switzerland (French)	1									1
England	Switzerland (Germ)	12	1	3			2				18
England	Wales	9	3				2				14
England	United States (Col)				1						1
England	Austria (Jew)	1		2			2				5
England	France (Jew)						1				1
England	Germany (Jew)	5	3	1			8				17
England	Hungary (Jew)	1		1			2				4
England	Rumania (Jew)	2									2
England	Russia (Jew)	1		1			6				8
England	Australia (Engl)	2									2
England	Philippines	1									1
Totals		**903**	**183**	**168**	**1**		**371**				**1626**
16—FINLAND											
Finland	Finland	350	1	1							352
Finland	Cuba (Span)	2									2
Finland	Denmark	5									5
Finlan	England	7					1				8

NATIONALITY		GENERATION									
Woman	Man	1st Gen. (FBFP) with 1st Gen. (FBFP)	1st Gen. (FBFP) with 2nd Gen. (NBFP)	2nd Gen. (NBFP) with 1st Gen. (FBFP)	1st Gen. (FBFP) with 3rd Gen. (NBNP)	3rd Gen. (NBNP) with 1st Gen. (FBFP)	2nd Gen. (NBFP) with 2nd Gen. (NBFP)	2nd Gen. (NBFP) with 3rd Gen. (NBNP)	3rd Gen. (NBNP) with 2nd Gen. (NBFP)	3rd Gen. (NBNP) with 3rd Gen. (NBNP)	Totals
				16—FINLAND—*Continued*							
Finland	France	3	1								4
Finland	Germany	5	3				1				9
Finland	Germany (North)	2		1							3
Finland	Germany (South)	3									3
Finland	Hungary (Germ)	2									2
Finland	Ireland	3	7								10
Finland	Italy		1								1
Finland	Italy (North)	1									1
Finland	Japan	2									2
Finland	Norway	10									10
Finland	Russia (Pol)	12	1								13
Finland	Scotland	1									1
Finland	Sweden	35	1								36
Finland	Switzerland (Germ)	4									4
Finland	Russia (Jew)	1									1
Totals		**448**	**15**	**2**			**2**				**467**
				17—FRANCE							
France	France	331	9	21			6				367
France	Austria (Germ)	2		1							3
France	Austria (Boh)	2									2
France	Austria (Pol)						1				1
France	Belgium	19									19
France	Canada (Engl)	3									3
France	Canada (French)	2					1				3
France	China	1									1
France	Cuba (Span)	1	1	1							3
France	Denmark	1					1				2
France	England	35	6	5			7				53
France	Germany	37	12	7			34				90
France	Germany (North)	1									1
France	Germany (South)	1		12							13

17—FRANCE—*Continued*

NATIONALITY		GENERATION									
Woman	Man	1st Gen. (FBFP) with 1st Gen. (FBFP)	1st Gen. (FBFP) with 2nd Gen. (NBFP)	2nd Gen. (NBFP) with 1st Gen. (FBFP)	1st Gen. (FBFP) with 3rd Gen. (NBNP)	3rd Gen. (NBNP) with 1st Gen. (FBFP)	2nd Gen. (NBFP) with 2nd Gen. (NBFP)	2nd Gen. (NBFP) with 3rd Gen. (NBNP)	3rd Gen. (NBNP) with 2nd Gen. (NBFP)	3rd Gen. (NBNP) with 3rd Gen. (NBNP)	Totals
France	Greece	5									5
France	Holland	12					1				13
France	Hungary (Germ)	1									1
France	Hungary (Sl)	2		1							3
France	Ireland	12	6	6			26				50
France	Italy	11	2	6			6				25
France	Italy (North)	14									14
France	Italy (South)	7		6							13
France	Japan	1									1
France	Mexico	2									2
France	Norway			1			1				2
France	Portugal	2									2
France	Scotland	4	1	3			1				9
France	Spain	7		1							8
France	Sweden	9	1				4				14
France	Switzerland (French)	10									10
France	Switzerland (Germ)	12					1				13
France	Turkey	1									1
France	Austria (Jew)	1		1							2
France	France (Jew)		1								1
France	Rumania (Jew)	2									2
France	Russia (Jew)	1		1							2
France	United States (Jew)							1			1
France	Brasil	1									1
France	Chile	1									1
France	Colombia (Span)	1									1
France	Corea	1									1
France	Peru			1							1
France	Venezuela (Span)	1									1
France	Luxemburg	3									3
Totals		560	39	74			90	1			764

NATIONALITY		GENERATION									
WOMAN	MAN	1st Gen. (FBFP) with 1st Gen. (FBFP)	1st Gen. (FBFP) with 2nd Gen. (NBFP)	2nd Gen. (NBFP) with 1st Gen. (FBFP)	1st Gen. (FBFP) with 3rd Gen. (NBNP)	3rd Gen. (NBNP) with 1st Gen. (FBFP)	2nd Gen. (NBFP) with 2nd Gen. (NBFP)	2nd Gen. (NBFP) with 3rd Gen. (NBNP)	3rd Gen. (NBNP) with 2nd Gen. (NBFP)	3rd Gen. (NBNP) with 3rd Gen. (NBNP)	TOTALS
18—GERMANY											
Germany	Germany	1863	278	699			1604				4444
Germany	Armenia			3			1				4
Germany	Austria (Boh)	12	1	7			7				27
Germany	Austria (Germ)	34	4	24			16				78
Germany	Austria (Ital)			1							1
Germany	Austria (Pol)	13		9			6				28
Germany	British West Indies (Engl)			4							4
Germany	Belgium	11		6			5				22
Germany	Canada (Engl)	4	1	22			23				50
Germany	Canada (French)	2	3	2			2				9
Germany	Cuba (Span)	1		4			3				8
Germany	Denmark	7	3	8			9				27
Germany	England	68	13	92			101				274
Germany	France	19	6	13			29				67
Germany	Greece	4		4			1				9
Germany	Holland	19		8			5				32
Germany	Hungary (Germ)	10		5							15
Germany	Hungary (Sl)	9		2			1				12
Germany	Ireland	25	38	78			437				578
Germany	Italy	31	7	43			45				126
Germany	Italy (North)	1		8							9
Germany	Italy (South)	11		30			3				44
Germany	Japan	1									1
Germany	Mexico (Span)	1		1							2
Germany	Norway	4		5			7				16
Germany	Porto Rico (Span)	2									2
Germany	Portugal						1				1
Germany	Rumania	1									1
Germany	Scotland	8	2	27			49				86
Germany	Spain	4		3			1				8
Germany	Sweden	11		10			26				47
Germany	Switzerland (Germ)	41	2	26			20				89

NATIONALITY		GENERATION									
WOMAN	MAN	1st Gen. (FBFP) with 1st Gen. (FBFP)	1st Gen. (FBFP) with 2nd Gen. (NBFP)	2nd Gen. (NBFP) with 1st Gen. (FBFP)	1st Gen. (FBFP) with 3rd Gen. (NBNP)	3rd Gen. (NBNP) with 1st Gen. (FBFP)	2nd Gen. (NBFP) with 2nd Gen. (NBFP)	2nd Gen. (NBFP) with 3rd Gen. (NBNP)	3rd Gen. (NBNP) with 2nd Gen. (NBFP)	3rd Gen. (NBNP) with 3rd Gen. (NBNP)	TOTALS
18—GERMANY—*Continued*											
Germany	Wales	1		2			5				8
Germany	United States (Col)							3			3
Germany	Austria (Jew)	3	1	3			2				9
Germany	England (Jew)						3				3
Germany	Germany (Jew)	1		4			8				13
Germany	Holland (Jew)			1							1
Germany	Hungary (Jew)			2							2
Germany	Russia (Jew)	1		3			8				12
Germany	United States (Jew)				1			6			7
Germany	Guatemala	1									1
Germany	Luxemburg	1									1
Totals		2225	359	1159	1		2428	9			6181
19—GERMANY (NORTH)											
Germany (North)	Germany (North)	209	2	3			5				219
Germany (North)	Austria (Germ)	5		1			1				7
Germany (North)	Austria (Boh)	3									3
Germany (North)	Austria (Pol)	1									1
Germany (North)	Canada (Engl)	1									1
Germany (North)	Canada (French)	2	1								3
Germany (North)	China	2									2
Germany (North)	Denmark	4									4
Germany (North)	England	9	3				8				20
Germany (North)	Finland	2					2				4
Germany (North)	France	1									1
Germany (North)	Germany (South)	77	1	2			2				82
Germany (North)	Greece	4									4
Germany (North)	Holland	1									1
Germany (North)	Hungary (Germ)	5									5
Germany (North)	Hungary (Sl)	1									1
Germany (North)	Ireland	13	7								20

NATIONALITY		GENERATION									
WOMAN	MAN	1st Gen. (FBFP) with 1st Gen. (FBFP)	1st Gen. (FBFP) with 2nd Gen. (NBFP)	2nd Gen. (NBFP) with 1st Gen. (FBFP)	1st Gen. (FBFP) with 3rd Gen. (NBNP)	3rd Gen. (NBNP) with 1st Gen. (FBFP)	2nd Gen. (NBFP) with 2nd Gen. (NBFP)	2nd Gen. (NBFP) with 3rd Gen. (NBNP)	3rd Gen. (NBNP) with 2nd Gen. (NBFP)	3rd Gen. (NBNP) with 3rd Gen. (NBNP)	TOTALS
19—GERMANY (NORTH)—*Continued*											
Germany (North)	Italy (North)	1									1
Germany (North)	Italy (South)	4									4
Germany (North)	Mexico	1									1
Germany (North)	Norway	3									3
Germany (North)	Russia (Pol)	12		5							17
Germany (North)	Scotland						2				2
Germany (North)	Sweden	7					1				8
Germany (North)	Switzerland (Germ)	3	1				1				5
Germany (North)	Turkey	1					1				2
Germany (North)	Wales		1								1
Totals		372	16	11			23				422
20—GERMANY (SOUTH)											
Germany (South)	Germany (South)	278	2	6			5				291
Germany (South)	Austria (Germ)	35		1			1				37
Germany (South)	Austria (Boh)	2	1								3
Germany (South)	Austria (Pol)	8									8
Germany (South)	British West Indies (Col)	1									1
Germany (South)	British West Indies (Engl)	1									1
Germany (South)	Canada (Engl)		1								1
Germany (South)	Canada (French)	1									1
Germany (South)	Cuba (Span)	1									1
Germany (South)	Denmark	4									4
Germany (South)	England	13	4	2							19
Germany (South)	Finland		1								1
Germany (South)	France	12	4								16
Germany (South)	Germany (North)	91	4	1							96
Germany (South)	Greece	2		4							6
Germany (South)	Holland	1	1				4				6
Germany (South)	Hungary (Germ)	9									9
Germany (South)	Hungary (Hung)	1									1

NATIONALITY		GENERATION									
WOMAN	MAN	1st Gen. (FBFP) with 1st Gen. (FBFP)	1st Gen. (FBFP) with 2nd Gen. (NBFP)	2nd Gen. (NBFP) with 1st Gen. (FBFP)	1st Gen. (FBFP) with 3rd Gen. (NBNP)	3rd Gen. (NBNP) with 1st Gen. (FBFP)	2nd Gen. (NBFP) with 2nd Gen. (NBFP)	2nd Gen. (NBFP) with 3rd Gen. (NBNP)	3rd Gen. (NBNP) with 2nd Gen. (NBFP)	3rd Gen. (NBNP) with 3rd Gen. (NBNP)	TOTALS
		20—GERMANY (SOUTH)—*Continued*									
Germany (South)	Ireland	14	8								22
Germany (South)	Italy	11	1	7			3				22
Germany (South)	Italy (North)	2					1				3
Germany (South)	Italy (South)	2									2
Germany (South)	Japan	2		1							3
Germany (South)	Mexico	1									1
Germany (South)	Scotland	3	2	1							6
Germany (South)	Spain	1		1			1				3
Germany (South)	Sweden	3									3
Germany (South)	Switzerland (Germ.)	16	3				1				20
Germany (South)	Austria (Jew)	2	1								3
Germany (South)	Germany (Jew)	2					1				3
Germany (South)	England (Jew)	2									2
Germany (South)	Russia (Jew)	1									1
Totals		**522**	**33**	**24**			**17**				**596**
		21—GREECE									
Greece	Greece	218									218
Greece	England	1									1
Greece	Holland	1									1
Greece	Italy	1									1
Greece	Turkey	5									5
Totals		**226**									**226**
		22—HOLLAND									
Holland	Holland	50	1	4							55
Holland	Austria (Germ.)	1									1
Holland	Belgium	3									3
Holland	Canada (Engl.)		1								1
Holland	Cuba (Span.)	1	1								2
Holland	England		1				2				3

NATIONALITY		GENERATION									
WOMAN	MAN	1st Gen. (FBFP) with 1st Gen. (FBFP)	1st Gen. (FBFP) with 2nd Gen. (NBFP)	2nd Gen. (NBFP) with 1st Gen. (FBFP)	1st Gen. (FBFP) with 3rd Gen. (NBNP)	3rd Gen. (NBNP) with 1st Gen. (FBFP)	2nd Gen. (NBFP) with 2nd Gen. (NBFP)	2nd Gen. (NBFP) with 3rd Gen. (NBNP)	3rd Gen. (NBNP) with 2nd Gen. (NBFP)	3rd Gen. (NBNP) with 3rd Gen. (NBNP)	TOTALS
				22—HOLLAND—*Continued*							
Holland	Finland	1									1
Holland	France	1									1
Holland	Germany	1		1			5				7
Holland	Germany (North)	2									2
Holland	Germany (South)	2									2
Holland	Greece	1									1
Holland	Ireland	2	2				4				8
Holland	Italy	2		2			4				8
Holland	Scotland	1		1							2
Holland	Sweden	1					1				2
Holland	Germany (Jew)	2	1				10				13
Holland	Russia (Jew)	2	2	3			6	3			13
Totals		73	9	11			32				125
				23—HUNGARY (GERM.)							
Hungary (Germ.)	Hungary (Germ.)	397	2	1			1				401
Hungary (Germ.)	Austria (Germ.)	14									14
Hungary (Germ.)	Austria (Pol.)	1									1
Hungary (Germ.)	Canada (Engl.)	2	1								3
Hungary (Germ.)	England	2									2
Hungary (Germ.)	Germany	55	5	2			4				66
Hungary (Germ.)	Germany (North)	13									13
Hungary (Germ.)	Germany (South)	37									37
Hungary (Germ.)	Greece	1									1
Hungary (Germ.)	Hungary (Sl.)	5									5
Hungary (Germ.)	Hungary (Hung.)	6									6
Hungary (Germ.)	Ireland	2	1	1							4
Hungary (Germ.)	Italy	3									3
Hungary (Germ.)	Sweden						1				1
Hungary (Germ.)	Switzerland (Germ.)	6									6
Hungary (Germ.)	Hungary (Jew)	2		1							3
Hungary (Germ.)	Bulgaria	1									1
Totals		547	9	5			6				567

NATIONALITY		GENERATION									
WOMAN	MAN	1st Gen. (FBFP) with 1st Gen. (FBFP)	1st Gen. (FBFP) with 2nd Gen. (NBFP)	2nd Gen. (NBFP) with 1st Gen. (FBFP)	1st Gen. (FBFP) with 3rd Gen. (NBNP)	3rd Gen. (NBNP) with 1st Gen. (FBFP)	2nd Gen. (NBFP) with 2nd Gen. (NBFP)	2nd Gen. (NBFP) with 3rd Gen. (NBNP)	3rd Gen. (NBNP) with 2nd Gen. (NBFP)	3rd Gen. (NBNP) with 3rd Gen. (NBNP)	TOTALS
24—HUNGARY (HUNG.)											
Hungary (Hung.)	Hungary (Hung.)	334		1							335
Hungary (Hung.)	Austria (Germ.)		1								1
Hungary (Hung.)	Austria (Pol.)	1									1
Hungary (Hung.)	Germany	4					1				5
Hungary (Hung.)	Germany (North)	2									2
Hungary (Hung.)	Germany (South)	1									1
Hungary (Hung.)	Greece	1									1
Hungary (Hung.)	Hungary (Germ.)	17									17
Hungary (Hung.)	Hungary (Sl.)	2									2
Hungary (Hung.)	Ireland	1					5				6
Hungary (Hung.)	Italy	2									2
Hungary (Hung.)	Italy (South)	2									2
Hungary (Hung.)	Sweden	4									4
Hungary (Hung.)	Germany (Jew)		1								1
Hungary (Hung.)	England	3									3
Totals		374	2	1			6				383
25—HUNGARY (SL.)											
Hungary (Sl.)	Hungary (Sl.)	1522	9	8			6				1545
Hungary (Sl.)	Armenia	1									1
Hungary (Sl.)	Austria (Boh.)	21					1				22
Hungary (Sl.)	Austria (Germ.)	12									12
Hungary (Sl.)	Austria (Pol.)	99	2	1							102
Hungary (Sl.)	British West Indies (Col.)	2									2
Hungary (Sl.)	Belgium	1	1								2
Hungary (Sl.)	Canada (Engl.)	2									2
Hungary (Sl.)	Denmark	2									2
Hungary (Sl.)	England	5	2				2				9
Hungary (Sl.)	Finland	1									1
Hungary (Sl.)	France	1									1
Hungary (Sl.)	Germany	75	10	2			2				89

NATIONALITY		GENERATION									
Woman	Man	1st Gen. (FBFP) with 1st Gen. (FBFP)	1st Gen. (FBFP) with 2nd Gen. (NBFP)	2nd Gen. (NBFP) with 1st Gen. (FBFP)	1st Gen. (FBFP) with 3rd Gen. (NBNP)	3rd Gen. (NBNP) with 1st Gen. (FBFP)	2nd Gen. (NBFP) with 2nd Gen. (NBFP)	2nd Gen. (NBFP) with 3rd Gen. (NBNP)	3rd Gen. (NBNP) with 2nd Gen. (NBFP)	3rd Gen. (NBNP) with 3rd Gen. (NBNP)	Totals
		25—HUNGARY (SL.)—*Continued*									
Hungary (Sl.)	Germany (North)	16									16
Hungary (Sl.)	Germany (South)	28									28
Hungary (Sl.)	Greece	10									10
Hungary (Sl.)	Holland	2									2
Hungary (Sl.)	Hungary (Germ.)	11									11
Hungary (Sl.)	Hungary (Hung.)	2									2
Hungary (Sl.)	Ireland	8	2				2				12
Hungary (Sl.)	Italy	18	5	1			1				25
Hungary (Sl.)	Italy (North)	2									2
Hungary (Sl.)	Italy (South)	10		1							11
Hungary (Sl.)	Norway	1		1							2
Hungary (Sl.)	Rumania	2									2
Hungary (Sl.)	Russia (Pol.)	32		1							33
Hungary (Sl.)	Servia	7									7
Hungary (Sl.)	Scotland	1									1
Hungary (Sl.)	Spain	1									1
Hungary (Sl.)	Sweden	3		1							4
Hungary (Sl.)	Switzerland (South)	5		1							6
Hungary (Sl.)	Switzerland (Ital.)	1									1
Hungary (Sl.)	Turkey	2									2
Hungary (Sl.)	United States (Col.)				1						1
Hungary (Sl.)	Austria (Jew)		1								1
Hungary (Sl.)	India			1							1
Hungary (Sl.)	Bulgaria	1									1
Hungary (Sl.)	Montenegro	1									1
Totals		**1908**	**32**	**18**	**1**		**14**				**1973**

NATIONALITY		GENERATION									
WOMAN	MAN	1st Gen. (FBFP) with 1st Gen. (FBFP)	1st Gen. (FBFP) with 2nd Gen. (NBFP)	2nd Gen. (NBFP) with 1st Gen. (FBFP)	1st Gen. (FBFP) with 3rd Gen. (NBNP)	3rd Gen. (NBNP) with 1st Gen. (FBFP)	2nd Gen. (NBFP) with 2nd Gen. (NBFP)	2nd Gen. (NBFP) with 3rd Gen. (NBNP)	3rd Gen. (NBNP) with 2nd Gen. (NBFP)	3rd Gen. (NBNP) with 3rd Gen. (NBNP)	TOTALS
					26—IRELAND						
Ireland	Ireland	4455	784	412			1620				7271
Ireland	Armenia	2		2							4
Ireland	Austria (Boh.)	3	3				4				10
Ireland	Austria (Germ.)	16		3			10				29
Ireland	Austria (Ital.)	1									1
Ireland	Austria (Pol.)	10	2	4			4				20
Ireland	British West Indies (Col.)	1									1
Ireland	British West Indies (Engl.)	12		6							18
Ireland	Belgium	6	1	2			1				10
Ireland	Canada (Engl.)	54	13	26			18				111
Ireland	Canada (French)	7	4	6			24				41
Ireland	China	1									1
Ireland	Cuba (Span.)		1	3			2				6
Ireland	Denmark	22	4	2			7				35
Ireland	England	284	58	100			110				552
Ireland	Finland	4		1							5
Ireland	France	23	14	15			26				78
Ireland	Germany	77	147	42			481				747
Ireland	Germany (North)	24	1	13							38
Ireland	Germany (South)	29	1	26							56
Ireland	Greece	23		5							28
Ireland	Holland	10	1	3			1				15
Ireland	Hungary (Germ.)	2					3				5
Ireland	Hungary (Hung.)	2									2
Ireland	Hungary (Sl.)		2	2							4
Ireland	Italy	35	12	20			24				91
Ireland	Italy (North)	5		3			36				44
Ireland	Italy (South)	19		20			2				41
Ireland	Japan	2									2
Ireland	Mexico (Span.)	2		2			1				5
Ireland	Norway	12	1	4			1				18
Ireland	Porto Rico (Span.)	3		2							5

NATIONALITY		GENERATION									
WOMAN	MAN	1st Gen. (FBFP) with 1st Gen. (FBFP)	1st Gen. (FBFP) with 2nd Gen. (NBFP)	2nd Gen. (NBFP) with 1st Gen. (FBFP)	1st Gen. (FBFP) with 3rd Gen. (NBNP)	3rd Gen. (NBNP) with 1st Gen. (FBFP)	2nd Gen. (NBFP) with 2nd Gen. (NBFP)	2nd Gen. (NBFP) with 3rd Gen. (NBNP)	3rd Gen. (NBNP) with 2nd Gen. (NBFP)	3rd Gen. (NBNP) with 3rd Gen. (NBNP)	TOTALS
		26—IRELAND—*Continued*									
Ireland	Portugal	3		2							5
Ireland	Rumania			1							1
Ireland	Russia (Pol.)	8		4			1				13
Ireland	Servia			1							1
Ireland	Scotland	115	14	37			50				216
Ireland	Spain	2		3			2				7
Ireland	Sweden	30	6	8			13				57
Ireland	Switzerland (French)	6		3							9
Ireland	Switzerland (Germ.)	11	3	4			9				27
Ireland	Switzerland (Ital.)		1	1							2
Ireland	Turkey	5	1	1							7
Ireland	Wales	4	1	5			7				17
Ireland	United States (Col.)				1			4			5
Ireland	Austria (Jew)	3	3	1			2				9
Ireland	England (Jew)						1				1
Ireland	Germany (Jew)	2	1	3			14				20
Ireland	Holland (Jew)			1							1
Ireland	Hungary (Jew)	1		1			1				3
Ireland	Russia (Jew)	7	6	3			10				26
Ireland	United States (Jew)				2			1			3
Ireland	Australia (Engl.)	1	1								2
Ireland	Brazil	1									1
Ireland	Chile	3									3
Ireland	Egypt	1									1
Ireland	Persia	1									1
Ireland	Canada (Jew)			1							1
Ireland	Luxemburg	2									2
Totals		**5352**	**1066**	**804**	**3**		**2485**	**5**			**9735**

NATIONALITY		GENERATION									
WOMAN	MAN	1st Gen. (FBFP) with 1st Gen. (FBFP)	1st Gen. (FBFP) with 2nd Gen. (NBFP)	2nd Gen. (NBFP) with 1st Gen. (FBFP)	1st Gen. (FBFP) with 3rd Gen. (NBNP)	3rd Gen. (NBNP) with 1st Gen. (FBFP)	2nd Gen. (NBFP) with 2nd Gen. (NBFP)	2nd Gen. (NBFP) with 3rd Gen. (NBNP)	3rd Gen. (NBNP) with 2nd Gen. (NBFP)	3rd Gen. (NBNP) with 3rd Gen. (NBNP)	TOTALS
					27—ITALY						
Italy	Italy	5279	107	650			129				6165
Italy	Austria (Germ.)	1									1
Italy	Austria (Boh.)						2				2
Italy	Austria (Ital.)	2									2
Italy	Austria (Pol.)						1				1
Italy	British West Indies (Engl.)	1									1
Itals	Belgium	1					1				2
Italy	Canada (Engl.)		1				3				4
Italy	Canada (French)						1				1
Italy	Cuba (Span.)	2									2
Italy	Italy (South)	7	1	7			1				16
Italy	France	13	2				1				16
Italy	Germany	10	9	6			28				53
Italy	Germany (North)	2		1							3
Italy	Greece	8		4							12
Italy	Holland			1							1
Italy	Ireland	5	6	15			24				50
Italy	Norway			1							1
Italy	Portugal	2									2
Italy	Scotland			1			1				2
Italy	Spain	3		1			1				5
Italy	Sweden	1									1
Italy	Switzerland (Germ.)	3					1				4
Italy	Switzerland (Ital.)	6		1							7
Italy	United States (Col.)							1			1
Italy	England (Jew)			1							1
Italy	Germany (Jew)						2				2
Italy	Hungary (Jew)			1							1
Italy	Russia (Jew)	1					1				2
Italy	United States (Jew)							1			1
Totals		5347	126	690			197	2			6362

NATIONALITY		GENERATION									
WOMAN	MAN	1st Gen. (FBFP) with 1st Gen. (FBFP)	1st Gen. (FBFP) with 2nd Gen. (NBFP)	2nd Gen. (NBFP) with 1st Gen. (FBFP)	1st Gen. (FBFP) with 3rd Gen. (NBNP)	3rd Gen. (NBNP) with 1st Gen. (FBFP)	2nd Gen. (NBFP) with 2nd Gen. (NBFP)	2nd Gen. (NBFP) with 3rd Gen. (NBNP)	3rd Gen. (NBNP) with 2nd Gen. (NBFP)	3rd Gen. (NBNP) with 3rd Gen. (NBNP)	TOTALS
28—ITALY (NORTH)											
Italy (North)	Italy (North)	861		115			1				977
Italy (North)	Austria (Germ.)	1									1
Italy (North)	Austria (Ital.)	1									1
Italy (North)	England	1		1							2
Italy (North)	Germany	1	4								5
Italy (North)	Germany (North)	3									3
Italy (North)	Greece	1									1
Italy (North)	Ireland	1	1								2
Italy (North)	Italy (South)	185		2							187
Italy (North)	Scotland	1									1
Italy (North)	Switzerland (Ital.)	1									1
Italy (North)	Russia (Jew)	1									1
Italy (North)	Cuba (Col.)	1									1
Totals		**1059**	**5**	**118**			**1**				**1193**
29—ITALY (SOUTH)											
Italy (South)	Italy (South)	3580		376			4				3960
Italy (South)	Canada (French)	2									2
Italy (South)	Cuba (Span.)	1									1
Italy (South)	England		1								1
Italy (South)	Germany	1					1				2
Italy (South)	Greece	3									3
Italy (South)	Hungary (Sl.)						1				1
Italy (South)	Ireland	1	4								5
Italy (South)	Italy (North)	58		5							63
Italy (South)	Norway	1									1
Italy (South)	Porto Rico (Span.)	2									2
Italy (South)	Scotland	1									1
Italy (South)	Spain	1		1							2
Italy (South)	Turkey	2									2
Italy (South)	Switzerland (French)	1									1
Totals		**3654**	**5**	**382**			**6**				**4047**

Nationality: Woman	Nationality: Man	1st Gen. (FBFP) with 1st Gen. (FBFP)	1st Gen. (FBFP) with 2nd Gen. (NBFP)	2nd Gen. (NBFP) with 1st Gen. (FBFP)	1st Gen. (FBFP) with 3rd Gen. (NBNP)	3rd Gen. (NBNP) with 1st Gen. (FBFP)	2nd Gen. (NBFP) with 2nd Gen. (NBFP)	2nd Gen. (NBFP) with 3rd Gen. (NBNP)	3rd Gen. (NBNP) with 2nd Gen. (NBFP)	3rd Gen. (NBNP) with 3rd Gen. (NBNP)	Totals
30—NORWAY											
Norway	Norway	206	3	2			2				213
Norway	Austria (Germ.)	2									2
Norway	Austria (Pol.)		1								1
Norway	British West Indies (Col.)	1									1
Norway	Canada (Engl.)	1									1
Norway	China	1									1
Norway	Denmark	16	2	1			1				20
Norway	England	9	3	2			2				16
Norway	Finland	1									1
Norway	Germany	7	4	2			9				22
Norway	Germany (North)	2	1	1							4
Norway	Greece	1									1
Norway	Holland						1				1
Norway	Ireland	9	5				8				22
Norway	Italy	3	1	1							5
Norway	Italy (South)	3		1							4
Norway	Japan	1									1
Norway	Portugal	1									1
Norway	Russia (Pol.)	1									1
Norway	Scotland	3					1				4
Norway	Sweden	36	1	1							38
Norway	Switzerland (Germ.)	2					1				3
Norway	Switzerland (French)	1									1
Norway	Turkey	1									1
Norway	Germany (Jew)		2								2
Norway	Russia (Jew)	1					1				2
Norway	Peru	1									1
Totals		310	23	11			26				370

NATIONALITY		GENERATION									
WOMAN	MAN	1st Gen. (FBFP) with 1st Gen. (FBFP)	1st Gen. (FBFP) with 2nd Gen. (NBFP)	2nd Gen. (NBFP) with 1st Gen. (FBFP)	1st Gen. (FBFP) with 3rd Gen. (NBNP)	3rd Gen. (NBNP) with 1st Gen. (FBFP)	2nd Gen. (NBFP) with 2nd Gen. (NBFP)	2nd Gen. (NBFP) with 3rd Gen. (NBNP)	3rd Gen. (NBNP) with 2nd Gen. (NBFP)	3rd Gen. (NBNP) with 3rd Gen. (NBNP)	TOTALS
31—PORTO RICO (SPAN.)											
Porto Rico (Span.)	Porto Rico (Span.)	15		1							16
Porto Rico (Span.)	Belgium	1									1
Porto Rico (Span.)	Cuba (Span.)	2									2
Porto Rico (Span.)	Germany	1									1
Porto Rico (Span.)	Spain	3									3
Porto Rico (Span.)	Russia (Jew)	1									1
Totals		23		1							24
32—RUMANIA											
Rumania	Rumania	15		1							16
Totals		15		1							16
33—RUSSIA (POL.)											
Russia (Pol.)	Russia (Pol.)	750		4			2				756
Russia (Pol.)	Armenia	2									2
Russia (Pol.)	Austria (Pol.)	33	1	1							35
Russia (Pol.)	Canada (Engl.)	1									1
Russia (Pol.)	Denmark	1									1
Russia (Pol.)	England	3									3
Russia (Pol.)	Germany	6	3				2				11
Russia (Pol.)	Germany (North)	4		1							5
Russia (Pol.)	Germany (South)	7									7
Russia (Pol.)	Greece	3									3
Russia (Pol.)	Holland	1									1
Russia (Pol.)	Hungary (Sl.)	5									5
Russia (Pol.)	Ireland		4				3				7
Russia (Pol.)	Italy	8	1	1			1				11
Russia (Pol.)	Italy (North)	1									1
Russia (Pol.)	Italy (South)	4									4
Russia (Pol.)	Russia (Jew)	1									1
Russia (Pol.)	Scotland						1				1
Russia (Pol.)	Switzerland (Germ.)	1									1
Totals		831	9	7			9				856

NATIONALITY		GENERATION									
WOMAN	MAN	1st Gen. (FBFP) with 1st Gen. (FBFP)	1st Gen. (FBFP) with 2nd Gen. (NBFP)	2nd Gen. (NBFP) with 1st Gen. (FBFP)	1st Gen. (FBFP) with 3rd Gen. (NBNP)	3rd Gen. (NBNP) with 1st Gen. (FBFP)	2nd Gen. (NBFP) with 2nd Gen. (NBFP)	2nd Gen. (NBFP) with 3rd Gen. (NBNP)	3rd Gen. (NBNP) with 2nd Gen. (NBFP)	3rd Gen. (NBNP) with 3rd Gen. (NBNP)	TOTALS
				34—SCOTLAND							
Scotland	Scotland	280	10	14			9				313
Scotland	Austria (Germ.)	2									2
Scotland	Austria (Boh.)		1								1
Scotland	Austria (Pol.)	2		2			1				5
Scotland	British West Indies (Engl.)	1		1							2
Scotland	Canada (Engl.)	10	2	6			4				22
Scotland	Canada (French)			1			2				3
Scotland	China						1				1
Scotland	Cuba (Span.)		1				1				2
Scotland	Denmark	2	1				1				4
Scotland	England	66	2	16			15				99
Scotland	Finland			1							1
Scotland	France	6	2	2			2				12
Scotland	Germany	10	22	3			35				70
Scotland	Germany (North)	2		1							3
Scotland	Germany (South)	4									4
Scotland	Greece	2									2
Scotland	Holland	1	2								3
Scotland	Hungary (Germ.)		2								2
Scotland	Ireland	55	33	19			33				140
Scotland	Italy	1	1	7			5				14
Scotland	Italy (South)			1							1
Scotland	Japan	2		1							3
Scotland	Norway	2									2
Scotland	Russia (Pol.)	1									1
Scotland	Sweden	4		1							5
Scotland	Wales	4									4
Scotland	Germany (Jew)			1							1
Scotland	Holland (Jew)		1								1
Scotland	Hungary (Jew)		1	1							2
Scotland	Russia (Jew)		2	1			1				4
Scotland	Switzerland (Germ.)						1				1

NATIONALITY		GENERATION									
WOMAN	MAN	1st Gen. (FBFP) with 1st Gen. (FBFP)	1st Gen. (FBFP) with 2nd Gen. (NBFP)	2nd Gen. (NBFP) with 1st Gen. (FBFP)	1st Gen. (FBFP) with 3rd Gen. (NBNP)	3rd Gen. (NBNP) with 1st Gen. (FBFP)	2nd Gen. (NBFP) with 2nd Gen. (NBFP)	2nd Gen. (NBFP) with 3rd Gen. (NBN P)	3rd Gen. (NBNP) with 2nd Gen. (NBFP)	3rd Gen. (NBNP) with 3rd Gen. (NBNP)	TOTALS
34—SCOTLAND—*Continued*											
Scotland	France (Jew)						2				2
Scotland	Canada (Col.)	1									1
Scotland	Mexico (Span.)	2									2
Totals		**460**	**83**	**79**			**113**				**735**
35—SPAIN											
Spain	Spain	102		1			1				104
Spain	China	1									1
Spain	Cuba (Span.)	6									6
Spain	England	3									3
Spain	France	3									3
Spain	Germany	1	1				2				4
Spain	Germany (South)	1									1
Spain	Ireland	1		2			1				4
Spain	Italy	1		2							3
Spain	Italy (North)	2									2
Spain	Italy (South)	5									5
Spain	Japan	1									1
Spain	Mexico (Span.)	3									3
Spain	Porto Rico (Span.)	1									1
Spain	Scotland	1									1
Spain	Turkey	1									1
Spain	Germany (Jew)						1				1
Spain	Russia (Jew)	1									1
Spain	Australia (Engl.)			1							1
Totals		**134**	**1**	**6**			**5**				**146**
36—SWEDEN											
Sweden	Sweden	681	17	16			10				724
Sweden	Armenia	1									1
Sweden	Austria (Germ.)	2	1								3
Sweden	Austria (Pol.)	1									1
Sweden	British West Indies (Engl.)	2									2

NATIONALITY		GENERATION									
WOMAN	MAN	1st Gen. (FBFP) with 1st Gen. (FBFP)	1st Gen. (FBFP) with 2nd Gen. (NBFP)	2nd Gen. (NBFP) with 1st Gen. (FBFP)	1st Gen. (FBFP) with 3rd Gen. (NBNP)	3rd Gen. (NBNP) with 1st Gen. (FBFP)	2nd Gen. (NBFP) with 2nd Gen. (NBFP)	2nd Gen. (NBFP) with 3rd Gen. (NBNP)	3rd Gen. (NBNP) with 2nd Gen. (NBFP)	3rd Gen. (NBNP) with 3rd Gen. (NBNP)	TOTALS
36—SWEDEN—*Continued*											
Sweden	Canada (Engl.)	1	2				3				6
Sweden	Canada (French)						1				1
Sweden	Denmark	20									20
Sweden	England	47	5	3			7				62
Sweden	Finland	10		1							11
Sweden	France	6		1							7
Sweden	Germany	31	23	5			32				91
Sweden	Germany (North)	9									9
Sweden	Germany (South)	10	1								11
Sweden	Greece	5									5
Sweden	Holland	6	1								7
Sweden	Hungary (Germ.)	2									2
Sweden	Ireland	20	13	5			9				47
Sweden	Italy	10	2				3				15
Sweden	Italy (North)	2									2
Sweden	Italy (South)	1		1							2
Sweden	Japan	2									2
Sweden	Mexico (Span.)	1									1
Sweden	Norway	24	2	2			1				29
Sweden	Porto Rico (Span.)	1									1
Sweden	Portugal		1								1
Sweden	Russia (Pol.)	3		1							4
Sweden	Scotland	24	1	2			1				28
Sweden	Spain	2									2
Sweden	Switzerland (French)	2									2
Sweden	Switzerland (Germ.)	1		1							2
Sweden	Syria	1									1
Sweden	Wales	1									1
Sweden	United States (Col.)				1						1
Sweden	Germany (Jew)			1			1				2
Sweden	Russia (Jew)	1	1				2				4
Sweden	Brazil	1									1
Totals		931	70	39	1		70				1111

NATIONALITY		GENERATION									
Woman	Man	1st Gen. (FBFP) with 1st Gen. (FBFP)	1st Gen. (FBFP) with 2nd Gen. (NBFP)	2nd Gen. (NBFP) with 1st Gen. (FBFP)	1st Gen. (FBFP) with 3rd Gen. (NBNP)	3rd Gen. (NBNP) with 1st Gen. (FBFP)	2nd Gen. (NBFP) with 2nd Gen. (NBFP)	2nd Gen. (NBFP) with 3rd Gen. (NBNP)	3rd Gen. (NBNP) with 2nd Gen. (NBFP)	3rd Gen. (NBNP) with 3rd Gen. (NBNP)	Totals
		37—SWITZERLAND (GERM.)									
Switzerland (Germ.)	Switzerland (Germ.)	103	3	8			2				116
Switzerland (Germ.)	Austria (Germ.)	8									8
Switzerland (Germ.)	Austria (Boh.)	2		1							3
Switzerland (Germ.)	Austria (Ital.)	1									1
Switzerland (Germ.)	Austria (Pol.)			1							1
Switzerland (Germ.)	British West Indies (Col.)	1									1
Switzerland (Germ.)	Belgium	1									1
Switzerland (Germ.)	Canada (Engl.)	2	1				1				4
Switzerland (Germ.)	Denmark	4	1								5
Switzerland (Germ.)	England	7	1	1			6				15
Switzerland (Germ.)	Finland	1									1
Switzerland (Germ.)	France	13		1							14
Switzerland (Germ.)	Germany	26	14	8			25				73
Switzerland (Germ.)	Germany (North)	8		4							12
Switzerland (Germ.)	Germany (South)	25	1	1			1				28
Switzerland (Germ.)	Holland	1		1			1				3
Switzerland (Germ.)	Hungary (Germ.)	1									1
Switzerland (Germ.)	Hungary (Sl.)	1									1
Switzerland (Germ.)	Ireland	3	3	2			17				25
Switzerland (Germ.)	Italy	2	1								3
Switzerland (Germ.)	Italy (South)			1							1
Switzerland (Germ.)	Japan	2									2
Switzerland (Germ.)	Mexico (Span.)	1									1
Switzerland (Germ.)	Porto Rico (Span.)	1									1
Switzerland (Germ.)	Russia (Pol.)	1									11
Switzerland (Germ.)	Scotland	1	3	4			3				6
Switzerland (Germ.)	Sweden	5		1							3
Switzerland (Germ.)	Switzerland (French)	3									1
Switzerland (Germ.)	Turkey	1									1
Switzerland (Germ.)	Germany (Jew)						1				1
Switzerland (Germ.)	Hungary (Jew)	1									1
Totals		226	28	34			57				345

NATIONALITY		GENERATION									
Woman	Man	1st Gen. (FBFP) with 1st Gen. (FBFP)	1st Gen. (FBFP) with 2nd Gen. (NBFP)	2nd Gen. (NBFP) with 1st Gen. (FBFP)	1st Gen. (FBFP) with 3rd Gen. (NBNP)	3rd Gen. (NBNP) with 1st Gen. (FBFP)	2nd Gen. (NBFP) with 2nd Gen. (NBFP)	2nd Gen. (NBFP) with 3rd Gen. (NBNP)	3rd Gen. (NBNP) with 2nd Gen. (NBFP)	3rd Gen. (NBNP) with 3rd Gen. (NBNP)	Totals
38—SWITZERLAND (FRENCH)											
Switz. (French)	Switzerland (French)	6									6
Switz. (French)	Belgium	1									1
Switz. (French)	Canada (Engl.)	1									1
Switz. (French)	France	20					1				21
Switz. (French)	Ireland						1				1
Switz. (French)	Italy (South)	1									1
Switz. (French)	Luxemburg	1									1
Switz. (French)	Switzerland (Germ.)	1									1
Switz. (French)	Syria	1									1
Totals		32					2				34
39—SWITZERLAND (ITAL.)											
Switzerland (Ital.)	Switzerland (Ital.)	6		1							7
Switzerland (Ital.)	Hungary (Germ.)	1									1
Switzerland (Ital.)	Italy	11									11
Switzerland (Ital.)	Italy (South)	2									2
Switzerland (Ital.)	Switzerland (Germ.)			1							1
Switzerland (Ital.)	Australia (Engl.)	1									1
Totals		21		2							23
40—SYRIA											
Syria	Syria	71		1							72
Syria	Canada (French)	1									1
Syria	Italy (South)	1									1
Syria	Spain	1									1
Totals		74		1							75

NATIONALITY		GENERATION									
WOMAN	MAN	1st Gen. (FBFP) with 1st Gen. (FBFP)	1st Gen. (FBFP) with 2nd Gen. (NBFP)	2nd Gen. (NBFP) with 1st Gen. (FBFP)	1st Gen. (FBFP) with 3rd Gen. (NBNP)	3rd Gen. (NBNP) with 1st Gen. (FBFP)	2nd Gen. (NBFP) with 2nd Gen. (NBFP)	2nd Gen. (NBFP) with 3rd Gen. (NBNP)	3rd Gen. (NBNP) with 2nd Gen. (NBFP)	3rd Gen. (NBNP) with 3rd Gen. (NBNP)	TOTALS
41—TURKEY											
Turkey	Turkey	99									99
Turkey	Germany (South)	1									1
Turkey	Persia	1									1
Totals		101									101
42—UNITED STATES											
United States	United States									9542	9542
United States	Australia (Engl.)					3					3
United States	Austria (Germ.)					26			18		44
United States	Armenia					6					6
United States	Argentina					1					1
United States	Austria (Boh.)					6			9		15
United States	Austria (Pol.)					18			11		29
United States	Brazil					4					4
United States	British West Indies (Col.)					2					2
United States	British West Indies (Engl.)					26			1		27
United States	Belgium					2			1		3
United States	Bolivia					1					1
United States	Bulgaria					1					1
United States	Canada (French)					23			15		38
United States	Chile					1					1
United States	China					5			3		8
United States	Colombia (Span.)					1					1
United States	Cuba (Span.)					13			3		16
United States	Denmark					22			28		50
United States	England					419			378		797
United States	Equador					1					1
United States	Egypt					3					3
United States	Finland					1			4		5
United States	Germany (South)					106			8		114
United States	Germany (North)					69			13		82

42—UNITED STATES—*Continued*

NATIONALITY		GENERATION									
Woman	Man	1st Gen. (FBFP) with 1st Gen. (FBFP)	1st Gen. (FBFP) with 2nd Gen. (NBFP)	2nd Gen. (NBFP) with 1st Gen. (FBFP)	1st Gen. (FBFP) with 3rd Gen. (NBNP)	3rd Gen. (NBNP) with 1st Gen. (FBFP)	2nd Gen. (NBFP) with 2nd Gen. (NBFP)	2nd Gen. (NBFP) with 3rd Gen. (NBNP)	3rd Gen. (NBNP) with 2nd Gen. (NBFP)	3rd Gen. (NBNP) with 3rd Gen. (NBNP)	Totals
United States	Germany					256			1674		1930
United States	Greece					21					21
United States	Holland					19			13		32
United States	Hungary (Sl.)					6			4		10
United States	Hungary (Germ.)					2					2
United States	Hungary (Hung.)					3					3
United States	India					2					2
United States	Ireland					364			1581		1945
United States	Italy					105			118		223
United States	Italy (North)					49			10		59
United States	Italy (South)					56			2		58
United States	Japan					5					5
United States	Mexico (Span.)					6					6
United States	Norway					21			18		39
United States	Portugal					2			1		3
United States	Russia (Pol.)					9			3		12
United States	Scotland					118			149		267
United States	Spain					16			7		23
United States	Sweden					59			36		95
United States	Switzerland (Germ.)					32			35		67
United States	Switzerland (French)					3					3
United States	Porto Rico (Span.)					6					6
United States	Porto Rico (Col.)					1					1
United States	Turkey					5					5
United States	Venezuela (Span.)					2					2
United States	Wales					9			23		32
United States	Australia (Jew)					1					1
United States	Austria (Jew)					11			9		20
United States	Canada (Jew)					1					1
United States	England (Jew)					1					1
United States	France (Jew)								1		1
United States	Germany (Jew)					7			41		48

NATIONALITY		GENERATION									
WOMAN	MAN	1st Gen. (FBFP) with 1st Gen. (FBFP)	1st Gen. (FBFP) with 2nd Gen. (NBFP)	2nd Gen. (NBFP) with 1st Gen. (FBFP)	1st Gen. (FBFP) with 3rd Gen. (NBNP)	3rd Gen. (NBNP) with 1st Gen. (FBFP)	2nd Gen. (NBFP) with 2nd Gen. (NBFP)	2nd Gen. (NBFP) with 3rd Gen. (NBNP)	3rd Gen. (NBNP) with 2nd Gen. (NBFP)	3rd Gen. (NBNP) with 3rd Gen. (NBNP)	TOTALS
42—UNITED STATES—*Continued*											
United States	Holland (Jew)								1		1
United States	Hungary (Jew)					5			1		6
United States	Portugal (Jew)								1		1
United States	Rumania (Jew)					1					1
United States	Russia (Jew)					8			15		23
United States	Turkey (Jew)					1					1
United States	United States (Jew)									19	19
United States	United States (Col.)									11	11
Totals						1973			4595	9572	16140
43—UNITED STATES (COL.)											
United States (Col.)	United States (Col.)									2194	2194
United States (Col.)	Canada (Engl.)					2			1		3
United States (Col.)	Denmark					2			2		4
United States (Col.)	Italy (South)					1					1
United States (Col.)	United States									1	1
United States (Col.)	Spain								1		1
United States (Col.)	British West Indies (Col.)					219			8		227
United States (Col.)	Canada (Col.)					7			2		9
United States	Cuba (Col.)					19			4		23
United States (Col.)	Danish West Indies (Col.)					18					18
United States (Col.)	Haiti (Col.)					1					1
United States (Col.)	India					1					1
Totals						270			18	2195	2483
44—WALES											
Wales	Wales	23	1	2			3				29
Wales	Canada (Engl.)						1				1
Wales	Denmark	1		1							2
Wales	England	3	1	1			2				7
Wales	Germany		5				3				8
Wales	Greece			1							1

NATIONALITY		GENERATION									
WOMAN	MAN	1st Gen. (FBFP) with 1st Gen. (FBFP)	1st Gen. (FBFP) with 2nd Gen. (NBFP)	2nd Gen. (NBFP) with 1st Gen. (FBFP)	1st Gen. (FBFP) with 3rd Gen. (NBNP)	3rd Gen. (NBNP) with 1st Gen. (FBFP)	2nd Gen. (NBFP) with 2nd Gen. (NBFP)	2nd Gen. (NBFP) with 3rd Gen. (NBNP)	3rd Gen. (NBNP) with 2nd Gen. (NBFP)	3rd Gen. (NBNP) with 3rd Gen. (NBNP)	TOTALS
		44—WALES—*Continued*									
Wales	Ireland	3	4	1			4				12
Wales	Scotland	3		2							5
Totals		33	11	8			13				65
		45—AUSTRIA (JEW)									
Austria (Jew)	Austria (Jew)	4465	31	60			56				4612
Austria (Jew)	Austria (Germ.)		1								1
Austria (Jew)	Austria (Boh.)						2				2
Austria (Jew)	England	2					1				3
Austria (Jew)	Germany	6	3	1			6				16
Austria (Jew)	Germany (South)	3									3
Austria (Jew)	Greece	1									1
Austria (Jew)	Hungary (Sl.)	1									1
Austria (Jew)	Ireland	2	2				5				9
Austria (Jew)	Italy	4	2				2				8
Austria (Jew)	Italy (North)	2									2
Austria (Jew)	Italy (South)	6		2			1				9
Austria (Jew)	Russia (Pol.)						1				1
Austria (Jew)	Scotland		1								1
Austria (Jew)	Wales	1									1
Austria (Jew)	United States				11			13			24
Austria (Jew)	Bulgaria (Jew)	3									3
Austria (Jew)	England (Jew)	12	3	5			10				30
Austria (Jew)	France (Jew)	3		1			6				10
Austria (Jew)	Germany (Jew)	82	28	26			91				227
Austria (Jew)	Holland (Jew)	11	1	1			1				14
Austria (Jew)	Hungary (Jew)	125	9	22			22				178
Austria (Jew)	Rumania (Jew)	195	1	15			4				215
Austria (Jew)	Russia (Jew)	1434	45	181			141				1801
Austria (Jew)	Spain			1							1
Austria (Jew)	Sweden	2					1				3
Austria (Jew)	Turkey (Jew)	3									3
Austria (Jew)	United States (Jew)				48			38			86
Totals		6363	127	315	59		350	51			7265

NATIONALITY		GENERATION									
WOMAN	MAN	1st Gen. (FBFP) with 1st Gen. (FBFP)	1st Gen. (FBFP) with 2nd Gen. (NBFP)	2nd Gen. (NBFP) with 1st Gen. (FBFP)	1st Gen. (FBFP) with 3rd Gen. (NBNP)	3rd Gen. (NBNP) with 1st Gen. (FBFP)	2nd Gen. (NBFP) with 2nd Gen. (NBFP)	2nd Gen. (NBFP) with 3rd Gen. (NBNP)	3rd Gen. (NBNP) with 2nd Gen. (NBFP)	3rd Gen. (NBNP) with 3rd Gen. (NBNP)	TOTALS
				46—ENGLAND (JEW)							
England (Jew)	England (Jew)	10		2			4				16
England (Jew)	Canada (French)		1								1
England (Jew)	England	1									1
England (Jew)	Italy	1					1				2
England (Jew)	Italy (South)	1									1
England (Jew)	United States							1			1
England (Jew)	Austria (Jew)	8	2	8			11				29
England (Jew)	Bulgaria (Jew)			1							1
England (Jew)	Germany (Jew)	1	4	2			37				44
England (Jew)	Holland (Jew)		1				1				2
England (Jew)	Hungary (Jew)	1					2				3
England (Jew)	Rumania (Jew)			1			1				2
England (Jew)	Russia (Jew)	30	4	13			20				67
England (Jew)	United States (Jew)				7			12			19
England (Jew)	Canada (Jew)			1							1
England (Jew)	Sweden (Jew)						1				1
Totals		53	12	28	7		78	13			191
				47—FRANCE (JEW)							
France (Jew)	France (Jew)		1								1
France (Jew)	France	1									1
France (Jew)	Austria (Jew)	2	1								3
France (Jew)	England (Jew)						3				3
France (Jew)	Germany (Jew)		3	5			13				21
France (Jew)	Hungary (Jew)		1	2			1				4
France (Jew)	Russia (Jew)		1	4			3				8
France (Jew)	Turkey (Jew)	1									1
France (Jew)	United States (Jew)				2			2			4
Totals		4	7	11	2		20	2			46

NATIONALITY		GENERATION									
WOMAN	MAN	1st Gen. (FBFP) with 1st Gen. (FBFP)	1st Gen. (FBFP) with 2nd Gen. (NBFP)	2nd Gen. (NBFP) with 1st Gen. (FBFP)	1st Gen. (FBFP) with 3rd Gen. (NBNP)	3rd Gen. (NBNP) with 1st Gen. (FBFP)	2nd Gen. (NBFP) with 2nd Gen. (NBFP)	2nd Gen. (NBFP) with 3rd Gen. (NBNP)	3rd Gen. (NBNP) with 2nd Gen. (NBFP)	3rd Gen. (NBNP) with 3rd Gen. (NBNP)	TOTALS
				48—GERMANY (JEW)							
Germany (Jew)	Germany (Jew)	213	117	61			329				720
Germany (Jew)	Austria (Ital.)	2									2
Germany (Jew)	China	1									1
Germany (Jew)	England			3			1				4
Germany (Jew)	Germany			1			1				2
Germany (Jew)	Ireland		2	1			6				9
Germany (Jew)	Italy	5		1			2				8
Germany (Jew)	Italy (South)	2		1							3
Germany (Jew)	Scotland			1							1
Germany (Jew)	Austria (Jew)	80	7	71			69				227
Germany (Jew)	Canada (Jew)	1									1
Germany (Jew)	England (Jew)	5	6	14			24				49
Germany (Jew)	France (Jew)	2	1	4			9				16
Germany (Jew)	Holland (Jew)	3	1	2			6				12
Germany (Jew)	Hungary (Jew)	44	5	35			33				117
Germany (Jew)	Russia (Jew)	101	25	141			101				368
Germany (Jew)	Turkey (Jew)			2							2
Germany (Jew)	United States (Jew)				15			97			112
Germany (Jew)	Rumania (Jew)	7		12			1				20
Germany (Jew)	United States				3			15			18
Germany (Jew)	Denmark (Jew)						1				1
Germany (Jew)	Palestine (Jew)			1							1
Totals		**466**	**164**	**351**	**18**		**583**	**112**			**1694**
				49—HOLLAND (JEW)							
Holland (Jew)	Austria (Jew)	1					1				2
Holland (Jew)	England (Jew)	2		1			1				4
Holland (Jew)	Holland (Jew)	6	1	2			1				10
Holland (Jew)	Hungary (Jew)	2	1	4			1				8
Holland (Jew)	Rumania (Jew)	2									2
Holland (Jew)	United States (Jew)				1			3			4
Totals		**13**	**2**	**7**	**1**		**4**	**3**			**30**

NATIONALITY		GENERATION									
Woman	Man	1st Gen. (FBFP) with 1st Gen. (FBFP)	1st Gen. (FBFP) with 2nd Gen. (NBFP)	2nd Gen. (NBFP) with 1st Gen. (FBFP)	1st Gen. (FBFP) with 3rd Gen. (NBNP)	3rd Gen. (NBNP) with 1st Gen. (FBFP)	2nd Gen. (NBFP) with 2nd Gen. (NBFP)	2nd Gen. (NBFP) with 3rd Gen. (NBNP)	3rd Gen. (NBNP) with 2nd Gen. (NBFP)	3rd Gen. (NBNP) with 3rd Gen. (NBNP)	Totals
		50—HUNGARY (JEW)									
Hungary (Jew)	Hungary (Jew)	1429	27	73			26				1555
Hungary (Jew)	Austria (Germ.)	15									15
Hungary (Jew)	Austria (Ital.)	1									1
Hungary (Jew)	British West Indies (Engl.)	1									1
Hungary (Jew)	Canada (Engl.)	1									1
Hungary (Jew)	Denmark	1									1
Hungary (Jew)	England	3		3			1				7
Hungary (Jew)	Finland	1									1
Hungary (Jew)	France	1	1	1							3
Hungary (Jew)	Germany	5	2								7
Hungary (Jew)	Germany (North)	2									2
Hungary (Jew)	Greece	2									2
Hungary (Jew)	Holland	3									3
Hungary (Jew)	Ireland	1		1							2
Hungary (Jew)	Italy	9	4								13
Hungary (Jew)	Italy (South)	8									8
Hungary (Jew)	Norway	1									1
Hungary (Jew)	Portugal	1									1
Hungary (Jew)	Scotland	1		2							3
Hungary (Jew)	Servia	1									1
Hungary (Jew)	United States				7			6			13
Hungary (Jew)	Wales	1									1
Hungary (Jew)	Austria (Jew)	328	16	32			22				398
Hungary (Jew)	Bulgaria (Jew)	1									1
Hungary (Jew)	England (Jew)	4	2				5				11
Hungary (Jew)	Holland (Jew)	2		1							3
Hungary (Jew)	Rumania (Jew)	36		13			2				51
Hungary (Jew)	Russia (Jew)	283	27	57			43				410
Hungary (Jew)	Turkey (Jew)	1									1
Hungary (Jew)	United States (Jew)				24			19			43
Hungary (Jew)	United States (Col.)				1						1
Hungary (Jew)	Germany (Jew)	65	31	15			37				148
Totals		**2208**	**110**	**198**	**32**		**136**	**25**			**2709**

NATIONALITY		GENERATION									
WOMAN	MAN	1st Gen. (FBFP) with 1st Gen. (FBFP)	1st Gen. (FBFP) with 2nd Gen. (NBFP)	2nd Gen. (NBFP) with 1st Gen. (FBFP)	1st Gen. (FBFP) with 3rd Gen. (NBNP)	3rd Gen. (NBNP) with 1st Gen. (FBFP)	2nd Gen. (NBFP) with 2nd Gen. (NBFP)	2nd Gen. (NBFP) with 3rd Gen. (NBNP)	3rd Gen. (NBNP) with 2nd Gen. (NBFP)	3rd Gen. (NBNP) with 3rd Gen. (NBNP)	TOTALS
51—RUMANIA (JEW)											
Rumania (Jew)	Rumania (Jew)	769	2	6			3				780
Rumania (Jew)	England	1					1				2
Rumania (Jew)	Italy			1			1				2
Rumania (Jew)	United States				3						3
Rumania (Jew)	Austria (Jew)	154	5	10			5				174
Rumania (Jew)	Germany (Jew)	8	5				5				18
Rumania (Jew)	Hungary (Jew)	19	1				3				23
Rumania (Jew)	Russia (Jew)	379	9	25			20				433
Rumania (Jew)	Turkey (Jew)	4									4
Rumania (Jew)	United States (Jew)				7						7
Rumania (Jew)	Palestine (Jew)	3									3
Rumania (Jew)	Scotland (Jew)	1									1
Totals		1338	22	42	10		38				1450
52—RUSSIA (JEW)											
Russia (Jew)	Russia (Jew)	14510	328	777			455				16070
Russia (Jew)	Austria (Germ.)	1	1								2
Russia (Jew)	Austria (Boh.)			1							1
Russia (Jew)	Belgium			1							1
Russia (Jew)	Canada (Engl.)	1	1								2
Russia (Jew)	China			1							1
Russia (Jew)	Denmark	1									1
Russia (Jew)	England	4		1							5
Russia (Jew)	France	5	2				1				8
Russia (Jew)	Germany	2	6	4			8				20
Russia (Jew)	Greece			1							1
Russia (Jew)	Ireland						8				8
Russia (Jew)	Italy	18	7	4			8				37
Russia (Jew)	Italy (North)	3	1								4
Russia (Jew)	Italy (South)	10		6							16
Russia (Jew)	Russia (Pol.)	1									1
Russia (Jew)	Spain			1							1

NATIONALITY		GENERATION									
WOMAN	MAN	1st Gen. (FBFP) with 1st Gen. (FBFP)	1st Gen. (FBFP) with 2nd Gen. (NBFP)	2nd Gen. (NBFP) with 1st Gen. (FBFP)	1st Gen. (FBFP) with 3rd Gen. (NBNP)	3rd Gen. (NBNP) with 1st Gen. (FBFP)	2nd Gen. (NBFP) with 2nd Gen. (NBFP)	2nd Gen. (NBFP) with 3rd Gen. (NBNP)	3rd Gen. (NBNP) with 2nd Gen. (NBFP)	3rd Gen. (NBNP) with 3rd Gen. (NBNP)	TOTALS
		52—RUSSIA (JEW)—*Continued*									
Russia (Jew)	Sweden		1								1
Russia (Jew)	Syria			1							1
Russia (Jew)	United States				14			12			26
Russia (Jew)	Austria (Jew)	876	44	133			77				1130
Russia (Jew)	Bulgaria (Jew)	1									1
Russia (Jew)	England (Jew)	28	7	13			16				64
Russia (Jew)	France (Jew)		2	2							4
Russia (Jew)	Germany (Jew)	74	69	26			103				272
Russia (Jew)	Hungary (Jew)	82	25	30			30				167
Russia (Jew)	Rumania (Jew)	245	8	29			15				297
Russia (Jew)	Turkey (Jew)	12		1							13
Russia (Jew)	United States (Jew)				109			69			178
Russia (Jew)	Holland (Jew)	4	3	1			3				11
Russia (Jew)	Canada (Jew)	1	1				1				3
Russia (Jew)	Luxemburg (Jew)			1							1
Russia (Jew)	Morocco (Jew)		1								1
Russia (Jew)	Palestine (Jew)	2									2
Russia (Jew)	Spain (Jew)	1					1				2
Russia (Jew)	Sweden (Jew)	1		3							4
Totals		**15883**	**507**	**1037**	**123**		**726**	**81**			**18357**
		53—TURKEY (JEW)									
Turkey (Jew)	Turkey (Jew)	166									166
Turkey (Jew)	Greece	1									1
Turkey (Jew)	Austria (Jew)	1									1
Turkey (Jew)	Bulgaria (Jew)	1									1
Turkey (Jew)	Germany (Jew)		1								1
Turkey (Jew)	Rumania (Jew)	1									1
Turkey (Jew)	Russia (Jew)	6									6
Turkey (Jew)	Palestine (Jew)	1									1
Totals		**177**	**1**								**178**

NATIONALITY		GENERATION									
WOMAN	MAN	1st Gen. (FBFP) with 1st Gen. (FBFP)	1st Gen. (FBFP) with 2nd Gen. (NBFP)	2nd Gen. (NBFP) with 1st Gen. (FBFP)	1st Gen. (FBFP) with 3rd Gen. (NBNP)	3rd Gen. (NBNP) with 1st Gen. (FBFP)	2nd Gen. (NBFP) with 2nd Gen. (NBFP)	2nd Gen. (NBFP) with 3rd Gen. (NBN P)	3rd Gen. (NBNP) with 2nd Gen. (NBFP)	3rd Gen. (NBNP) with 3rd Gen. (NBNP)	TOTALS
54—UNITED STATES (JEW)											
United States (Jew)	United States (Jew)									155	155
United States (Jew)	British West Indies (Engl.)					1					1
United States (Jew)	France					1					1
United States (Jew)	Germany								4		4
United States (Jew)	Ireland								2		2
United States (Jew)	Italy					1			4		5
United States (Jew)	Italy (North)					1					1
United States (Jew)	United States									14	14
United States (Jew)	Austria (Jew)					76			56		132
United States (Jew)	England (Jew)					10			16		26
United States (Jew)	France (Jew)					4			5		9
United States (Jew)	Germany (Jew)					51			151		202
United States (Jew)	Hungary (Jew)					49			22		71
United States	Rumania (Jew)					17			2		19
United States (Jew)	Russia (Jew)					61			69		130
United States (Jew)	Holland (Jew)					3			11		14
United States (Jew)	Honduras					1					1
Totals						**276**			**342**	**169**	**787**

NATIONALITY		GENERATION									
WOMAN	MAN	1st Gen. (FBFP) with 1st Gen. (FBFP)	1st Gen. (FBFP) with 2nd Gen. (NBFP)	2nd Gen. (NBFP) with 1st Gen. (FBFP)	1st Gen. (FBFP) with 3rd Gen. (NBNP)	3rd Gen. (NBNP) with 1st Gen. (FBFP)	2nd Gen. (NBFP) with 2nd Gen. (NBFP)	2nd Gen. (NBFP) with 3rd Gen. (NBNP)	3rd Gen. (NBNP) with 2nd Gen. (NBFP)	3rd Gen. (NBNP) with 3rd Gen. (NBNP)	TOTALS
55—MARRIAGES OF WOMEN OF VARIOUS NATIONALITIES, FIRST AND SECOND GENERATIONS, TO MEN NATIVE-BORN OF NATIVE PARENTS (UNITED STATES)											
Austria (Boh.)	United States				20			29			49
Austria (Germ.)	United States				31			18			49
Austria (Pol.)	United States				37			31			68
B. W. I. (Engl.)	United States				8						8
Belgium	United States				6			2			8
Canada (Engl.)	United States				152			126			278
Canada (French)	United States				11			18			29
Cuba (Span.)	United States				10			7			17
Denmark	United States				25			24			49
England	United States				264			417			681
Finland	United States				17			6			23
France	United States				43			81			124
Germany	United States				193			1489			1682
Germany (North)	United States				44			13			57
Germany (South)	United States				78			6			84
Holland	United States				6			20			26
Hungary (Germ.)	United States				10			1			11
Hungary (Sl.)	United States				29			6			35
Ireland	United States				694			1662			2356
Italy	United States				34			83			117
Italy (North)	United States				8			1			9
Italy (South)	United States				14			4			18
Norway	United States				26			17			43
Portugal	United States							1			1
Russia (Pol.)	United States				6			9			15
Scotland	United States				124			157			281
Spain	United States				5			9			14
Sweden	United States				70			53			123
Switzerland (Germ.)	United States				20			49			69
Wales	United States				9			16			25
Totals					1994			4355			6349
Grand Total		57383	3348	6091	2345	2723	8514	4697	4628	12038	101767

TABLE VI
Groups Represented by less than 10 Cases.

NATIONALITY		GENERATION									
WOMAN	MAN	1st Gen. (FBFP) with 1st Gen. (FBFP)	1st Gen. (FBFP) with 2nd Gen. (NBFP)	2nd Gen. (NBFP) with 1st Gen. (FBFP)	1st Gen. (FBFP) with 3rd Gen. (NBNP)	3rd Gen. (NBNP) with 1st Gen. (FBFP)	2nd Gen. (NBFP) with 2nd Gen. (NBFP)	2nd Gen. (NBFP) with 3rd Gen. (NBNP)	3rd Gen. (NBNP) with 2nd Gen. (NBFP)	3rd Gen. (NBNP) with 3rd Gen. (NBNP)	TOTALS
56—ALGERIA											
Algeria	Spain	2									2
Totals		2									2
57—ARGENTINA											
Argentina	Germany		1								1
Totals			1								1
58—AUSTRALIA (ENGL.)											
Australia (Engl.)	Germany (North)	1									1
Totals		1									1
59—BULGARIA											
Bulgaria	Bulgaria	1									1
Bulgaria	Turkey	1									1
Totals		2									2
60—CHILE											
Chile	France						1				1
Totals							1				1
61—CHINA											
China	China	5		1			2				8
Totals		5		1			2				8

NATIONALITY		GENERATION									
Woman	Man	1st Gen. (FBFP) with 1st Gen. (FBFP)	1st Gen. (FBFP) with 2nd Gen. (NBFP)	2nd Gen. (NBFP) with 1st Gen. (FBFP)	1st Gen. (FBFP) with 3rd Gen. (NBNP)	3rd Gen. (NBNP) with 1st Gen. (FBFP)	2nd Gen. (NBFP) with 2nd Gen. (NBFP)	2nd Gen. (NBFP) with 3rd Gen. (NBNP)	3rd Gen. (NBNP) with 2nd Gen. (NBFP)	3rd Gen. (NBNP) with 3rd Gen. (NBNP)	Totals
62—COLOMBIA (SPAN.)											
Colombia (Span.)	Colombia (Span.)	1									1
Totals		1									1
63—COREA											
Corea	Corea	1									1
Totals		1									1
64—DALMATIA											
Dalmatia	Dalmatia	3									3
Totals		3									3
65—EGYPT											
Egypt	Turkey	1									1
Egypt	Egypt	1									1
Totals		2									2
66—EQUADOR											
Equador	Equador	1									1
Totals		1									1
67—GUATEMALA											
Guatemala	Guatemala	1									1
Totals		1									1

NATIONALITY		GENERATION									
WOMAN	MAN	1st Gen. (FBFP) with 1st Gen. (FBFP)	1st Gen. (FBFP) with 2nd Gen. (NBFP)	2nd Gen. (NBFP) with 1st Gen. (FBFP)	1st Gen. (FBFP) with 3rd Gen. (NBNP)	3rd Gen. (NBNP) with 1st Gen. (FBFP)	2nd Gen. (NBFP) with 2nd Gen. (NBFP)	2nd Gen. (NBFP) with 3rd Gen. (NBNP)	3rd Gen. (NBNP) with 2nd Gen. (NBFP)	3rd Gen. (NBNP) with 3rd Gen. (NBNP)	TOTALS
68—HAITI (COL.)											
Haiti (Col.)	United States (Col.)							2			2
Totals								2			2
69—JAPAN											
Japan	Japan	8									8
Totals		8									8
70—LUXEMBURG											
Luxemburg	Luxemburg	1									1
Luxemburg	Belgium	1									1
Luxemburg	France	1									1
Luxemburg	Holland			1							1
Luxemburg	Italy	1									1
Luxemburg	Spain	1									1
Luxemburg	Sweden	1									1
Totals		6		1							7
71—MEXICO (SPAN.)											
Mexico (Span.)	Mexico (Span.)	2		1							3
Mexico (Span.)	Japan	1									1
Mexico (Span.)	Spain	1									1
Totals		4		1							5
72—MONTENEGRO											
Montenegro	Montenegro	1									1
Totals		1									1

NATIONALITY		GENERATION									
WOMAN	MAN	1st Gen. (FBFP) with 1st Gen. (FBFP)	1st Gen. (FBFP) with 2nd Gen. (NBFP)	2nd Gen. (NBFP) with 1st Gen. (FBFP)	1st Gen. (FBFP) with 3rd Gen. (NBNP)	3rd Gen. (NBNP) with 1st Gen. (FBFP)	2nd Gen. (NBFP) with 2nd Gen. (NBFP)	2nd Gen. (NBFP) with 3rd Gen. (NBNP)	3rd Gen. (NBNP) with 2nd Gen. (NBFP)	3rd Gen. (NBNP) with 3rd Gen. (NBNP)	TOTALS
73—PHILIPPINE ISLANDS											
Philippine Islands	Philippine Islands	1									1
Totals		1									1
74—PORTO RICO (COL.)											
Porto Rico (Col.)	British West Indies (Col.)	2									2
Porto Rico (Col.)	United States (Col.)				1						1
Porto Rico (Col.)	Cuba (Col.)	2									2
Totals		4			1						5
75—PORTUGAL											
Portugal	Portugal	2									2
Portugal	Canada (Engl.)						1				1
Portugal	Germany		1								1
Portugal	Ireland						1				1
Portugal	Spain	1									1
Portugal	Russia (Jew)	1									1
Totals		4	1				2				7
76—SERVIA											
Servia	Sweden			1							1
Totals				1							1

NATIONALITY		GENERATION									
WOMAN	MAN	1st Gen. (FBFP) with 1st Gen. (FBFP)	1st Gen. (FBFP) with 2nd Gen. (NBFP)	2nd Gen. (NBFP) with 1st Gen. (FBFP)	1st Gen. (FBFP) with 3rd Gen. (NBNP)	3rd Gen. (NBNP) with 1st Gen. (FBFP)	2nd Gen. (NBFP) with 2nd Gen. (NBFP)	2nd Gen. (NBFP) with 3rd Gen. (NBNP)	3rd Gen. (NBNP) with 2nd Gen. (NBFP)	3rd Gen. (NBNP) with 3rd Gen. (NBNP)	TOTALS
77—VENEZUELA (SPAN.)											
Venezuela (Span.)	Cuba (Span.)	1									1
Venezuela (Span.)	France	1									1
Venezuela (Span.)	Germany	2									2
Venezuela (Span.)	Germany (North)			1							1
Venezuela (Span.)	Ireland			1							1
Totals		4		2							6
78—AUSTRALIA (JEW)											
Australia (Jew)	Russia (Jew)						2				2
Totals							2				2
79—CANADA (JEW)											
Canada (Jew)	Austria (Jew)	1									1
Canada (Jew)	Germany (Jew)		1				1				2
Canada (Jew)	Hungary (Jew)	1									1
Canada (Jew)	United States (Jew)				1						1
Totals		2	1		1		1				5
80—BULGARIA (JEW)											
Bulgaria (Jew)	Bulgaria (Jew)	3									3
Bulgaria (Jew)	Rumania (Jew)	1									1
Bulgaria (Jew)	Russia (Jew)	1									1
Bulgaria (Jew)	Turkey (Jew)	1									1
Totals		6									6

NATIONALITY		GENERATION									
Woman	Man	1st Gen. (FBFP) with 1st Gen. (FBFP)	1st Gen. (FBFP) with 2nd Gen. (NBFP)	2nd Gen. (NBFP) with 1st Gen. (FBFP)	1st Gen. (FBFP) with 3rd Gen. (NBNP)	3rd Gen. (NBNP) with 1st Gen. (FBFP)	2nd Gen. (NBFP) with 2nd Gen. (NBFP)	2nd Gen. (NBFP) with 3rd Gen. (NBNP)	3rd Gen. (NBNP) with 2nd Gen. (NBFP)	3rd Gen. (NBNP) with 3rd Gen. (NBNP)	Totals
81—FINLAND (JEW)											
Finland (Jew)	Rumania (Jew)	1									1
Totals		1									1
82—PALESTINE (JEW)											
Palestine (Jew)	Rumania (Jew)	2									2
Palestine (Jew)	Russia (Jew)	1									1
Totals		3									3
83—SCOTLAND (JEW)											
Scotland (Jew)	Germany (Jew)						1				1
Totals							1				1
84—SERVIA (JEW)											
Servia (Jew)	Servia (Jew)	1									1
Totals		1									1
85—SPAIN (JEW)											
Spain (Jew)	Austria (Jew)						1				1
Totals							1				1
86—SWEDEN (JEW)											
Sweden (Jew)	Germany (Jew)						1				1
Sweden (Jew)	Russia (Jew)	1					1				2
Totals		1					2				3

NATIONALITY		GENERATION									
Woman	Man	1st Gen. (FBFP) with 1st Gen. (FBFP)	1st Gen. (FBFP) with 2nd Gen. (NBFP)	2nd Gen. (NBFP) with 1st Gen. (FBFP)	1st Gen. (FBFP) with 3rd Gen. (NBNP)	3rd Gen. (NBNP) with 1st Gen. (FBFP)	2nd Gen. (NBFP) with 2nd Gen. (NBFP)	2nd Gen. (NBFP) with 3rd Gen. (NBNP)	3rd Gen. (NBNP) with 2nd Gen. (NBFP)	3rd Gen. (NBNP) with 3rd Gen. (NBNP)	Totals
87—SWITZERLAND (JEW)											
Switzerland (Jew)	England (Jew)			1							1
Switzerland (Jew)	Germany (Jew)	1					1				2
Switzerland (Jew)	Hungary (Jew)			1							1
Switzerland (Jew)	Russia (Jew)	1	1	2							4
Totals		2	1	4			1				8
88—VENEZUELA (JEW)											
Venezuela (Jew)	United States (Jew)							1			1
Totals								1			1
Totals for groups represented by less than 10 cases		67	4	10	2		13	3			99
Totals for all groups		57448	3350	6103	2345	2726	8519	4697	4628	12038	101854

Table VII

PERCENTAGE OF INCREASE IN
INTERMARRIAGE OF 2ND GENERATION OVER 1ST GENERATION

	CLASS																					
	Class I Increase of 100%-199.9%		Class II Increase of 200%-299.9%		Class III Increase of 300%-499.9%		Class IV Increase of 500%-699.9%		Class V Increase of 700%-999.9%		Class VI Increase of 1000%-1499.9%		Class VII Increase of 1500%-2499.9%		Class VIII Increase of 2500%-5000%		Class IX Decrease of 100%-199.9%		Class IX Decrease of 200%-300%	
	M	W	M	W	M	W	M	W	M	W	M	W	M	W	M	W	M	W	M	W
China																	X			
Germany (North)	X	X																		
Holland	X			X																
England (Jew)	X																			X
Portugal	X																			
Germany (South)	X	X																		
Holland (Jew)	X																			
Canada (Engl.)	X	X																		
Cuba (Span.)	X	X																		
Germany	X	X																		
England	X	X																		
Canada (Fr.)	X	X																		
Belgium	X	X																		
Switzerland (Germ.)	X	X																		
Wales	X	X																		
Austria (Boh.)	X			X																
Scotland	X	X																		
Porto Rico (Span.)	X																			
Austria (Germ.)	X	X																		
Germany (Jew)	X	X																		
Denmark	X					X														
Austria (Pol.)	X			X																
Germany (Not located)	X			X																
France		X	X																	
Norway			X	X																
Spain			X			X														
Russia (Pol.)			X					X												
Hungary (Jew)		X	X																	
Ireland				X	X															
Greece					X															
Sweden				X	X															
Hungary (Germ.)				X	X															
Turkey					X															
Hungary (Slovak)				X			X													
Armenia							X													
Italy (S.)							X											X		
Italy (Combined groups)				X			X													
Jews (Combined groups)						X	X													
Italy (N.)									X											X
Italy (Not located)									X	X										
Austria (Jew)									X			X								
Finland						X					X									
Russia (Jew)								X			X									
Switzerland (Ital.)																		X		
Hungary (Hung.)										X										
Roumania (Jew)												X								
D.W.I.																X				

TABLE XIII

PROPORTION OF INTERMARRIAGE AMONG MEN OF VARIOUS NATIONALITIES IN NEW YORK CITY ACCORDING TO OCCUPATION AND GENERATION

(1908-1912)

MEN

Culture Level	Occupation Group	1st Gener. (FB FP)	% Grand Total	2nd Gener. (NB FP)	% Grand Total
High	Professional service	378	11.1	285	11.3
Medi-ocre	Commerce and trade	679	19.9	674	26.6
	Manufacturing and mechanical pursuits	1175	34.4	886	34.9
	Personal and domestic service	597	17.6	103	4.1
Low	Public service	151	4.5	123	4.9
	Agriculture	74	2.3	20	.8
	Transportation	31	.9	28	1.1
	Navigation	50	1.5	14	.6
Very Low	Unskilled	265	7.8	399	15.7
	Grand Total	3400	100.0	2532	100.0

Table XV

PROPORTION OF SEXES IN THE 1ST AND 2ND GENERATIONS AMONG VARIOUS NATIONALITIES IN NEW YORK CITY

(Boroughs of Manhattan and Bronx)

(Compiled from Figures in Statistical Sources for Demographic Studies Greater N. Y., 1910, Vol. I. p. II-III Edited by Walter Laidlaw, Ph.D.)

NATIONALITY	GENERATIONS															
	1ST GENERATION (FBFP)								2ND GENERATION (NBFP)							
	Manhattan		Bronx		Total		No. of Men per 100 Women	No. of Women per 100 Men	Manhattan		Bronx		Total		No. of Men per 100 Women	No. of Women per 100 Men
	M.	F.	M.	F.	M.	F.			M.	F.	M.	F.	M.	F.		
Canada (Engl.)	446	6136	974	987	5471	7095	77	129	905	925	252	243	1157	1166	99	100
England	19061	17473	3538	3534	22599	20737	108	91	5493	5906	1559	1695	7052	7601	92	107
Scotland	5702	4933	1305	1102	7007	6035	116	87	2128	2287	735	719	2863	3006	91	105
Wales	463	440	107	84	570	524	108	91	214	260	59	57	273	317	86	116
Ireland	62217	88835	8499	9770	70716	98605	77	111	73845	78977	13727	14743	87572	93720	93	107
Norway	1730	2296	718	481	2448	2777	88	113	494	519	254	237	748	756	98	101
Sweden	5112	8103	1619	1558	67..	9661	69	143	1870	1914	1011	1019	2881	2933	98	101
Denmark	1559	1195	416	353	1975	1548	127	78	259	269	170	138	429	407	105	95
Finland	1240	2364	394	443	1643	2807	58	170	356	338	207	214	563	552	101	98
Holland	1311	798	220	174	1531	972	157	63	415	444	122	113	537	567	96	103
Germany	60822	57168	18433	18159	79225	75327	105	96	55999	59726	21180	23275	77179	83001	92	107
Switzerland	3038	2757	694	661	3732	3418	109	91	617	634	297	274	814	908	89	111
France	5966	7092	502	597	6468	7689	84	118	1717	1841	246	259	1963	2100	93	106
Canada (Fr.)	804	805	154	147	958	952	100	99	315	393	125	122	440	515	85	117
Italy	111286	88471	15819	9351	127105	97822	129	85	51316	51371	753	7135	58847	98506	105	98
Greece	5743	894	191	69	5934	963	616	16	259	191	28	26	287	217	132	75
Roumania	11476	11946	1059	1108	12533	13054	96	104	3417	3413	506	516	3923	3929	99	101
Canada (others)	359	429	87	73	446	507	87	113	28	39	2	6	30	45	66	150
Austria	69615	67786	5037	5290	74652	73076	102	97	33100	33141	3013	2997	36113	36158	99	100
Hungary	26788	32119	2814	3442	29602	35561	85	120	11005	11443	1482	1549	12487	12992	96	104
Russia	151631	133563	14566	13225	166197	146788	113	88	60177	59200	892	9009	69098	68209	101	98
Turkey - Europe	2321	769	93	58	2414	817	296	33	106	310	10	9	116	325	92	280
Turkey - Asia	2725	1360	113	67	2838	1427	128	50	271	283	32	27	303	310	97	102
At Sea	71	83	14	20	85	103	82	121	--	2	--	--	--	--	--	--
Other Countries	6144	4583	582	469	6726	5052	111	75	704	709	89	84	793	793	100	100

1910 - 1914						1910 - 1914						1915 - 1917				1915 - 1917				MEN	WOMEN	No. of Men per 100 Women (1910 - 1914)	No. of Women per 100 Men (1910-1914)	No. of Men per 100 Women (1915-1917)	No. of Women per 100 Men (1915-1917)	No. of Men per 100 Women 1910-1917
1910	1911	1912	1913	1914	Total 1910-1914	1910	1911	1912	1913	1914	Total 1910-1914	1915	1916	1917	Total 1915-1917	1915	1916	1917	Total 1915-1917	1910-1917	1910-1917					
2080	2806	2595	2513	3340	13502	1511	1680	1938	1920	2549	9598	2017	1875	2028	6536	1694	1502	2605	5801	19818	15049	145	69	112	86	152
2622	1457	2857	4154	3387	14157	387	200	380	616	884	2466	370	424	635	1430	112	70	66	248	15595	2334	678	14	579	17	668
2585	2760	2294	3517	2551	13464	1851	1865	2016	2424	2290	10436	365	117	86	566	410	176	49	637	14080	11063	129	78	90	119	126
4707	3217	3899	3301	5086	19610	153	175	266	285	439	1298	1178	1086	584	2764	66	23	15	104	22374	1409	1502	5	2615	4	1587
660	526	781	785	798	3546	12	25	21	27	29	124	760	711	643	2114	30	26	30	106	5660	220	5110	3	1990	6	2572
18731	6609	8184	14570	11704	54797	5156	336	2687	6581	5121	17879	676	165	85	864	280	89	20	396	55631	17777	338	31	309	47	312
1519	1797	1511	1414	1569	7810	335	428	486	432	417	2096	1236	1568	1455	4247	442	445	465	1352	11787	3380	375	26	316	32	382
2719	2502	1968	2136	2255	11580	208	385	299	385	404	1677	143	46	61	180	47	5	4	56	11708	1585	739	13	867	37	716
4764	4565	5491	4844	3850	21762	1166	1426	1286	1575	1288	6686	2028	1065	1642	5832	830	730	564	2174	27394	8829	327	30	284	39	309
1065	512	104	119	99	1689	2	1	4	1	4	12	45	46	44	135	3	5	2	10	1822	22	14075	.7	1350	7	8281
16502	16865	14002	16112	15019	78498	7298	8803	9897	10487	9969	46454	9725	8484	7157	25297	8658	7800	7455	23893	103795	70547	148	69	196	92	147
6876	3804	2813	8901	5190	25884	3229	2792	2513	3289	3430	15225	1440	2259	2371	6080	705	1114	1191	3010	30074	18255	157	71	202	49	164
5632	5475	5159	8965	5456	27676	3299	3444	3610	3860	3282	17495	3644	5899	8646	18191	2684	3339	3421	9444	45867	27150	158	62	180	55	168
21445	20135	19167	22899	22195	105859	13634	15909	14014	15862	17071	76190	6557	2915	2799	12271	4321	2252	1681	8254	118110	82444	142	73	148	67	143
24425	25245	19974	24206	26076	117926	1158	1378	1315	1675	2727	8267	5676	8524	11879	26079	1577	2961	2593	7131	144005	15578	1420	6	365	27	956
20454	25190	20661	27550	36642	128477	15906	19992	17535	20732	31067	105029	6297	4475	3626	16596	5443	1595	2704	9742	144873	114771	122	82	168	65	126
16324	16642	13471	15008	13242	74487	12558	15014	13700	14412	15608	70299	10211	7875	4351	22435	7875	6588	6467	20930	97122	91219	106	94	107	91	106
15149	13138	10266	17502	17580	71225	2542	2951	3140	3551	3886	16070	3034	1297	1180	5611	1503	788	797	3088	76836	19158	443	22	182	55	401
65642	52725	43882	79458	79899	359046	12638	14799	14775	18851	23462	84705	9470	5432	4442	19344	7295	5268	8590	21151	358410	105854	400	24	91	109	38
549	912	1117	1480	1613	5671	75	282	189	321	320	1187	1786	1915	1959	5660	349	370	445	1164	11331	1351	478	20	486	20	838
6	—	10	7	38	61	2	2	4	5	15	28	51	55	57	161	2	10	12	24	222	32	218	45	670	14	693
9687	7362	5861	11595	8754	43459	4570	4385	4265	6115	6632	25695	787	250	192	1229	913	57	30	1000	44648	26695	167	59	122	81	166
4498	3656	4154	4669	5397	22364	3075	3534	3942	5720	7638	23909	522	60	70	652	616	129	32	777	25016	24686	95	106	84	119	95
5222	5828	7328	2742	2344	23464	1640	1856	1802	1241	1905	8526	2029	2872	2903	7804	1760	3101	2940	7801	31268	16327	275	36	100	99	191
32	1	1	4	—	38	—	2	1	1	—	4	2	—	3	5	—	—	1	1	43	5	950	1000	500	20	860
44585	24427	29056	61945	37443	197454	22744	2478	23255	35738	13144	97357	2121	928	864	3913	2510	606	386	3502	201247	100839	202	49	111	89	199
2161	2279	2489	3701	2787	13417	1109	1106	1364	2162	1584	7325	1459	3786	1937	7162	640	2111	3013	5764	20579	15088	185	54	124	80	137
2956	1334	1939	2611	3675	12515	441	289	486	1009	1430	3654	289	210	212	711	95	83	35	213	13226	3867	342	29	333	29	341
6415	7426	8803	20441	16625	59710	760	1072	1437	3019	3116	9404	1662	2015	1378	5025	424	164	195	783	62935	10187	613	15	641	15	617
6284	5954	6776	8369	8108	37491	4624	4590	6617	7704	8875	32490	689	465	329	1483	612	39	43	694	38974	33164	115	86	213	47	117
26449	22654	15032	20282	18472	102889	11635	12067	9054	9743	9251	51760	11178	8615	8610	28398	6908	4797	4594	16299	151287	68039	198	50	176	57	192
8930	8309	5973	6509	6032	35753	4057	5305	5116	5157	4672	24307	4014	3419	3291	10724	4860	3702	3576	12138	44477	36456	147	65	88	112	127
7293	5807	6207	6472	4277	29556	4369	4387	5253	5195	5303	24506	219	29	40	288	433	59	18	510	29844	25015	120	84	56	180	119
5286	3936	4119	4326	5111	20778	398	565	668	658	838	3127	2984	4447	7682	15113	585	555	660	1880	35891	4807	664	15	899	11	746

TABLE XVI
PROPORTION OF MARRIAGEABLE PERSONS IN NEW YORK CITY ACCORDING TO GENERATION
1910

(Adapted from U. S. Census, 1910, Vol. 3 Pop. Stat. p. 222, Table 16.)

Generation	Single Men	% Grand Total	Single Women	% Grand Total	Number of Men per 100 Women	Number of Women per 100 Men
1st Generation (Foreign born white)	298,096	42.9	231,066	38.2	129	77
2nd Generation (Native white of foreign or mixed parentage)	257,869	37.1	243,857	40.4	105	94
3rd Generation (Native white of native parentage)	139,117	20.0	129,668	21.4	107	93
Grand Total	695,082	100.0	604,591	100.0		

TABLE XVII

PROPORTION OF MARRIAGEABLE PERSONS IN MANHATTAN AND BRONX BOROUGHS IN NEW YORK CITY ACCORDING TO GENERATION—1910

(Adapted from U. S. Census, 1910, Vol. 3 Pop. Stat. p. 222, Table 16.)

GENERATION	SINGLE MEN				SINGLE WOMEN				No. of Men per 100 Women	No. of Women per 100 Men
	Manhattan	Bronx	Total	% Grand Total	Manhattan	Bronx	Total	% Grand Total		
1st Generation (Foreign born white)....	191,173	19,140	210,313	49.3	157,110	12,487	169,597	45.7	124	80
2nd Generation (Native white of foreign parentage)........................	119,271	26,177	145,448	34.1	112,610	24,919	137,529	37.0	105	94
3rd Generation (Native white of native parentage)........................	58,091	12,806	70,897	16.6	52,399	11,638	64,037	17.3	110	90
Grand Total.....................	**368,535**	**58,123**	**426,658**	**100.0**	**322,119**	**49,044**	**371,163**	**100.0**		

VITA

Julius Drachsler, born September 5, 1889, in Northwestern Hungary, now part of the Republic of Checko-Slovakia; attended royal gymnasium at Rosenberg, 1900-1903. Came to the United States in 1903; graduated from Townsend Harris Hall High School, 1908, and from the College of the City of New York, 1912, with degree of Bachelor of Science; received certificate from New York School of Social Work in 1914; M. A. in sociology from Columbia University, in 1915.

Entered the field of social service in 1913; assistant secretary of the Jewish Big Brother Association, 1913-1915; secretary of the Faculty of The School for Jewish Communal Work, 1915-1918; assistant executive director of the Bureau of Jewish Social Research, 1918-1919; during the latter part of the war served as special expert and assistant executive director of the New York office of the Bureau of War Risk Insurance.

Lecturer on immigration and problems of race fusion, in New York Training School for Community Workers, 1918; lecturer in Sociology, College of the City of New York, 1920; assistant professor of economics and sociology in Smith College, Northampton, Mass., September, 1919

www.ingramcontent.com/pod-product-compliance
Lightning Source LLC
LaVergne TN
LVHW010601110826
845149LV00003B/723
9781418187491